CRUSADE TE
IN TRANSLA'

About the volume:

This is the first translation into English of Ralph of Caen's *Gesta Tancredi*. This text provides an exceptionally important narrative of the First Crusade and its immediate aftermath, covering the period 1096–1105, but is often neglected, due in no small part to the difficulties of its Latin. A native of the Norman city of Caen where he was a student of Arnulf, the future patriarch of Jerusalem, in 1107 Ralph joined Bohemond of Taranto's army as a military chaplain. After arriving in the East, Ralph took service with Bohemond's nephew Tancred, who ruled the principality of Antioch from 1108 to 1112.

Although dedicated to Arnulf, the *Gesta Tancredi* focuses on the careers of Bohemond and, especially, of Tancred. It is one of the most important sources – indeed the most important Latin source – for the Norman campaigns in Cilicia (1097–1108), and for the early Norman rule of Antioch. The work as a whole has a striking Norman point of view and contains details found in no other source, providing a corrective to the strong northern focus of most of the other narrative sources for the First Crusade.

About the translators:

Bernard S. Bachrach is Professor of History at the University of Minnesota, USA and David S. Bachrach is Assistant Professor of History at the University of New Hampshire, USA.

To Deborah and Elyse

The *Gesta Tancredi* of Ralph of Caen

Crusade Texts in Translation

The *Gesta Tancredi* of Ralph of Caen

A History of the Normans on the First Crusade

Translated and with an introduction
by
BERNARD S. BACHRACH and DAVID S. BACHRACH

ASHGATE

Reprinted in 2007
First published in paperback 2010

Published by
Ashgate Publishing Limited
Wey Court East
Union Road
Farnham
Surrey, GU9 7PT
England

Ashgate Publishing Company
Suite 420
101 Cherry Street
Burlington
VT 05401-4405
USA

www.ashgate.com

British Library Cataloguing in Publication Data
Bernard S. Bachrach and David S. Bachrach
    Ralph, of Caen
    The Gesta Tancredi of Ralph of Caen: A History of the Normans on the First
    Crusade. – (Crusade Texts in Translation)
    1. Tancred, ca. 1075–1112. 2. Crusades – First, 1096–1099. 3. Antioch
    (Principality) – History. I. Title. II. Bachrach, Bernard S., 1939– . III. Bachrach,
    David Steward, 1971– .
    940.1'8

Library of Congress Cataloging-in-Publication Data
Raoul, de Caen, 1080–1120
    [Gesta Tancredi, English]
    The Gesta Tancredi of Ralph of Caen: A History of the Normans on the First
    Crusade / translated by Bernard S. Bachrach and David S. Bachrach.
        p.   cm. – (Crusade Texts in Translation; 12)
    Includes bibliographical references (p.) and index.
    1. Tancred, ca. 1075–1112. 2. Crusades – First, 1096–1099 – Sources. I. Bachrach,
    Bernard S., 1939– . II. Bachrach, David Steward, 1971– . III. Title. IV. Series.
    D181.T3R3613 2005
    956'.014–dc22   2005041040

ISBN 9780754637103 (hbk)
ISBN 9781409400325 (pbk)
ISBN 9780754682004 (ebk)

Reprinted 2012

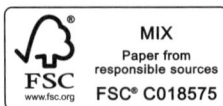

MIX
Paper from
responsible sources
FSC
www.fsc.org   FSC® C018575

Printed and bound in Great Britain by
the MPG Books Group, UK

Contents

Acknowledgments

We would like to thank Professor Bernard Hamilton for his helpful suggestions as Ashgate's reader of this translation. We would also like to thank Professor R. Scott Smith for his valuable observations. We, of course, take full responsibility for any infelicities in the text and translation.

Maps

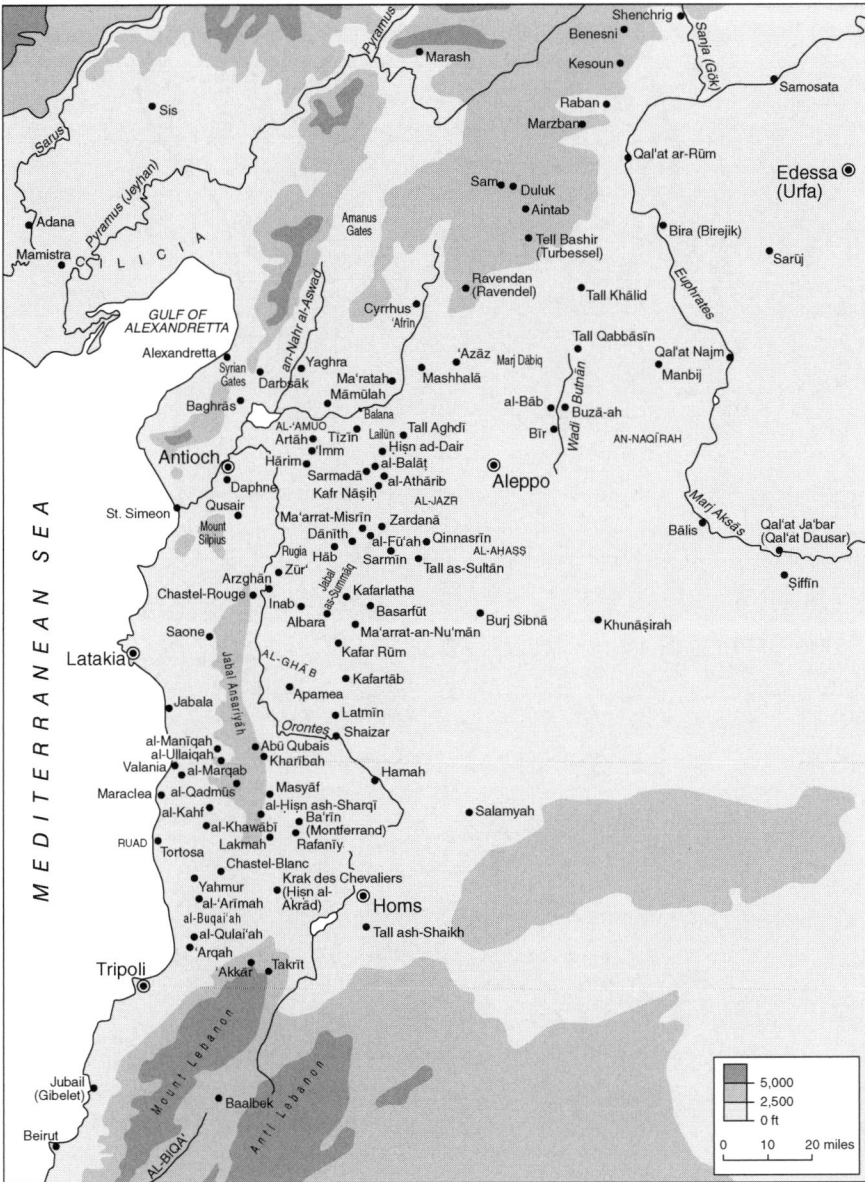

Shenchrig

Benesni
Kesoun

Marash

Raban
Marzban

Samosata

Sarja (Gök)

Qal'at ar-Rūm

Sis

Sarus

Edessa ◉
(Urfa)

Pyramus

Pyramus (Jeyhan)

Adana

Amanus
Gates

Sam
Duluk
Aintab

Tell Bashir
(Turbessel)

Bira (Birejik)

CILICIA

Mamistra

Sarūj

ar-Nahr al-Aswad

GULF OF
ALEXANDRETTA

Cyrrhus
'Afrīn

Ravendan
(Ravendel)

Tall Khālid

Euphrates

Tall Qabbāsīn

Alexandretta

Yaghra

'Azāz
Marj Dābiq

Qal'at Najm

Syrian
Gates
Darbsāk

Ma'ratah
Māmūlah

Mashhalā

al-Bāb

Wadi Butnān

Manbij

Baghrās

Balana

AL-'AMŪ
Artāh Tizīn
'Imm

Tall Aghdī
Lailūn
Hisn ad-Dair

Buzā-ah

Bīr

AN-NAQĪRAH

Antioch

Hārim

Sarmadā
al-Balāt
al-Athārib

◉
Aleppo

Daphne

Kafr Nāsih

AL-JAZR

St. Simeon

Qusair

Ma'arrat-Misrīn
Dānith
al-Fū'ah Qinnasrīn

Zardanā

Marj Aksās

Mount
Silpius

Rugia Hāb

Arzghān

Zūr'

Jabal as-Summāq

Sarmīn
Tall as-Sultān

AL-AHASS

Bālis

Qal'at Ja'bar
(Qal'at Dausar)

Chastel-Rouge

Inab

Kafarlatha

Basarfūt

Sıffīn

Saone

Albara

Ma'arrat-an-Nu'mān

Burj Sibnā

Khunāsirah

MEDITERRANEAN SEA

Latakia

AL-GHĀB

Jabal Ansariyah

Kafar Rūm

Kafartāb

Aparnea

Latmīn

Jabala

Orontes

Shaizar

al-Manīqah
al-Ullaiqah
Valania
al-Marqab

Abū Qubais
Kharibah

Hamah

Maraclea

al-Qadmūs

Masyāf
al-Hisn ash-Sharqī

Salamyah

al-Kahf

al-Khawābī
Ba'rīn
(Montferrand)

RUAD

Tortosa

Lakmah

Rafanīy

Chastel-Blanc

Yahmur

Krak des Chevaliers
(Hisn al-
Akrād)

◉ **Homs**

al-'Arīmah

al-Buqai'ah

al-Qulai'ah

Tall ash-Shaikh

'Arqah

Tripoli ◉

'Akkār

Takrīt

Mount Lebanon

Anti Lebanon

Jubail
(Gibelet)

Baalbek

Beirut

AL-BIQĀ'

5,000
2,500
0 ft

0   10   20 miles

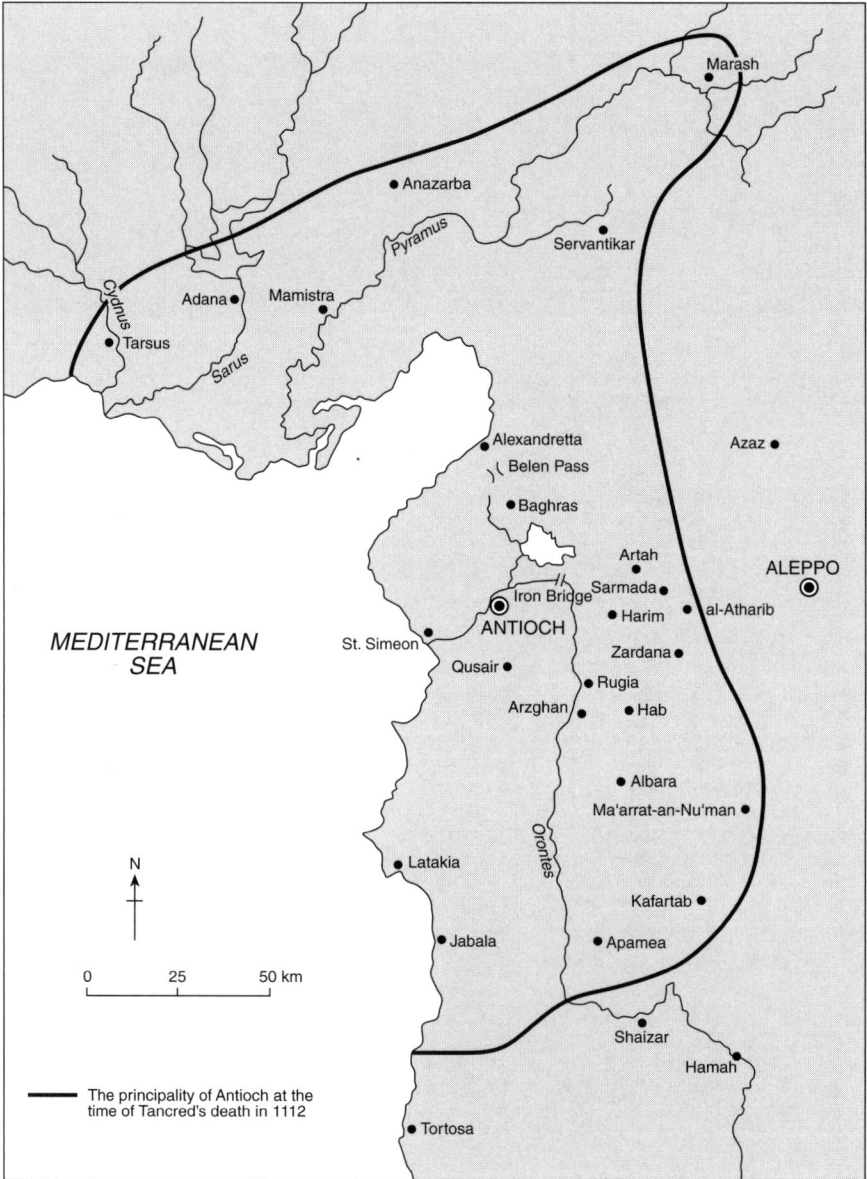

Marash

Anazarba

Pyramus

Servantikar

Cydnus

Adana

Mamistra

Tarsus

Sarus

Azaz

Alexandretta

Belen Pass

Baghras

Artah

ALEPPO

Sarmada

al-Atharib

Harim

Iron Bridge

St. Simeon

ANTIOCH

Zardana

MEDITERRANEAN
SEA

Qusair

Rugia

Arzghan

Hab

Albara

Ma'arrat-an-Nu'man

N

Latakia

Orontes

Kafartab

0   25   50 km

Jabala

Apamea

Shaizar

Hamah

The principality of Antioch at the
time of Tancred's death in 1112

Tortosa

Introduction

Our Knowledge of Ralph

Among the half-dozen or so Latin accounts of the First Crusade written by participants and those with substantial access to participants, the *Gesta Tancredi* by Ralph of Caen is the least studied and least well known.[1] However, by contrast with the authors of several of these other texts, Ralph's biography is not particularly obscure. His family probably came from Caen or the region (*pagus*) administered from this flourishing Norman city. This is suggested by the fact that Ralph spent his youth studying in the city, likely at the cathedral school, where Arnulf of Chocques, who later was to become patriarch of Jerusalem, served as young Ralph's teacher. The two men were to maintain a close life-long relationship.[2]

Ralph's course of study under the direction of Arnulf ended no later than early 1096 and probably some time before that date because the latter departed for the crusade in the entourage of Duke Robert of Normandy.[3] Arnulf, who judging from his career was a prominent figure in the Norman church prior to the First Crusade (see below), either was appointed the duke's personal chaplain, a very prestigious position, at the start of the crusade or was given that role at a somewhat later date, that is, well before Robert's departure from the Holy Land in 1099 in order to return to Normandy.[4] Arnulf was elevated to episcopal rank during the course of the crusade and played a noteworthy role in the ecclesiastical leadership of this pilgrimage in arms following the death of Adhemar of Le Puy (1 August 1098), the papal legate who led the crusade, at least from a spiritual perspective. Arnulf

---

[1] See Susan Edgington, 'The First Crusade: Reviewing the Evidence', in *The First Crusade: Origins and Impact*, ed. Jonathan Phillips (Manchester, 1997), 57–77.

[2] As will be seen below, Ralph asked Arnulf to act as the editor of the *Gesta Tancredi*, some time after 1112, thereby indicating the continuing relationship of the two men over this period.

[3] On this point, see Charles Homer Haskins, *Norman Institutions* (New York, 1918, repr. 1967), 74–5.

[4] The basic biography of Robert Curthose remains, Charles Wendell David, *Robert Curthose, Duke of Normandy* (Cambridge, Mass, 1920, New York, repr. 1982).

remained in the Holy Land and ultimately became patriarch of Jerusalem (1099, 1112–15, 1116–18).[5]

Whether Ralph had completed both his academic studies and his training for the priesthood in Caen prior to Arnulf's departure with Duke Robert is not clear and perhaps unlikely. However, it is certain that Ralph was ordained a priest by 1106, at the latest, because it was in that year that he was recruited by Bohemond (*c.*1056–1111), during the latter's tour of Francia, to serve as a chaplain in the entourage of the erstwhile ruler of Antioch.[6] In the reform milieu of late eleventh and early twelfth-century Normandy, it is almost certain that no later than 1106 Ralph had reached the age of 25, which was required by canon law for priestly ordination.[7]

It is not clear whether it was Ralph's prior association with Arnulf which brought him to the attention of a man of Bohemond's lofty status or the priest's social connections generated as a result of family background. Although virtually nothing is known directly either of Ralph's paternal or maternal lineage, it is clear that they were of sufficient importance to have him placed as a student with Arnulf of Chocques, who, as noted above, was a very prominent Norman cleric closely associated with the Norman ducal family. Indeed, early in his career, that is, the later 1060s and early 1070s, Arnulf was chosen to serve as a tutor to William the Conqueror's daughter Cecilia (1056–1126).[8] For Ralph, as a youth, to have touched even tangentially on the circle which included an Anglo-Norman princess and a future duke may well permit the inference that his family was of considerable importance.

After joining Bohemond's entourage as a chaplain, Ralph accompanied his principal on his return to the eastern Mediterranean in 1107. There, he

---

[5] Arnulf was the first man to be selected as patriarch (1 August 1099). However, following the arrival of a large Pisan fleet in the autumn of that year, Daimbert, archbishop of Pisa, who accompanied this fleet, was appointed with the support of Bohemond. Concerning Daimbert's appointment and the role played by the leaders in the kingdom of Jerusalem in selecting the patriarchs of Jerusalem, see J. G. Rowe, 'Pascal II and the Relation between the Spiritual and Temporal Powers in the Kingdom of Jerusalem', *Speculum*, 32 (1957), 470–501.

[6] Concerning Tancred's service with Bohemond, see Luigi Russo, 'Tancredi e i Bizantini. Sui *Gesta Tancredi in expeditione Hierosolymitana* di Rodolfo di Caen', *Medio evo greco* 2 (2002), 193–230, here 195.

[7] Russo, 'Tancredi e i Bizantini', 193–4, suggests that Ralph's mention of bright lights in the sky in his home of Caen during his youth (ch. 57) may also permit the conclusion that Ralph was born during the 1080s. Russo notes that the *Chronographia* of Sigebert of Gembloux and the *Chronica* of Frutolf and Ekkehard both record the appearance of comets, which might be identified with Ralph's 'terrible red light in the sky', during the 1080s.

[8] In this regard, see Charles Homer Haskins, *Norman Institutions*, 74–5; and David, *Robert Curthose*, 217–20.

seems to have served the Norman prince on campaign during the latter's efforts, unsuccessful in the end, to recapitulate the earlier campaign under Robert Guiscard (1080–85) in the Balkans.[9] Following an initial victory at Avlona, in modern Albania, during the autumn of 1107, Bohemond was forced by Emperor Alexios Comnenos to break off his siege of Durazzo and then to end his campaign. In September 1108, in return for permission from Alexios to withdraw his forces from Albania, Bohemond concluded a treaty with the Byzantine emperor in which he agreed to take an oath that made explicit the subordination of Antioch to the empire and to return to Apulia.[10] Whether Ralph rose to a position as Bohemond's personal chaplain during this period cannot be established. It is clear, however, that Ralph wants his readers to believe that he had a close conversational relationship with Bohemond and that the latter provided him with a considerable quantity of information concerning the First Crusade. Nevertheless, it should be emphasized, in this context, that Ralph's casting of the situation in this manner may have been a rhetorical artifice that was intended to provide credibility for the corpus of information regarding operations during the crusade, much of it unique to the <i>Gesta</i>, that he implies or, in some cases, says he obtained from the prince.

Some time prior to Bohemond's death (1111), and indeed likely soon after the prince's defeat at Durazzo, Ralph left his patron and journeyed to Antioch where he joined the staff of Tancred who had succeeded Bohemond as the prince of Antioch. Ralph intentionally leaves vague the conditions under which he moved from the entourage of Bohemond to that of Tancred. Throughout his text, Ralph maintains obvious loyalty to both men and never gives the impression that his movement to service at Antioch was the result of a falling out with Bohemond or that the latter opposed or even resented the move. It is clear from his narrative, however, that from the time he left Bohemond's service for that of Tancred until the death of the latter on 12 December 1112, Ralph remained a loyal supporter and close confidant of the prince of Antioch. At least, this is the picture that Ralph conveys to his readers which serves to undergird the credibility of his account.

Throughout his association with both Bohemond and Tancred, Ralph makes it clear that he sought and obtained detailed information from both men and from their followers regarding a wide spectrum of events during the

---

[9] Concerning this campaign, see John W. Birkenmeier, <i>The Development of the Komnenian Army: 1081–1180</i> (Leiden, 2002), 60–70.

[10] Bohemond's final campaign and his defeat at the hands of Alexios are dealt with in considerable detail by Anna Comnena, <i>Alexiad</i>, trans. E. R. A. Sewter (London, 1969), 388–434. In this context, Anna offers what purports to be the text of the agreement between Bohemond and Alexios (433).

crusade.[11] It seems very likely that both men knew of Ralph's aim to write a history and cooperated with him in providing information personally and making additional information accessible. It also seems probable that Ralph informed his principals, or at least Tancred, that he would not write while they were still living because he did not wish to have his account challenged as being biased by their patronage.[12] Thus, only after Tancred's death did Ralph begin to write the *Gesta Tancredi*, probably while living in Jerusalem, where his former teacher Arnulf, was patriarch having been elected to this position in the same year that Tancred died.[13] It is possible that Arnulf made Ralph a canon of the cathedral church so that the latter would have the leisure time and resources; for example, supplies of parchment, ink and quills, work space, and perhaps even a scribe to take his dictation.[14] Patriarch Arnulf took a strong interest in both Ralph and the *Gesta* as he would appear to have promised Ralph that he would edit the completed work. Indeed, this suggests an ongoing and very positive relationship between the two men. Given Ralph's dedication of the work to Arnulf, it seems likely that it was completed before the latter's death in April 1118.

Ralph's education, likely at the cathedral school of Caen, provided a strong focus in continuing work on the trivium and quadrivium while concentrating heavily on the study of both the Hebrew bible and the New Testament, both, of course, in Latin translation.[15] However, Ralph spent a considerable period studying classical literature. Among the poets, he was very well versed in Vergil, which was not unusual, but he also had a good acquaintance with Ovid, who did not become very popular until later in the twelfth century. In addition, he had read Horace, who never was much of a favorite during the

---

[11] In his preface, Ralph makes explicit reference to his relationship with both of the princes of Antioch, emphasizing that he knew Tancred even better than he knew Bohemond.

[12] In this context, it should be emphasized that Ralph makes reference in his preface to the sneers of men who would claim that a positive account of the deeds of Bohemond and Tancred, while these men were alive, was purchased rather than earned.

[13] Rowe, 'Pascal II', 472–6; and R. Foreville, 'Un chef de la première croisade: Arnoul Malecouronne', *Bulletin Philologique et Historique du comité des travaux historiques et scientifiques* (1953–54), 377–90.

[14] Concerning Ralph's effort to gain Arnulf as a patron following the death of Tancred, see Russo, 'Tancredi e i Bizantini', 214.

[15] Ralph has been identified by specialists in both crusading and Norman literary texts as an exceptionally well-educated man. See Laetitia Boehm, 'Die "Gesta Tancredi" des Radulf von Caen. Ein Beitrag zur Geschichtsschreibung der Normannen um 1100', *Historisches Jahrbuch*, 75 (1956), 47–72; and H. Glaesener, 'Raoul de Caen historien et écrivain', *Revue d'histoire ecclésiastique*, 46 (1951), 5–21, here 16ff.

High Middle Ages.[16] While these works are found frequently quoted or alluded to in the *Gesta*, it was Ralph's study of classical historians, particularly Livy, Caesar, Lucan, and Sallust, which indicates the depth of his classical learning and preparation for writing the *Gesta*. It remains to be seen, as a great deal more research would be necessary, if Ralph had studied the Latin translations of Josephus' *History* and *Jewish Antiquities*.[17] These works were widely dispersed throughout the libraries of Normandy during this period and had considerable importance for the writing of history as illustrated by Ralph's contemporary Baudri of Bourgueil.[18]

Ralph as a Historian

Both in his preface to the *Gesta Tancredi* and throughout the body of the work, Ralph demonstrates that he is self-aware as a historian who is shaping a particular view of the past for posterity. The purpose of history, as Ralph envisioned it, was consistent with the views of both Livy and Caesar, two of the classical writers upon whom he modeled some of his writing, as well as being consistent with the aims of much Christian historiography. In this context, Ralph's aim was to encourage good deeds and to discourage bad deeds by providing appropriate examples of both from the past. In terms of his own writing and as advice to posterity, Ralph expresses the view that '[w]e should, therefore, press forward with the greatest effort to read what has been written' (Preface).[19]

In this context, Ralph emphasizes that the writing of history is a 'noble discipline' and recounting the deeds of princes must be done accurately (*honeste*).[20] The historian must 'write down what ought to be read' and not simply what people like to hear or read. It seems clear that to Ralph, history was a subject from which people were to learn and that it was not simply a form of entertainment. Thus, Ralph emphasizes that he is dismayed and, in fact, recoils in disgust that his contemporaries are not reading what ought to be read and, more importantly, were not writing what ought to be written. He

---

[16] Concerning the availability and reading of Horace during the eleventh century, see Maria Barbara Quint, *Untersuchungen zur mittelalterlichen Horaz-Rezeption* (Frankfurt, 1988), esp. 29–31 and 89–104.

[17] See Franz Blatt, *The Latin Josephus 1: Introduction and Text* (Aarhus, 1951).

[18] See Baudri of Bourgueil, *Historia Hierosolymitana*, Recueil des historiens des croisades, IV (Paris, 1879).

[19] Ralph's comment here would seem to indicate his view that it is historians, that is, those who relayed what actually happened in the past, using the Isidorian sense of the historian's task, who should provide the basis for understanding the contemporary world.

[20] Preface, 'nobile est studium res probe gestas principum recensere'.

attacks those who set out 'fabulous inventions' and ignore the real victories achieved by Christ's armies. Ralph's task, as he sees it, is to rectify this situation because no one more suitable has taken up the burden. This is particularly true of the deeds carried out by Tancred.

In defending his suitability to write the *Gesta Tancredi*, Ralph does not depart from the ubiquitous modesty-humility topos and avers that other men more talented than he undoubtedly could be found to do this work. Nevertheless, Ralph defends his efforts not only because no one better has undertaken the burden of carrying out this task with regard to Bohemond and especially Tancred, but *tempus fugit* and much that is known will be lost due to deficient memories and the death of witnesses. Even more important in justifying his decision to write is Ralph's special relationship with Bohemond and Tancred. It is in this context that Ralph discusses what would appear to have been his most important criterion for gathering and transmitting accurate information, the sine qua non, in his view for the writing of history. He avers, that despite his limited talents, he had a very close personal connection to Bohemond and an even closer relationship with Tancred. These connections enabled him to obtain information from eyewitnesses concerning events and, indeed, information from participants at a high level who had access to more information than the mere soldier in the battle line.

Ralph, as noted above, was very much aware that having a close, personal relationship with his eyewitness sources was a two-edged sword. On the one hand, these men could provide the best and most accurate information. On the other hand, however, this information potentially was subject to bias, what modern scholars characterize as the memoir effect, in so far as there is a tendency for actors to 'remember' the past in a way that puts the person recalling the situation in a positive light. While source bias was a potential problem for Ralph, he also understood that he could be accused of authorial bias insofar as he enjoyed a very close, indeed a patron–client, relationship with his principals. As a consequence, as indicated earlier, Ralph made clear that he would not write his *Gesta* while either of his principals was living. In this manner, he worked to avoid the potential charge that he was currying favor with his patrons for future advancement.

In looking more closely at Ralph's historical method, it is clear that a reliance and, indeed, a preference for eyewitness information was central to his approach. Not only did he gather information from Bohemond and Tancred he also questioned the members of their entourages and their soldiers. However, simply because someone provided information did not mean that Ralph accepted it without question. A careful reading of Ralph's work makes clear that he often gave more than one version of an event or an aspect of an event and in doing so encouraged his reader through his rhetoric to favor one reading of events over another. One particularly compelling example of this practice is Ralph's discussion of a legal dispute between

Tancred and Arnulf of Chocques concerning the disposition of booty acquired from the temple complex during the assault on Jerusalem (chs 135–6). In both cases he had direct personal access to both men with whom he had good personal relationships. However, since the situation was part of a court proceeding and Ralph presents the arguments of both Arnulf and Tancred as direct discourse, it is possible that there was a written record that survived and was made available to Ralph.

As will be seen below in more detail, a second element of Ralph's historical–rhetorical style was to use poetry and prose for different purposes with regard to indicating to his audience the firmness or accuracy of his information. In using poetry to describe, for example, the action of the non-Norman commanders at the battle of Dorylaeum (chs 27–32) Ralph appears to have been signaling his readers or listeners that this information was not as soundly based in fact as he would have liked. By contrast, when discussing the death of Tancred's brother, William, in the battle (chs 25–6), about which Ralph could obtain exact, detailed information from both Tancred and his officers, the author of the *Gesta* moves from poetry to prose. The only sustained description in verse of Tancred's participation in the crusade (chs 128–9, 131) concerns his capture and despoliation of the Dome of the Rock complex, which the crusaders thought was Solomon's temple. Ralph's treatment in verse of Tancred's Rolandesque effectiveness as a killing machine turns to prose, however, (ch. 130) when dealing with the mundane facts regarding the amount of booty taken in the Dome of the Rock, thereby leading his audience to accept that this information is factual.

In a more subtle manner, Ralph's arguments evidence what modern scholars characterize as source criticism. Here, we can see how the author's education in logic, a key subject of the trivium, plays a role in the examination of efficient causes. In his discussion of the Holy Lance, one of the most dramatic episodes depicted in the *Gesta*, Ralph demonstrates both his skills in logic and his ability as a rhetorician to develop a persuasive argument. Ralph indicates that Bohemond believed that the discovery of the Holy Lance in the church of Saint Peter at Antioch by Bartholomew, a member of Raymond of Toulouse's entourage, was 'an empty and false discovery'. He goes on to condemn the man who had made the discovery as having acted in a duplicitous manner in making this untrue claim (ch. 102).

In order to sustain the view that Bartholomew had not found the Holy Lance, Ralph, as author, following the technique often advocated by Cicero, used Bohemond to attack the credibility of the protagonist. First, Bartholomew is assailed as a person imbued with *levitas* rather than *gravitas*, that is, 'he was not a serious man' (ch. 102). Indeed, he was prone to excessive drinking, carousing, and had a reputation for spouting nonsense. After undermining Bartholomew's reputation and thereby calling into question his credibility, Ralph has Bohemond ask a series of rhetorical questions meant to

undermine the likelihood that the Holy Lance could possibly have found its
way to Antioch. First, the rationale for moving the Lance from the Holy
Land to Syria is rendered suspect. Why, Ralph has Bohemond ask, would one
of Christ's followers have carried the Lance so far away rather than hiding it
in Jerusalem? He follows up by asking, if a Jew or a pagan Roman had taken
the Lance from the Holy Land, why would he have hidden it in a church?
Finally, Ralph recalls the tradition that the Holy Lance belonged to one of
the soldiers serving Pontius Pilate and asks where one could find evidence that
the Roman procurator had ever visited Antioch? In short, Ralph implies that
research would not provide evidence that the Roman officer had traveled to
Antioch.

Ralph's emphasis on eyewitness accounts is particularly important because
it sets his work in a long tradition of history writing in the West going back to
Herodotus and Thucydides. Indeed, the very root of the word history in
Greek, *istoria*, meant research among contemporaries who had participated
in the events the historian wished to describe. For the would be historian of
the Middle Ages, these values were solidified in the work of Isidore of Seville
(d. 635).[21] The view that information provided by eyewitnesses was
exceptionally important was adopted by Christian historians from their
pagan predecessors and continues today in a variety of fields, but particularly
in law. Indeed, the exceptional importance of eyewitness accounts for Ralph's
reconstruction of the past helps explain why he felt compelled to write this
history despite what would seem to have been a keen understanding of his
own limitations as a writer.[22] The longer he waited, the fewer witnesses would
be available to supply him with information.

Despite these clear indications that Ralph intended his work to be
understood as history, the fact cannot be avoided that significant portions of
the *Gesta* demonstrate qualities that are more reminiscent of contemporary
entertainment literature, the *chansons de geste*, which did not carry with them
the same generic demands for describing real events in the past.[23] In
particular, as noted earlier, Ralph's *Gesta* is a prosimetric narrative meaning
that he wrote in both prose and in verse, a genre often used in contemporary
heroic literary composition.[24]

---

[21] Isidore of Seville, *Etymologiarum sive originum libri xx*, 2 vols, ed. W. M. Lindsay
(Oxford, 1911, repr. 1957), 1.41–4.

[22] Not only does Ralph ask Arnulf of Chocques to act as an editor for the completed
Gesta, thereby indicating that his composition would need to be improved, but also his
topological claim to be a poor writer would seem to be borne out by the relative
neglect of this text by modern scholars.

[23] On this point, see Bernard S. Bachrach, 'Dudo of Saint Quentin as an Historian of
Military Organization', *Haskins Society Journal*, 12 (2002), 165–85, particularly 184–5.

[24] In the tradition of writing about the history of the Normans, Dudo of Saint
Quentin's *De moribus et actis primorum Normaniae ducum*, written during the early

About one-fourth (36 of 157) of the chapters of the *Gesta* are written in verse, and these fall into five distinct sections of 6, 22, 1, 4, and 3 chapters respectively.[25] The subjects of these verse sections are the battle of Dorylaeum, the suffering of the Christian forces within Antioch and their subsequent victory over Kerbhoga, Tancred's song of praise for Jerusalem, the assault on Jerusalem by the crusaders, and finally the fighting in the streets of Jerusalem, respectively.

How then are we to understand Ralph's stated goal of relating true events in the past with his deployment of a generic form, verse, that often was associated with ahistorical epic compositions such as the *Song of Roland*?[26] It is first necessary to recall that Ralph's focus is on Tancred and that the *Gesta* is intended to be a historical account of Tancred's career. In this context, it is striking that only five of the 36 verse chapters have Tancred as their subject or even mention him. Of these five chapters, one (ch. 85) simply notes Tancred's place in the order of attack against Kerbhoga's troops beneath the walls of Antioch, and provides no information regarding his role in the subsequent battle. In the second verse chapter to mention Tancred (ch. 111), Ralph explicitly directs the audience to expect a poetic interpretation of the protagonist's first glimpse of Jerusalem. Here the romantic element does not directly concern Tancred, but is intended to glorify the Holy City, the goal of the crusade itself. Ralph records,

> when he arrived at Jerusalem, he circled the walls, but only after he had freed Bethlehem from the enemy. Getting his first view of Jerusalem from a distance, Tancred greeted her, placed his knees on the ground, fixed his eyes on the city, his heart on heaven, and this is the image of his salvation placed into poetic meter. (ch. 111)

As noted above, the only sustained description in verse of Tancred's participation in the crusade (chs 128–9, 131) concerns his capture and despoliation of the Dome of the Rock complex. Moreover, even here, as mentioned earlier, in the midst of a lengthy verse description of Tancred, Ralph turned to prose (ch. 130), that is, a style intended to portray actual events that took place in the past, to describe the specific quantity of silver taken from the complex and Tancred's use of it to support additional

---

eleventh century may have served as a model for Ralph. See the treatment of Ralph by Emily Albu, *The Normans in their Histories: Propaganda, Myth and Subversion* (Woodbridge, 2001), 16–66, and 176–7.

[25] We have indicated the verse sections of the *Gesta* by displaying them on the page.

[26] In this context, it should be emphasized that Dudo of Saint Quentin, who also wrote his history of the dukes of Normandy in the prosimetric style, provided factual details about Norman military organization in the prose rather than in the verse portions of his text. See Bachrach, 'Dudo', 167–84.

troops. In particular, Ralph notes that Tancred took 7000 marks' weight of silver from the walls. This silver had been beaten into sheets that were about a finger's width in thickness and had been used to cover up the images carved into the walls of the structure. These details, including the amount of booty taken and the artwork uncovered in the process of moving the silver would have been well known to an audience living in Jerusalem and therefore subject to critical comment if Ralph got these details wrong.

In contrast to the very rare appearances of Tancred in versified chapters, he is the subject of or mentioned in just over half of the prose chapters (63 of 121). Moreover, in every instance that Ralph describes Tancred's career as a military commander or territorial prince, he does so in prose. It therefore seems likely that Ralph wished to incorporate certain possibly fictional epic elements into his *Gesta*, particularly heroic battle scenes concerning which he had no reliable or very little eyewitness information. Nevertheless, he did not wish to have his audience perceive either the narrative as a whole or the account of Tancred, in particular, as some sort of fiction of the type traditionally found in epic poetry.

Ralph's Subject Matter

In his preface, Ralph of Caen addresses the question of his subject matter in a straightforward manner, insisting that the deeds (*Gesta*) of princes were a worthy topic in general, and that the recent expedition resulting in the capture of Jerusalem (15 July 1099), carried out by the noble Tancred and, to a lesser extent, Bohemond was of particular merit. In the body of the text, overwhelmingly in the prose sections, Ralph carries through on both of these goals. Ralph's primary interest is Tancred's career and he only focuses on other princes when Tancred holds a subordinate position in military operations under their command. Moreover, even in these circumstances, Ralph stresses his primary obligation to record Tancred's deeds. After, for example, noting the courage of Duke Godfrey of Lotharingia, Count Robert of Flanders, Bohemond, and Count Stephen of Blois during the siege of Antioch, Ralph abruptly changes course emphasizing: 'Normandy and Flanders celebrated their Roberts. The Remainder of the West celebrated their leaders. One son of a marquis (Tancred) is enough for me, although I am not adequate or sufficiently thorough in my treatment of him' (ch. 53). In considering the second point, it should be emphasized that the body of the narrative, as it survives, is focused overwhelmingly on the military campaigns of the First Crusade. It is the subject of 134 of the 157 chapters of the text. By contrast, the period after the capture of Jerusalem on 15 July 1099 through *c.*1105 is covered by only 23 chapters.[27] It should be noted here, however, that Ralph either did not complete the work or the final chapters have not survived.

The primary focus of the *Gesta* on Tancred's career during and after the crusade campaign can be divided into five parts. The primary focus of the first section is on Tancred's service as Bohemond's second in command. This covers the period up to the battle of Dorylaeum on 1 July 1097 (chs 1–32). Ralph begins with an account of Tancred's personal virtues of military valor and profound piety that lead him to give up his life in Norman-dominated southern Italy to take part in Pope Urban II's call for an armed pilgrimage (ch. 1). Ralph then considers in detail Tancred's reaction to a variety of military and moral challenges that, in one instance, bring him into direct conflict with his relative and commander Bohemond. Here (chs 9–13, 17–18), Tancred rejects the decision made by Bohemond and the other crusade commanders to do homage to Emperor Alexios in return for military support and personal wealth, arguing that they are selling themselves into the emperor's service.

The second element in the arc of Ralph's narrative is Tancred's experience as an independent commander operating in eastern Anatolia and Armenia after leaving the main body of crusaders behind (chs 33–47). According to Ralph, Tancred left the main crusader force because he wished to pursue a more direct route to Antioch than the course followed by the larger army, which relied much more heavily on fixed supply lines (ch. 33). During the course of his independent campaign, Tancred successfully captures several cities from their Turkish garrisons, including Tarsus and Mamistra, and also establishes an alliance with Ursinus, the Armenian ruler of the city of Adana, all of which later would be incorporated into the principality of Antioch. During this initial campaign, however, Tancred's efforts repeatedly were undermined by Baldwin, the younger brother of Duke Godfrey and the future king of Jerusalem, who sought to establish his own principality and eventually succeeded in doing so at Edessa. Ralph, however, focuses here on Tancred and virtually ignores the far larger and more successful campaign conducted at this time by Baldwin.[28]

After the relative freedom of action he enjoyed as an independent commander following the battle of Dorylaeum, the siege of Antioch again brings Tancred under the control of the military council composed of the leading princes, including Bohemond and the papal legate Adhemar of Le Puy (chs 48–96). Ralph takes advantage of the siege to portray Tancred's

---

[27] The narrative breaks off during Tancred's siege of Apamea which fell in 1106.

[28] Baldwin, the younger brother of Duke Godfrey and the future king of Jerusalem, founded the first of the crusader states with its capital at the city of Edessa in March 1098.

extraordinary military exploits. However, he does not seek to exaggerate Tancred's importance by depicting him as a member of the crusader leadership. Rather, Ralph portrays his protagonist during this stage of the crusade as a subordinate figure. Bohemond is depicted as more important in this section of the narrative. In addition, Raymond of Toulouse, Robert of Flanders, Godfrey of Bouillon, Robert of Normandy, and even Stephen of Blois are credited with significant military achievements, as well as playing the key leadership roles.

The fourth section of Ralph's narrative takes the crusaders, including Tancred, from the victory over Kerbhoga, the atabeg of Mosul and the leader of the Muslim relief force, beneath the walls of Antioch on 28 June 1098 to the fall of Jerusalem and the subsequent Christian victory at the battle of Ascalon on 12 August 1099 (chs 96–138). Bohemond's decision to consolidate his position at Antioch rather than proceed south to Jerusalem paved the way for Tancred to establish himself as an independent commander. First, Bohemond's action undermined the cohesion of the princes' military council, which had governed the expedition up to this point by alienating Raymond of Toulouse. As a result, Tancred, who up to this point had been subservient to the wishes of the major princes, now had an opportunity to assert himself more freely. This independence was enhanced by the fact that Bohemond was no longer in the field and thus could not exercise directly his earlier claims to Tancred's obedience. Ralph's account of the subsequent campaign, which focuses on the sieges of Marra, Archas and Jerusalem, portrays Tancred as an independent commander, who is the equal of Robert of Flanders, Godfrey of Bouillon, and Raymond of Toulouse. In fact, Ralph describes in some detail Tancred's successful humiliation of Raymond on behalf of Bohemond which led to the complete consolidation of Antioch under the latter's control (ch. 98).

The final surviving section of Ralph's account considers the military and political affairs of the crusader states in the half-dozen years following the crusader victory at Ascalon on 12 August 1099 (chs 139–57). Even more so than in the campaign leading to the capture of Jerusalem, it is here, according to Ralph, that Tancred comes into his own, first as a military commander in the service of Godfrey, the ruler of Jerusalem, and subsequently as the ruler of Antioch and Edessa in place of Bohemond and Baldwin le Bourg. In these roles, Tancred fights a series of campaigns against both Muslim and Byzantine adversaries in which he attempts to undo the damage caused by the capture of Bohemond and Baldwin by the Muslims. Ralph's chronicle breaks off following Bohemond's final departure from the Levant in 1105 and Tancred's subsequent campaigns against the cities of Apamea and Latakia. Either the later chapters, encompassing the final six years of Tancred's career, have been lost or Ralph died before he was able to complete the *Gesta*. It is clear, however, that Ralph was still alive and writing in 1130 since he alludes to the death of Bohemond the Younger who died in that year (ch. 71).

Ralph as an Independent Source

As noted above, Ralph emphasized that he obtained much, if not most, of his information from Tancred, Bohemond, and their men. It is therefore quite reasonable to presume that his account, more so than any of the other Western crusade narratives, provides details about Tancred's campaigns, and his relationships with the other crusade leaders, including his complex association with Bohemond. However, in addition to this focus on Tancred, Ralph also treats a variety of other topics in a manner that is significantly different from the other contemporary Latin histories, written either by those who came to the Levant or by those who remained at home. In this context, Ralph is one of the few authors to pay significant attention to the problems of logistics, in general, and, in particular, to the crucial logistical support that the Byzantines provided to the crusaders.

Ralph first makes note of this help with a subtle reference regarding the capture of Nicaea (ch. 16). Here, when the city was forced to surrender 'it was Gaul which assured it, Greece which helped, and God who brought it about'. Ralph again makes reference to the support provided by the Byzantines in the context of the siege of Antioch (ch. 54). Not only did Byzantine territories such as Cyprus send food but 'Emperor Alexios' herald was there as well urging people to bring grain by land and by sea.' In one final example, Ralph recounts that Duke Robert of Normandy, who took command of the Byzantine garrison at Latakia, was able to use his position to send supplies to the crusader camp at Antioch because the city was being used by the Byzantines as a transshipment point for grain from Cyprus (ch. 58).

Nevertheless, despite his recognition of Byzantine aid to the crusaders, it would not be accurate to describe Ralph either as pro-Byzantine or pro-Alexios. As noted above, much of the first section of Ralph's narrative is dedicated to showing Tancred's firm resolve in rejecting Alexios' blandishments to accept Byzantine leadership and affirm this through oaths of faithfulness while the other crusade leaders, including Bohemond succumbed. When Tancred finally is forced to swear to be faithful to Alexios (ch. 17), Ralph makes clear that his protagonist did so under duress, which, in juridical terms, nullified the oath and absolved Tancred of any obligations he had sworn to undertake. Moreover, Ralph sets the stage for Tancred's later campaigns against the Byzantines by recording the existence of an 'agreement' between the Latins and Alexios in which the latter swore to lead an army to Jerusalem. According to Ralph's quote of Tancred, if Alexios did not do so: 'soon a material breach will occur either because you resent their successes or because you do not aid them in their misfortunes. Let it never happen that I am bound by an oath to anyone who breaks his own word to others' (ch. 58).

In addition to his rather forthcoming discussion of Byzantine support, Ralph also provides a more nuanced view of many of the crusade leaders than is found in the other contemporary accounts. Perhaps most striking in this regard is Ralph's treatment of Stephen of Blois. The *Gesta* does provide an account of Stephen's desertion from the crusade force during the siege at Antioch and his subsequent role in convincing Alexios to abandon the Byzantine relief effort (ch. 72). Nevertheless, Ralph goes out of his way to emphasize several of Stephen's valuable contributions during the siege of Antioch, particularly during a battle against a Muslim relief force (chs 53 and 55). Moreover, even when Stephen does leave the crusader force, before the capture of Antioch, Ralph indicates that the count of Blois was ill and went to Cilicia to regain his health, rather than in order to desert (ch. 58). It may perhaps be suggested that Ralph's restraint in dealing with Stephen was influenced by his Norman connection, namely that the count of Blois was married to Adele, the daughter of William the Conqueror.

Ralph as a Norman Historian

Ralph was, himself, a Norman by birth and his protagonist Tancred was a Norman of the pre-eminent line of Robert Guiscard, which gained its prestige in southern Italy and Sicily. The *Gesta* is not, however, dominated by an interest in 'Normanness' as a positive construct and, indeed, is as much concerned with Gaul (France) as it is with Normandy.[29] This is not to say that Ralph is without praise for Normandy and Normans. Tancred is described explicitly as an 'offshoot of Normandy' (but also of Calabria) when praised for his bravery in battle against Byzantine troops on the Vardar River (ch. 7). Ralph also emphasizes the proud military history of Normandy when discussing the first division of the crusader army as it marched from Nicaea to the fateful battle of Dorylaeum fought on 1 July 1097 (ch. 20). Here, Ralph suggests that Robert of Normandy, Bohemond and Tancred had marched out ahead of the main forces 'as if with one common thought they sought to propagate the unique glory of their fatherland'. It is noteworthy, in this context, that Ralph fails to mention the presence of Robert of Flanders and the Byzantine general Tatikios in this operation, thereby indicating the author's desire to emphasize further the 'Norman' quality or composition of

---

[29] Albu, *The Normans*, 176–7, suggests that Ralph did present a specifically Norman view of the crusade.

the vanguard. On a negative note, Ralph bemoaned the desertion from the siege of Antioch by William, Albert and Ivo of Maisnil because they were from Normandy, which, before this disgrace, had victory everywhere and was the glory of the world (ch. 79). This may be considered the rhetoric of the panegyric effect by which a figure or figures are depicted negatively so that another could be elevated.[30]

In addition, however, to his praise for Norman success before the crusade, and of the Normans who served in the crusade, Ralph repeatedly glorifies the role played by 'Gaul' and the 'Gauls' in the campaign. Peter the Hermit, the enigmatic spiritual leader of the People's Crusade, is made to say in a speech to Kerbhoga, the atabeg of Mosul, that the crusaders would never surrender Antioch because: 'The nobility of Gaul, the pilgrims of Christ, seek the holy sepulcher, and fear nothing because they hold this city [Antioch]' (ch. 81). In describing the preparations of the crusader army for battle against Kerbhoga beneath the walls of Antioch, Ralph makes no mention of Normandy but stresses: 'Then, the bold hearts of Gaul girded themselves for war' (ch. 82). In this vein, during the battle in the streets of Jerusalem, it was the 'Gallic sword' that struck down the Muslim defenders (ch. 132). No mention is made of Norman sword or spear or axe. Similarly, in characterizing the crusader army fighting in the streets of Jerusalem, Ralph records that: 'The strength of the Gauls was both huge and small. They were a small swarm, but a robust swarm' (ch. 133). Again, Ralph does not offer an equivalent characterization of the army using the Normans as synecdoche for the entire force. In one final example, which makes clear Ralph's decision to blur the distinction between Gaul and crusader, Tancred and Arnulf of Chocques, both of whom were 'Norman' are compared with Hector and Aeneas in Vergil's classic formulation of heroic character.[31] In this context, Ralph asserts: 'If the land of Gaul had sent out two other men such as these, the Gauls would hold Memphis (Egypt) and Babylon as kings' (ch. 137).

Principles of Translation

Ralph's style in both his prose and verse sections is characterized by an almost Tacitean brevity, particularly with respect to explanatory phrases and verbs in subordinate clauses. For example, while discussing the attacks on the crusader position by the Turkish garrison holding the citadel of Antioch following the capture of the city, Ralph addressed the problem in a laconic

---

[30] Ibid. 176, Albu characterizes Ralph as a 'Norman chauvinist'.
[31] Vergil, *Aeneid*, 11.285.

verse formulation. Here is his description of the crusaders' efforts to obtain supplies:

> Si sit opus lignis, ut materiam petat ignis,
> Illuc ad sparsas juga mitte bis octo sagittas
> Accipias reduces fluidos sudore jugales.
> Nemo redit vacuus, pharetras implere paratus.
> Ergo aliquam nactos, sed vix utcunque quietam
> Serius infigunt jam Parthica spicula Francos.

> When it was necessary to collect wood for a fire, they had to go a distance of 16 flights of an arrow to do so, and the yoked animals became soaked with sweat. None went without obtaining some arrows for his quiver. Therefore, the [Christians] gained some measure of sleep, but it was hardly ever quiet. Parthian arrows struck at the Franks now in earnest.

As is clear from this passage, it has frequently been necessary to interpret the meaning underlying Ralph's text to a greater extent than is the case with rhetorically more generous authors such as Fulcher of Chartres. In this vein, we have undertaken throughout to provide an account that relies on the principle of *sensus pro sensu* rather than *verbum pro verbo*. In the text, we have marked additions to the text with square brackets []. We have used parentheses () to mark off additional information that will aid the reader's understanding of the text.

In addition to his rather laconic style, Ralph also favored several methods of enlivening his narrative through poetic means in the composition of his prose sections. In particular, Ralph frequently repeated phrases, practiced alliteration, and emphasized his points through the use of parallel phrases. In chapter 10, for example, Ralph wrote concerning Bohemond's decision to accept Emperor Alexios' offer of rewards in return for swearing an oath of loyalty: 'And while the promises weighed on his spirit, and his spirit pressed on the horseman, and the horseman pushed his horse, Bohemond arrived at Constantinople in a few days.'[32]

Both personal and place names present great difficulties in all translations, both because of the multiple orthographic variants in medieval languages (Latin, German, French, Arabic, Turkish and Armenian), and different forms in modern usage, for example, Philip and Philippe. Our principle throughout has been to use those forms that will be the most easily recognizable to Anglophone readers. Thus, most prominently, we have chosen to discuss Ralph of Caen rather than Raoul or Radulfus. In those cases where there is

---

[32] *Gesta Tancredi*, 612, 'dumque fatigant promissa animum, animus equitem, eques caballum, infra dies paucos [Bohemond] Contantinopolim venitur'. Concerning these stylistic devices, see Russo, 'Tancredi e i Bizantini', 209.

no common English usage, particularly in place names, we have chosen the modern form of the name that is current in that location. Thus, for example, we have used Beit She'an for Ralph's Besan (ch. 132). In some cases, however, where there are competing names, we have chosen to use both, including one within parentheses, for example, Suweidijeh and Seutunijeh (ch. 44).

As noted earlier, Ralph wrote his account in a combination of prose and verse. We have indicated the verse portions of the text by centering them on the page. We have not, however, attempted to render the Latin verse into meter.

We have based our translation on the edition of Tancred in *Recueil des historiens des croisades: historiens occidentaux*, vol. III (Paris, 1866). The original edition of the text was established in 1717 by Edmund Martene and Ursinus Durand on the basis of the sole surviving manuscript of the *Gesta* discovered in the monastery of Gembloux in Belgium following a fire that destroyed the library there in 1716.[33] L. A. Muratori produced a second edition of the text in *Scriptores rerum Italicarum*, 5. It was this second edition that served as the basis for the *Recueil* edition of 1866.[34] There is a French translation of the *Gesta* by M. Guizot in Collection des mémoires relatifs a l'histoire de France, 23 (Paris, 1825).[35] This translation, which relies on the earlier edition by Martene and Durand, fails to take note of the improvements to the addition made by Muratori using more advanced codicological techniques.

---

[33] Ms. 5373 Bruxellensis, ol. Gembleaux. The edition is in *Thesaurus novus anecdotorum* 3 (Paris, 1717). Concerning the discovery and edition of the manuscript, see Jean-Charles Payen, 'Une légende épique en gestation: les "gesta Tancredi" de Raoul de Caen', in *La chanson de geste et le mythe Carolingien: mélanges René Louis*, 2 vols, (Saint-Père-sous-Vézelay, 1982), vol. II: 1051–62, here 1058 n. 2.

[34] Although largely the same as Muratori's text, the *Recueil* edition does make some improvements. The manuscript of the *Gesta* suffered some damage between Muratori's edition and the publication of the *Recueil* text, so that the French editors were required to undertake extensive repair efforts which led, in their estimation, to improved readings of several passages, including most prominently chapter 34.

[35] *Faits et gestes du Prince Tancrède*, trans. M. Guizot in Collection des mémoires relatifs a l'histoire de France, 23 (Paris, 1825).

The *Gesta Tancredi*

Preface

It is a noble exercise to recount accurately the deeds of princes. To do so is to consider generously all that is subject to time, to celebrate the dead, to entertain the living, and to set out a past life as a model for later generations. It is to bring back what has happened in the past. When it displays victories, it confers them on the victorious. It eliminates sloth, conveys honesty, presents virtues and draws a crowd. We should, therefore, press forward with the greatest effort to read what has been written and to write down what ought to be read. Thus, in reading old things and writing new, antiquity may be able to satisfy our needs and we may be able to nourish to the fullest the requirements of our posterity.

When considering these matters, I have frequently turned my mind to that joyous pilgrimage, that glorious labor that restored to us our inheritance, that is our mother Jerusalem. That pilgrimage extinguished idolatry and restored the faith (Christianity). Indeed, it would not have been absurd for someone to exclaim, 'behold your sons, o Jerusalem, they have come from afar, and have lifted out of obscurity your daughters namely Joffa and many other places that have suffered ruin'. It is fitting for me to battle on behalf of those who participated in this glorious labor, that is on behalf of Bohemond when he besieged Durazzo, and on behalf of Tancred when a short time later he freed Edessa from a Turkish siege.[1] Both of these men recalled daily the fleeing Turks and the approaching Franks. Sometimes they discussed the deadly enemies and sometimes the captured cities: Antioch that was captured by night through guile and Jerusalem that was captured by day through force of arms.[2] They both called out, 'o fathers, how much has sloth cost us? When was it the highest desire for the old prophets to write? Today, they relate fabulous inventions. Today, they pass over the victories of the army of Christ in silence. Truly a despicable herd, one that should be covered in excrement.' The Norman leaders said these things publicly and often turned their eyes

---

[1] Bohemond defeated Alexios Comnenos at the battle of Durazzo on 18 October 1081.

[2] Antioch was captured on 3 June 1098 and Jerusalem was captured on 15 July 1099.

toward me, for what reason I do not know, as if to say: 'we are speaking to you, we trust you'. Thus, I grew to know both of them, but especially Tancred. No one had a kinder lord, or one who was more generous or charming. In the presence of this very vigorous man, my quiet spirit responded in this manner: 'What you seek as a living man, you will receive once you have been buried, if I should survive. I will not praise you while you live. I will praise you after your death. I will praise you after all is complete. For in this case it will not happen that Tancred will rise up in elation after being praised and that [Ralph] shall fall into the trap of flattering his subject while praising him. The envious man will be silent and the murmurer will become muted when you are dead and when the gifts, which the living use as reward, cease to come to you. So too will fall silent the poisonous voices of the rumor mongers who would cast me in the role of seller and you as the buyer.'

It is for this reason that I delay, and for another as well. Since I am not confident in my skills, I was waiting to see if anyone with a more adept style might address these matters, if anyone more beholden to Tancred might pursue this course. But I have found that some neglect this topic, others are lazy, and still others are whisperers, and, horrible as it is to say, this last group tries to keep the story from being told. Fathers, where is the reverence, where is the liberty, where are the gifts, by which this glory of princes continually illuminated the dark places, absolved the guilty, and enriched those who were without hope? Therefore, I have taken up the burden that was left to me, not because I am worthy of it, but rather because those who were worthy scorned it as unworthy. Indeed, since it is necessary for someone to proceed if he is no longer bound, it is permissible for me to pass on this crude work to later generations.[3]

I predict that benevolent posterity will beautify the plain material which the present has left to me. On this account, o reader, it is fitting for me to beg you for forgiveness and for you, in turn, to pardon me. The language which is now spare will become full and vibrant. Minerva (agriculture), as they say, has degenerated through long neglect.[4] Indeed, since Maro's (Vergil) works have hardly sufficed to reach the summit, my useless tongue fairly babbles.[5] I recognize that I have a poor style. I depend entirely on His strength, that is of Christ, whose standard bearer and triumphs I intend to describe. Therefore, I have chosen you Arnulf,[6] most learned patriarch, as the physician who will cut the excess from my pages, fill in the gaps, illuminate the obscure points,

---

[3] Cf. Horace, *Epistolae*, 1.1.23–6.
[4] Cf. Columella, *On Agriculture, Preface to book 1.*
[5] Maro was the family name of Vergil.
[6] He sent his work to Patriarch Arnulf of Jerusalem. Arnulf obtained the see of Jerusalem after the death of Gibelinus in 1112 and held it until 1118.

and water the dry sections. We know that you are learned in all of the liberal arts. Whatever corrections you make will be particularly sweet to me since as a boy I had you as a teacher when you were in your youth, and now as a man I have chosen you as an old man to be my corrector.

Chapter 1

Tancred's parents, Tancred's royal character, Tancred prepares himself for holy war

Tancred, the most glorious descendant of a renowned clan had extraordinary parents, the marquis[7] and Emma. From his father's side, he was hardly an undistinguished son. However, he was an even more lofty nephew to the brothers of his mother. This second line of his ancestors had earned praise beyond the borders of their region. The brothers of his mother had demonstrated the glory of their military prowess beyond the boundaries of their homeland, that is Normandy. For who has not considered the virtue of Guiscard at the sight of whose victorious banner, they say, both the Greek and the German emperors quailed on the same day?[8] When he was in Rome, he freed her from the German emperor.[9] When Guiscard's son Bohemond conquered the king of the Greeks, Guiscard subjugated the region to his own rule. Guiscard's eleven brothers conquered Campania, Apulia, and even Calabria. Particular mention should be made of Roger who gained the greatest glory among the remaining brothers and took his place second only to Guiscard when pagan Sicily fell to him.[10] But the narrative which has caused me to discuss these matters no longer permits me to delay.

Now I return to Tancred. The wealth of his father's family did not lead him toward wantonness nor did the power of his mother's relatives make him arrogant. As a youth, he surpassed his elders in the practice of arms and in the seriousness of his conduct. He regularly offered new demonstrations of strength of character to both the young and to the old. From this point on, as a zealous adherent to God's commands, he strove to gather and to keep the Lord's commands. Moreover, in so far as his dealings with those of his own

---

[7] Tancred was the son of Marquis Odo the Good. The region that Odo ruled is not known.

[8] This is Robert Guiscard (*c.*1015–85) the Norman conqueror of Sicily.

[9] In 1084, Emperor Henry IV of Germany drove Pope Gregory VII from the city of Rome. Robert Guiscard, the ruler of Sicily and the most important Norman leader in southern Italy, gave sanctuary to Pope Gregory and subsequently drove the German forces out of Rome.

[10] Roger first invaded Sicily in 1061. The final Norman–Lombard subjugation of the island came in 1091.

age permitted, he put into practice the things that he had learned. He did not deign to disparage anyone even when he himself was maligned. For as the herald of hostile action was accustomed to say, 'an enemy is to be borne not to be slandered'.[11] He refused to say anything about himself, but had an insatiable longing to be talked about. He disregarded sleep in favor of watchfulness, quiet in place of labor, satiaty in place of hunger, leisure in favor of work, and indeed everything that was superfluous in favor of what was needed. It was only the glory of praise that moved the spirit of this young man. But in regularly pursuing glory he brought frequent suffering on himself, for he did not spare his own blood or that of his enemy.

Over time, however, his prudent soul raised concerns that caused him anxiety. It seemed that his military life contradicted the Lord's command. The Lord had commanded that after one cheek had been struck the other was to be offered as well. But a secular military life did not even permit the sparing of a relative's blood. The Lord admonished that it is necessary to give over one's cloak, as well, to the one asking for a tunic.[12] By contrast, the necessity of military life urges that once these two garments have been seized, the rest are to be taken as well. These two principles opposed one another and undermined the bravery of a man full of wisdom, if, indeed, they ever permitted him to sleep. But when Pope Urban's decision granted a remission of all sins to all of the Christians setting forth to fight against the pagans, then finally it was as if the vitality of the previously sleeping man was revived, his powers were roused, his eyes were opened and his boldness set in motion.[13]

Earlier, as is noted above, his soul was at a crossroads. Which of the two paths should he follow: the Gospels or the world? His experience in arms recalled him to the service of Christ. This two-fold opportunity for struggle energized the man. Therefore, once the task of going forth had been set, the necessary preparations were quickly made. Nor, indeed, did this man, whose custom it had been from boyhood to have others administer his inheritance, require great expenses. He furnished the military arms, horses, mules, and other goods of this type in quantities sufficient for the number of his fellow soldiers.

---

[11] It is not clear to whom Ralph is referring here.

[12] Cf. Matthew 5:39–40.

[13] Pope Urban II's sermon at Clermont on 27 November 1095 has been the subject of considerable scholarly debate, particularly concerning the content of the pope's promises regarding the spiritual benefits that would accrue to the participants in the expedition to the East. Translations of the five most contemporary accounts of the council at Clermont and Pope Urban's sermon are available in *The First Crusade*, 2nd edn, ed. Edward Peters (Philadelphia, 1998), 25–37.

Chapter 2

Eulogy for Bohemond

There was in those days a hero of great stature whose youth was discussed above. This was Bohemond, the son of that distinguished soldier Robert surnamed Guiscard, who was a vigorous emulator of his father's daring. The same apostolic sermon that stirred the souls of other princes around the world to free Jerusalem from the yoke of the infidels also moved him. The area he ruled included all of the towns and cities from Siponto to Oriolo on the sea. In addition, all of the flatlands and mountainous areas also served him. Moreover, many of the cities and towns of Apulia as well as the highland areas of Calabria also supported him. While serving under his father, he had twice forced the Greek emperor Alexios to retreat. The first time was in the presence of his father beneath the walls of Durazzo.[14] The second time, however, occurred when his father had returned to Rome and he had been left in command of his father's army at Larissa.[15] This victory, just as had been true of the first, brought him a double glory since it permitted the victor, who had been fighting sharply, to pass over the straits in peace.

[Now in this new campaign]he feared the ambushes of the Greeks since they had a habit of attacking even those whom they had earlier invited as guests, and moreover guests who were worthy of receiving gifts. What did these exasperating people want? For what did these people so often defeated strive? For what could their conquerors hope after defeating them? Either destruction had to be wrought on these miserable people, or they had to be made to end their struggle because they feared their own lack of strength. These concerns delayed Bohemond's crossing.[16] Before he left, he immediately forbade anyone to fortify his own property or to leave from any of the ports.[17]

Burning with the same desire as Bohemond, when he heard the news, Tancred's concern both diminished and increased. His fear was diminished because he thought he would be adding his strength to that of another. His

---

[14] The Normans under the command of Robert Guiscard and Bohemond fought the Byzantines under the command of Alexios in June 1081 at Durazzo.

[15] The siege of Larissa took place in 1082–83. Bohemond's victory over Alexios permitted the former to carry out an orderly withdrawal first toward the region of Kastoria and then back to Italy.

[16] This is Bohemond's passage from southern Italy to territories ruled by the Byzantine empire as he marched toward Constantinople to join the other crusaders gathered there.

[17] Bohemond was prohibiting the erection of adulterine fortifications in his territory during his absence, and requiring that all those going on crusade leave from the same port.

fear grew as he considered how to acquire provisions along a path so lacking in supplies.

Chapter 3

Tancred enters into an agreement with Bohemond

After Bohemond made many rich and flattering promises, Tancred agreed that he would fight under Bohemond as his second-in-command, just like a duke under a king. But in addition to these flatteries and rich gifts, two other matters urged him on, namely their close family ties and the difficulty of making the crossing [from Italy to Byzantine territory]. As they shared wine with one another, it was clear that the first of these reasons was bound up in their love for one another and that the second was based on fear. If Tancred did not obey Bohemond, he might easily be accused of jealousy and seem to be worthy of being sent away from the expedition. Finally, because of his gifts and prayers to God, they earned a safe passage.

When both of the Guiscardian offshoots, who exceeded their entire family in energy, were joined together, they set out for Epirus in a loosely arranged fleet.[18] It was Tancred's role to exercise his valor. When he served in the vanguard, he came upon ambushes. When he served in the rearguard of the army, he gave battle to brigands. Whether he proceeded [the army] or followed it, he was always ready, always armed, and took pleasure in being exposed to danger. While others were buried in wine or sleep, he kept watch along the road to temper the heavy snows and hailstorms with his shield. It was a fortunate old woman, weakened by starvation, who was found by Tancred, just as she was about to set her feet on the banks of a flooded river. Food was immediately made available to the starving woman. She was given a horse in place of a boat, and a horseman in place of an oar. Tancred, I say, freely offered himself to serve as this horseman.

Chapter 4

Tancred crosses the Vardar river with his troops. He defeats the Greeks

Under such leadership, this blessed people happily was led to a river which is called the Vardar. After establishing a camp there, they delayed for many

---

[18] Epirus lies on the north-western coast of Greece.

days. The flooding river blocked their advance and the opposite bank, filled with threatening enemies, frightened many [of the Latins]. There seemed to be a fear that those who crossed first would have the turcopoles in front of them and those who delayed would have the turcopoles behind them.[19] But when Tancred saw that the army was muttering, he placed his own life in danger and crossed the river with only a few of his followers. They were forced to go, he went willingly. They were coerced because they feared that a great number of the enemy might fall upon their meager squadron. By contrast, Tancred was worried that while he went into battle the enemy would turn in flight. Boldness brought victory, but they went without spoils, that other prize of victory. Once they had crossed the river, they stopped both because of their desire to gather spoils and because of their foreboding regarding another fear.

When the small size of the Latin force became clear to the multitude of ambushers, it seemed to the Greeks that the Latins were ignorant of their hiding places and had come to collect booty rather than to fight. The Greeks therefore came out from their hiding places and shot a terrible flight of arrows. While the arrows flew they had the appearance of a cloud, when they fell it seemed like hail, and where they stood, they seemed like a field of grain. But the Greeks, despite having launched many attacks, did not reach the Franks. Tancred, who was familiar with every manner of fighting, did not resist them quickly, rapidly, or all at once, but rather step by step. When an arrow struck about a spear's throw away he headed toward it so that the others might fall behind his back. Tancred was well versed in this type of battle from many contests and therefore recognized how to gain victory. So, he held back the unbridled spirits of his men through his prudence.

After they had borne the enemy attacks, his men redeemed their patient delay. They loosened their reins, they used their spurs, they shook their spears. Their morale undermined by this demonstration, the lightly armed Greeks were not able to withstand the charge. As the spears charged on, the bows of the Greeks, which had been their means of protection, now were transformed into a burden. For when it came to fighting with swords, the archers lost their value. Lacking shields and spears, the Greeks suffered wounds and did not inflict them in return. Without any doubt and without any mediation, these pitiable men were headed for immediate flight or to their deaths. They were pitiable. But just as they had not shown mercy to anyone, now they were not worthy of pity by anyone. This weak people was struck down and was taught not to make any further assumptions based on the small number of Franks. Rather, they learned that 100 of them were not equal to one.

---

[19] Turcopoles were light cavalry, often of Middle Eastern origin.

Tancred opened the path with his sword. He cut down anyone whom he intended to kill. The markers left in his wake made it easy for those following him. Half-dead bodies filled the banks on both the right and left with a middle channel of blood. There was no room to maneuver. Rather, [Tancred's men] could only follow along in the path of the killer. Here was the killer himself although it seemed that he had poured out his own blood rather than that of his enemies. Covered in blood, his appearance denied that this was Tancred but his work spoke for him. In the same manner, his young companions followed his lead in pursuing the enemy, in killing them, and cutting them down so that each one bloodied the field according to his own abilities.

Chapter 5

The Greeks attack the part of Bohemond's army that had not yet crossed the river

Therefore, Bohemond's army, which up to this point had remained inactive on the opposite bank of the river after sending Tancred ahead, finally ended its delay when it saw that the Greeks were retreating. Some swam across the river and others, having been taught to row, crossed in boats. Still others, who were ignorant of both these arts, used the tails of their horses in place of oars. Thus, this whole multitude crossed in a short period of time with the exception of about 600 who waited to be carried across.[20] These were not the heavily armed mounted troops or the heavily armed infantry, that is those who could charge into the enemy's ranks or who could repel such a charge. This was a lightly armed crowd with the exception of those heavily armed infantry whom old age or sickness had debilitated. Then the Greeks, who had been sent to follow the trail of the Latins, stumbled onto this place and rushed upon the remaining men in order to wet their swords with blood just as wolves slaughter sheep who have been deprived of their shepherd and dogs.

There was a clamor and grieving on both banks and there was no lack of cries or groans in either place. On the closer shore, the men suffered for their delay, on the further shore the men suffered for their speed. The men on the further shore were shamed by their inability to attack. The chagrin was even greater for those on the closer shore because it was not possible for them to escape. Tancred, who was at this time closely pursuing the fleeing Greeks, received an urgent message from those who rushed after him. There was no way to offer resistance, there was no means of offering support. The heavily

---

[20] It seems likely that Bohemond's army was well equipped with boats, probably confiscated from local villages along his line of march.

armed troops were on this side of the river and the lightly armed were on the other. Moreover, Tancred's men were scattered about almost as if they had been routed.[21] After these matters were brought quickly to the attention of the most pious and manifest leader, he bravely moved among the groups of men. He was like a lioness who has come upon prey, but who having left her young behind, catches sight of the traps that have been set for her. Thus, having turned from her path toward the poacher, she leaves the prey, as her gullet is already dry with worry.

Chapter 6

Jumping into the river, Tancred puts the Greeks to flight

Tancred therefore returned to the river and, spurning a boat, jumped into the whirling water. His horse took the place of a boat and oars. It seemed to him that it would be a foul delay and a recognition of fear should he expect his heavily armed mounted troops to follow while he prepared a ship. Therefore, just as noted earlier, the leader entered the river as if it were a field. The waters rose around the exceptional man with a rapid current. But soon, he reached the opposite bank unharmed. The battle line of his fellow soldiers followed on the heels of their pathbreaking lord using boats. The Greek foot soldiers, who were terrified both by the approach and by the name of Tancred for the men on both banks were calling out his name, ended their killing because of their fear of death. Thus, they took flight toward their accustomed refuge. They fled over broken ground and into pathless areas, to anywhere that seemed to offer a place of hiding for those who had been defeated and seemed to deny access to their conquerors. The victor nevertheless pursued them closely thirsting even more for the blood of those whose feet carried them rapidly over the broken ground. For none of those who had been vanquished wished to turn around unless, having been caught, he found it necessary to beg for mercy at the knees of the victor.

Thus, anger weakened, rage slackened, and all hope turned from arms to the swiftness of feet. The Greeks found their greatest solace in throwing aside their bows, casting off their quivers, dropping their shields, and stripping off their body armor. As a consequence, a vast quantity of polished goods, ransomed at great price, borne with enduring effort, whose workmanship enriched both the roads and the trackless areas, waited for victorious hands to seize them without any price or struggle. Nor was there any lack of those to

---

[21] Ralph is commenting here on the breakdown in discipline among Tancred's troops as they broke ranks to pursue the fleeing Byzantine soldiers.

pick up these items and pursue the fleeing mob once Tancred's name was heard. Since the survivors of the aforementioned slaughter, whom the arriving defenders had liberated, were still present, those who fled in disorder were followed in disorder, and those who were unburdened followed those who were burdened, and those who were stripped naked followed those who were armed, and those who had been set free pursued those who were exhausted. Many were led into servitude. Those whose bonds had been broken now bound those who had been their captors. Some sought after the goods that had been stolen from them. Others sought out both their own goods and those that had been thrown away by their ravagers. Still others, while they sought for the goods they had lost, also looked to make gains and kept what they found. Still others threw away things they had taken so that they might gather something better. However, whether burdened with his own goods or with those of another, no one returned to camp without carrying a full load.[22]

Chapter 7

News of Tancred's victory spreads

After avenging the wounds suffered by his fellows, obtaining booty, and having been blessed by grace, Tancred ordered everyone to cross the river. He followed, the last of all. How great was the praise that he received! How much more would he be in the hearts of everyone! How much was he revered by nobles and the commons alike! Certainly, this was the view of everyone and the talk that went around: 'Where and when, and who among the sons of man is equal to you Tancred! Who is so far removed from sloth, from rest, and fear? Who has so rid himself of arrogance and lust? Who can be summoned faster, from whom can requests be made with more ease, who is easier to placate after he has been offended? They are happy with your ancestor's token, they are pleased with the ancestor of such a successor, they are pleased with this student of Calabria and with this offshoot of Normandy!

'Those whom you have touched with your glory are happy. But we are happier still, we for whom your boldness has stood as a wall. Your boldness is a shield against our attackers, a bow and a sword against those assailing us. If danger precedes us, you go ahead. If it follows us, you remain behind. Blessed is the Lord who keeps you as the citadel for his people, and you are blessed who protect his people with the strength of your arm.' And everyone

---

[22] This victory took place on Ash Wednesday on 18 February 1097.

frequently repeated this magnificent praise in order to give thanks to the victor both while on the march and while in camp.

They even continued in the presence of Tancred himself. From this point on, Tancred seemed to mix freely and to act in an easygoing manner. It seemed that to be without him in the army was to be alone rather than in an army. As a result, many were expecting even greater things than the great things that they already had seen and transferred both themselves and their followings to his command. He gained the boldness and strength of the youths for a price, he attracted them by his merit and earned them by his example. He was so wealthy that no one who fought for him was in want. When he was in need, he sought a loan from his richer supporters. Then, he alleviated the indigency of the poor men with the money he had sought. If someone asked for the return of what had been loaned, he sought out other creditors. And so, he was in a position of begging on behalf of others, so to speak, even when war and booty had enriched him. In this manner, this prudent man showed himself to be generous to the poor and as truthful to the creditors, and thus as generous and as truthful to all.

Chapter 8

The approach of Bohemond and Tancred to Emperor Alexios and the announcement of victories

In the meantime, a messenger who had been dispatched earlier, returned and disturbed Emperor Alexios with the following account or something like it:

'Bohemond, the son of Guiscard, has crossed the Adriatic and taken possession of Macedonia. You have often experienced the great power of this man. However, his strength today surpasses that of former times no less than the strength of an eagle surpasses that of the sparrow. Now, at the same time, he provided himself with heavily armed mounted troops from Normandy and with foot soldiers from Lombardy. The Normans who were accustomed to gain victory and the Lombards, who increased their numbers, could be drawn up in battle. The first of these peoples came as fighting men while the latter came as levies. Both were warlike, but there were only two groups and only a few men in each. Moreover, they had come for pay, or had been obligated by law rather than by their freewill. They fought, but they were not avid for glory.[23]

---

[23] This passage refers to Robert Guiscard's campaign against the Byzantines 1080–85.

'Now, by contrast, all of Gaul has been roused and Bohemond has arrived after gaining the support of all of Italy. No region on this side of the Alps from Illyricum to the ocean refused arms to Bohemond. Heavily armed mounted soldiers, archers, slingers, as well as his own large force left no room in his army for crowds of noncombatants. The bread on this side of the sea was insufficient for his troops. Stores were seized from the warehouses of this land, not to mention that the lightly armed people passed from leisure to labor and that abundance passed into privation.[24] All of the troops, all of the fighting men, all of the craftsmen, all of them waited in the Guiscardian camp. Add in as well the Guiscardians, Tancred and his brothers William and Robert, who have the same ferocity as Phoenician lions, related to Bohemond both by their common ancestry and by their eagerness for war. This time, moreover, he did not coerce any of them as had been true in the past. This time, Bohemond came here after having been coerced by all of their requests. And it rarely happens, if ever, that those whom one will, one intention and one desire, have brought together, can be split apart.'

Chapter 9

Alexios' letters to Bohemond

After the shrewd emperor was stunned by this news, new schemes turned in his breast as a result of the new suffering in his heart.[25] He strove to tangle in nets the lions whom he dared not attack with a hunting spear. Therefore, he loaded his messengers with ruses and they went with blandishments of the following type to meet Bohemond who was approaching [Constantinople].

'King Alexios to Bohemond, greetings. I have received news of your arrival with paternal pleasure since you have now undertaken a task worthy of your heritage by turning your eagerness for war against the barbarians. As I see it, God has favored the undertaking of the Franks since he undertook to strengthen them with such a great companion. Your approach promises in its own right an answer to my desires. For although I shall remain silent on other matters, the very prophets of the Turks foretell your victory over their people. It is well, therefore, for you to hurry my son and by coming thereby bring an end to the delays of those leaders here with me who await you. The leaders and the magnates and all the people long for you.

---

[24] Likely a reference to the recruiting of peasants to serve in the army as lightly armed troops.

[25] Cf. Vergil, *Aeneid*, 1.657, 'But Cythera conceives new schemes, new plans in her breast' (*At Cytherea novas artes, nova pectore versat consilia*).

'The Latin heroes are with me and they have been granted generous gifts. But as you are so much better known to me than they, so too you, who have remained behind, will receive even greater gifts. Here, there are garments, gold, horses and all the remaining abundance of the treasury for you. Whatever you have seen anywhere else, it is as nothing in comparison to what is collected here. You should know that everything here is ready for you as if for a son if you are ready to be good and faithful to me like a son. You will find a font of gold such that however much you seek to consume, you will find this much again and it can be consumed over and over again without any difficulty. Should you begin to set a faster pace, content with only a few men, you will finish your journey more easily. Leave behind the other forces and commanders, the road will be easier and should be taken by him who is the more senior.'[26]

Chapter 10

Bohemond, who has been seduced by Alexios' promise, is forced to offer him homage

The legates, who were instructed by Alexios in lies beyond their own skills, left Constantinople, arrived at Bohemond's camp, delayed there, and spoke to the Norman leader. Bohemond, who was captivated by the superficial sweetness of these words, did not sense the poison hidden below the surface. Furthermore, the promise of the riches of Constantinople, for which he had long shed blood on land and sea, led him astray. He was pleased that these things had been offered so easily since he had not gained them in his long struggles against the Greeks. Thus, it was agreeable to him that he proceed with a few men, in the manner that had been suggested, and that Tancred should follow after with the remaining large force. What had happened was not displeasing to the ears of the son of the marquis. For he shuddered at these events as being the familiar deceit of the Greeks with the same zeal that the sparrow hawk rejects its bonds and the fish rejects the hook. After rejecting the king's gifts, Tancred contrived a means of escaping the king's presence.

Bohemond, after he had decided whom he found worthy of bringing with him and whom he would leave behind, departed from a town that is called Ipsala. And while the promises weighed on his spirit, and his spirit pressed on the horseman, and the horseman pushed his horse, Bohemond arrived at

---

[26] Ralph would seem to be indicating here that he had access to letters that were written by Emperor Alexios to Bohemond some two decades before Ralph wrote the *Gesta*.

Constantinople in a few days. There, he was brought to Alexios and was subjected to him by a yoke that commonly is called homage. He was forced to accept this yoke. However, he was given a portion of the Roman empire as a gift which was so large that a horse would require 15 days to cross its length and eight to cross its breadth.[27] There was no delay then in the speeding of the news to Tancred about what happened with the additional note: 'There is a similar gift waiting for you who are following along. There is a lesser reward for those whose wages are lower.'

Chapter 11

Tancred secretly groans at Bohemond's situation

When he heard what had happened, Tancred felt sorrow for Bohemond and feared for himself. Seeing that unbroken line of fire that lay nearby, he did not doubt that it would soon threaten him.[28] So he considered, and thought, and reflected on the means by which he could avoid this danger, and by which arts he might deceive the emperor, and with which of his strengths he might punish the suffering that this perfidious king had caused. As he set out, on one side were his men and on the other the emperor's deceits, here boldness, there power; here his soldiers, there riches; here the few, there the multitude. What could he work out? Should he fight? But the enemy was stronger. Should he seek an accommodation? But the enemy was inexorable. Should he retreat? But the sea blocked his path.

Seeing that the leaders of the Franks had been corrupted by gifts and that Bohemond similarly had been ensnared, he struggled with himself and turned these matters over in his heart. 'O evil fate! Where is the faithfulness? Where is the prudence? O heart of man! What perfidy and improvidence! Not ashamed to do harm, unheedful of knowledge, the man leaves having been summoned as a son to receive riches, to be embraced in paternal favor. He comes to the kingdom and finds a yoke. He comes so that he might rise higher. But he is forced to subsume himself among others. He has been made more humble. Certainly, he was ignorant of the fraud. He believed the fraudulent

---

[27] The details of this offer, if Alexios really made it, are not repeated in other crusade accounts. The territory envisioned here, if we estimate an average of 30 miles per day traveled on horseback, would comprise 94 500 square miles – an absurdly large territory for the emperor to have promised any subordinate, much less one who had been engaged just ten years before in an effort to conquer the Byzantine empire.

[28] Cf. Horace, *Epistolae*, 1.18.83–4; 'For your own property is equally at risk when your neighbor's is burning, and neglected fires are accustomed to spread' (*nam tua res agitur paries cum proximus ardet et neglecta solent incendia sumere viris*).

blandishments. But he was ordered to proceed with a few men leaving his army behind as if it were fitting for him to be freed from the burden of a mob. Surely this alone should have been sufficient for us to have seen through the emperor's words as coming from the font of iniquity. If the mind had not been perverse, it would have avoided the traps and the blocked roads.'[29] However, Bohemond had only a few companions. And those under his leadership were lightly armed even if they did not lack arms entirely.

But what shall I say of the leaders of Gaul who found it fitting not only to subject their own large forces to the yoke of homage but who even subjugated those who had rebelled against this yoke? I ought to have pity for such people and feel shame for those who lack both pity and shame. I see the end of this thing. Having accepted these treasures, punishments, poverty and suffering are to follow. There will be suffering for the people. When the present money runs out there will be no renewal of the emperor's promises. There will be suffering when the people see that they are forced to commit unjust acts, that they are coerced into accepting burdens, and that they are not able to escape them.

Then, I say, there will be suffering. But what is the purpose of this suffering when there is no means of correction? For what further means of correction are there? Was it ever possible to abjure an oath once it has been sworn? Was it ever the case that those who subjected themselves to a foreign will were able to live by their own law? Are those who have been sold ever freed? Is it more just for one to serve who was purchased after serving as his own seller, or would it be more just if he were produced as an item for sale after being collected as booty? It is therefore fitting that those who are content for the present and unconcerned about the future to pay the penalty.

Chapter 12

Tancred flees from meeting Alexios

After bemoaning Bohemond's situation, Alexios' schemes, and the yoke imposed on the leaders of Gaul, Tancred wisely discerned that to flee would comfort the former and punish the latter. Therefore, when he approached Constantinople, he did not come to the king as the others had done, nor did he send out trumpeters before him, nor did he have the horns sounded. He crossed [the Bosporus] in secret. He took off the equipment of a heavily armed mounted soldier and dressed like a foot soldier. Thus, dressed in rustic clothing he disguised Tancred and fooled Alexios. After he left Europe on a

---

[29] Vergil, *Aeneid*, 2.54.

boat, the north wind filled the sails with driving urgency and he arrived in Asia. The Guiscardian summoned his sailors to their oars and passed by ship from the cerulean Hellespont. Nor, as the helm was fixed on the desired shore, was there any delay among those hurrying since speed favored the desired course of those hurrying along. Having reached the Asian shore, the son of the marquis took back his clothing and his name since he was now safer. And thus, the count added himself to the other leaders who were heading to Nicaea.[30]

Bohemond had not yet left the Thracian shore. He delayed at the request of Count Raymond of Saint-Gilles. Necessity compelled the latter to delay and interrupt his journey, because the aforementioned king wished to impose on the count, who had arrived later, the same law by which he had obligated those who had come before. But the count responded in a good-natured manner that he refused this condition even at the cost of his own life. Bohemond's arrival was very helpful to him in maintaining this view. Therefore, when Alexios learned from his scouts that Tancred had secretly crossed over, he was annoyed that he had been fooled and demanded from those who were present that he see the one who was absent. He reckoned that Tancred had cleverly escaped him through their deceit. His eyes, which his anger had made hostile, were turned especially toward Bohemond. As these thunderbolts were falling and as he was making threats in his throat, Bohemond, whether he wished to or not, swore that he would bring Tancred's hands to do homage to the king, and that Bohemond would not remain safe or leave until he had done this.[31]

Chapter 13

Tancred sends messengers to Bohemond

While these events were going on, Tancred sent two heavily armed mounted soldiers named Attropius and Guarinus back to Constantinople. They rebuked Bohemond for his delays and reported that the Turkish forces were approaching. Unless he hurried, his hopes would be dashed and they would certainly be overcome by the enemy. This message could not be delivered without Alexios finding out. He summoned the messengers into his presence so that he might deal with them concerning their lord. It was as if he thought that he might extract something new because of their fear of being in his presence. The men were asked whom they served, whence they had come, and

---

[30] This is one of only two times that Tancred is called a *comes* in the text.

[31] Cf. *Gesta Francorum et aliorum Hierosolymitanorum*, ed. and trans. Rosalind Hill (London, 1962), 12.

for what purpose they had been sent. They confidently responded that they were Normans who had been sent by Tancred to summon Bohemond. When the king saw that he could not frighten the brave messengers, he sent them away unpunished because he realized that imposing a punishment on them would be useless to him.

When Tancred heard what had happened, first from the returning messengers, and then from Bohemond who followed after them, Tancred took the news so badly that it is not easy to discuss or to believe. This illness came about because of the indolence of others that ruined his own painstaking vigilance. A blazing furnace could not contain the flames of his anger. They surged as if through the rapid whirlwind motion of rumor. The present quarrel led him to groan: 'Alas, the minds of mortals are blind to the future! Since they seemed to have destroyed themselves it is fitting to begin anew. Prudence is in vain when opposed by hostile fortune. It is pointless to struggle against those whom the fates favor. I thought that I had made sufficient provision for myself and that nothing had been left to laziness or folly. I spurned the money, set out alone, fooled the guards and avoided the traps. I was able to do what others were not. What a great feat it was to pass as an enemy unharmed through the snares which even the innocent were not able to pass without some injury.

'I saw noblemen, some from ducal and others from royal lineage who had left their kingdom in voluntary exile. These peaceful men had come to frightful places and barbarian kingdoms which were turned against them. Neither the land nor the sea stood in their way. At the same time a wind arose which was a monster no less cruel than the triform chimera.[32] There was no Pegasus to set free those who were trapped nor was there anyone who could carry away the bewildered.[33] All were forced to cross as if under the threat of a divine spear, to swear all of those things which they were ordered. If I might return to my own experience, I feared the strict exactor of merit, the strictest avenger. Thus, it was fitting for me who had been saved that the more vigilant I became the more that a great zeal for vengeance burned in me. It was for this reason that I rejected the routine of the army camp, and I even disguised myself so that I would not give in as the others had done. Thus, I would remain free to avenge their anger. For what is gained by complaining about a man who leads me back to the shackles I have broken? It was not enough that he has bound his own neck, he would bind mine as well. His mouth perhaps denies that he is jealous of my good fortune, but it is evident from his lips that this oath trickles out from the font of jealousy and the end proves it.

---

[32] The chimera was the mythic beast composed of parts from a lion, goat and serpent, which was killed by Bellerophon.
[33] Pegasus was the winged horse of Greek mythology.

'Some question remains in this matter whether it was sloth or ignorance which drove me into sadness. Certainly, both were great and both were the stepmothers of my unhappiness. But Bohemond swore that he had been forced to participate in my ruin, as if he could hide his jealousy with these words, mitigate my indignation, excuse the deed and absolve the actor. He said these things so that they might demonstrate his innocence. But they could not make his delays innocent nor could they defend from their crime those who were somnolent in their delays. Truth be known, I will keep my oath and redeem my perjury. And, at a danger to myself, I will redeem the perjury of another. After having escaped, I was overcome but not by my own carelessness. Rather, I was captured by the weakness of another, by the liberation of a relative. Should I survive, the victor in this struggle has brought out my hatred and there is no room for peace. I consider it a small matter to violate that which I did not seek to swear but which was rather forced on me unwillingly by the violence of a tyrant, especially as the keeping of this promise would be a public scandal and worthy of general condemnation.'

Chapter 14

The siege of Nicaea and the first mention of the besieging dukes: Godfrey of Bouillon

After the son of the marquis had gone over the matters about which he had reason to complain, he rested for a short time. It is therefore fitting to mention that Nicaea was ringed by a siege and that camps had been laid out, and to recall the names, families and practices of the princes who were attacking the city. They were men of the sort who would not exclude the types of praise discussed above, but who also offer further material for writers. These were very famous leaders who provided instruction in war to those who refused to learn from any others. These men were as follows: Duke Godfrey, son of old Count Eustace of Bouillon.[34] Godfrey, received from his father the dignity of the ducal title and the name Bouillon. Bouillon is a town in the kingdom of Lotharingia and the capital of the nearby duchy that the old Duke Godfrey, his uncle, had left to the younger Godfrey.[35] The nobility of the younger man was marked by many virtues, both secular and divine. These included, charity to the poor, mercy to wrongdoers, humility, clemency,

---

[34] This is Eustace II, count of Bouillon from 1049–93.

[35] The older Godfrey, also known as Godfrey the Hunchback, was the brother of Duke Godfrey's mother Ida. The elder Godfrey died in 1076, and the duchy was granted to the younger Godfrey by King Henry IV of Germany.

sobriety, justice and chastity. In fact, the duke demonstrated more of the qualities of a monk than he did of a soldier. However, he was not less experienced in secular virtues. He knew how to wage war, to arrange a line of battle and to find glory in arms. As a youth, he was first or among the first in learning to kill the enemy. He grew more skilled as a young man and did not give up his practice as a mature man. Thus, as the son of a fighting count and a most religious countess, even when he had been observed by a rival he deserved to hear: 'in his eagerness for war look to the father, in his cultivation of God behold the mother'.[36] Innumerable fighting men undertook the siege at the walls of the aforementioned city at the side of this duke who was marked by these traits. He was the first one there.

Chapter 15

Count Robert of Normandy, Bohemond, Hugh the Great, Count Stephen of Blois, Count Robert of Flanders, Count Raymond of Saint-Gilles, a survey of the leaders of the expedition

Next came Count Robert of Normandy,[37] the son of King William the Conqueror of England. He was not inferior to the duke in family, wealth, or eloquence, rather he was his superior. He was his equal in those matters pertaining to Caesar, but inferior to him in those matters pertaining to God. His piety and his generosity were certainly marvelous. But because he was moderate in neither, he erred in all other aspects of life. Indeed, Normandy understood that his mercy was no mercy. While he ruled he spared neither man nor God but rather gave free rein to rapine and robbery. For as count he judged that he owed the same respect to the hands of murderers, to the gullet of thieves and to the salacious desire of the adulterous as he did to his own affairs. As a result, no one was brought to the count bound and in tears without an immediate order for the bound man to be released as tears poured from the ruler. Thus, as I said, Normandy complained at this time that there was no brake on evildoers and, in fact, they had been given an additional incentive. But it is also clear that largess was a little sister of this sense of mercy so that he would purchase a sparrow hawk or dog for any amount of silver. At the same time, the count's treasury was supported by plundering his citizens. These things, however, happened within his own territory. When he went beyond his borders, he tamed the great part of his luxurious lifestyle on which he had earlier spent a great deal of his wealth.

---

[36] Godfrey's mother was named Ida.
[37] Robert II, duke of Normandy, 1087–1106

Third in this order shines Bohemond. It would be superfluous to repeat his genealogy and premature to discuss his pattern of behavior and personality. This is especially true since the pages above dealt with his family and those below will deal with both his fortunes and misfortunes just as if the whole work turned on a hinge.

Hugh the Great, the brother of King Philip of France and the son of Henry (King Henry I of France) holds fourth place.[38] He was great in his family, in his sobriquet, in his honesty, and he was also great and powerful because of the military forces provided both by himself and by his brother the king. Nevertheless, he was more venerable for his royal blood than because of the extent of his wealth, the excellence of his large body of troops, or by the merits of his military victories.

Fifth is the count of Blois, Stephen by name, who was himself a relative of kings, a great-grandson of the king of the Gauls and of the family of the kings of the English.[39] And if he took more joy in his generosity and he was more fervent in his audacity than was required, these factors make clear that he lacked nothing necessary for leadership and nothing required of an exceptionally vigorous soldier.

Following after him was Count Robert of Flanders – Flanders the nurturer of horsemen, Flanders the fertile home of horses, Flanders of Ceres, Flanders home of cultivators, Flanders which excelled in her maidenly beauty and merited the royal lineages of Gaul, England and Denmark.[40] This present count, who was bound by family ties with those mentioned earlier, was praised above all the other leaders of the army for his skill with the sword and spear. But he shrank from taking a leadership role. As a result, he gained much more renown than the other leaders as a soldier but much less as a leader since he avoided the worries of command.

The last of all to appear at the siege was Count Raymond of Saint-Gilles.[41] He was last, I say, in time, but not in wealth, nor power, nor wisdom, nor in the great strength of his large military force. For of all of them, he was distinguished from the beginning among the leaders. And soon, when the money of the others had given way, his increased, and he excelled the others in wealth as well. His family was too frugal and was not generous. They served parsimony rather than fame. His family was frightened by the example of others and, unlike the Franks, strove to increase its wealth rather than give

---

[38] King Henry I of France, Hugh's father, reigned 1031–60. King Philip I of France, Hugh's elder brother, reigned 1060–1108.

[39] Stephen of Blois had married Adel, the daughter of William the Conqueror.

[40] Count Robert II of Flanders (1065–1111), succeeded his father Count Robert I (d. 1093).

[41] Raymond IV of Saint-Gilles (*c.*1043–1105), succeeded his brother William as count of Toulouse in 1088.

it away. Thus, wise in useful matters and understanding of the future, this people did not permit the country to be in want. He was a man who cultivated justice, who was an avenger of injustice, he was a lamb to the timid and a lion to the arrogant.

Chapter 16

The city is surrounded. Tancred is the first one of all to kill a Turk and to pursue the others

Thus, when Nicaea was surrounded, attacked and finally forced to surrender by the attackers, it was Gaul that assured it, Greece that helped and God who brought it about. While the most recent arrival Count Raymond, as I mentioned, established his camp before the eastern gate this was the only area that was open after the others had been occupied, behold a Turkish army appeared descending through a pass in a nearby mountain as if it intended to enter the city through this gate and wished to overcome the besiegers with a swift assault. A clamor went up. The count, as the closest one to the spot, was the first to offer resistance. Soon the other leaders arrived. Some were in armor and others were only partially armed. As the ardor of battle drove them on, they hurried forward. Tancred, who was far off, flew there on his horse burning for action since the location of his camp denied him the glory of inflicting the first wound. But whatever distance had taken away, his spirit returned to him, for during his absence, retreat and attack caused both fear and hope, first among them and then among us. But when he, who as one man was taken for a multitude and as a single soldier was taken for and actually was an entire battle line, rushed upon the scene, the neck of the Turks was broken at that spot. Tancred raised up the morale of the soldiers of Christ and transformed the enemy into women. Thus, losing their will, the Turks headed toward the mountains in retreat with the Franks at their back.

Boldness, the count (Tancred), the flight of the enemy, and fear of delay drove the emboldened troops to pursue those who were fleeing. If the asylum of the nearby mountain had not suddenly received the refugees, a short time later the spear tips of the Latins would have drunk their fill of barbarian blood. Because they were suddenly taken by a fear of death, whose characteristic it is to add wings to the feet, it was easy to evade pursuit by ascending those paths which they had used in their attack, with the exception of that soul that Tancred had sent down into Hell as an example of his bravery.

Many returned home, however, with dishonorable wounds on their backs. The Christians returned joyfully to camp. Some had bloody blades, others blades that were curved [taken as booty]. Some carried broken spears and still others held blunted swords. The Turk's head was presented as a spectacle to the crowd. Tancred was celebrated by all the people of the army, whatever their language, age, sex or profession, both as the first taker of a Turkish head and as the pursuer of countless others. This was not without some premonition of the future for Tancred. Anyone who paid close attention might see what would happen. It was fitting that heavenly signs of this sort be given for this man since he was now, or rather, long since had been chosen to go forth as the most indomitable of all in war and never to be overcome in battle.

Chapter 17

The city is surrendered. Tancred is brought before Alexios. Tancred's words to the emperor

After the brave deeds of the besiegers, the besieged saw that they had been deprived of the aid which they long had sought. At the same time they grew terrified because Count Raymond, as the last one to have begun mining the walls, was causing the undermined foundation to shake even more strongly. As a result, the Turks would hand over the city under this condition, namely that they be permitted to keep the booty they had taken on previous occasions. This condition was acceptable to both sides and so a message was sent to the emperor for him to send a body of troops to garrison the city.[42] However, the emperor was disturbed by this happy report. He sent out reinforcements and personally followed them up to the gulf which commonly is called the arm of Saint George.

After the city had been garrisoned, Bohemond, who was bound by agreements, pacts of friendship and by a sworn oath of homage, sailed to [Alexios]. Furthermore, just as he had promised, he brought the son of the marquis with him. However, since this homage brought Alexios more fear than comfort, and made him more dejected than elated, he appeared exaggerated in his anger rather than as a figure who would command reverence. For just as he had been instructed by the divine oracle, this prudent man feared those events which were to come rather than the results of the matters already settled.[43] The great strength of the Greek kingdom would not capture Jerusalem. The cities of this great area that were captured from the Turks would be given back to the care of Christ. But it was not appropriate to

---

[42] The city was captured on 20 June 1097.
[43] Ralph's use here of the expression 'divine oracle' is probably designed to give a further classicizing cast to his work.

hand over these captured cities to such defenders as the Greeks. It was the Franks who alone were capable of this type of protection. It was not possible to serve two lords, namely the common good and the king of the Greeks.[44]

Turning these matters over in his mind, the prudent man [Tancred] filled the king's ears with similar types of complaints: 'My blood relative Bohemond, compelled by your power, o emperor, forced me to come back here. If your promises and your gifts and your friendship had bound me, there would be no dearth of paths for my return. But when these other efforts fail, trying to please me by being in your presence is a vain effort. Considering these matters, I strove to pass beyond your power and to be free of you. But, after having been freed by my own efforts, your violence brought me back here unwillingly. As a consequence, you may know and must believe that I will regret whatever it is I am forced to do today. Having warned you in these matters, it is fitting to bring your attention to the following as well. Behold, it has come to this that I break the oath of alliance sworn by my relative. The law stands between us, that you set out for Jerusalem and provide aid, as it states in the agreement, or that soon a material breach will occur either because you resent their successes or because you do not aid them in their misfortunes. Let it never happen that I am bound by an oath to anyone who breaks his own word to others. Therefore, if you wish to rule, strive to serve and you can be certain of Tancred's service when you have made clear that the army of Christ is your own. If you are the common leader, in the interest of everyone I will not refuse to serve you. This short discussion sets out the most important of these matters. To the extent that your devotion precedes the Franks, the Greeks will see that my own devotion shall follow them.'

After these statements were drawn from the depths of his heart, from the tabernacle of his prudence and from the abode of his wisdom, this spirit that faithfully interceded for the common good was praised on all sides because it did not fear to intercede on his own behalf and did not shrink from justice. A great clamor of support arose among the Gauls, and the murmurs of the Greeks did not shrink from giving him the favor he deserved.

---

[44] It would appear that Tancred is saying here that Alexios stands opposed to the *res publica* and is therefore a tyrant, as the emperor is called earlier in the text in chapter 13. This passage is important for understanding Ralph's views about the nature of political authority.

Chapter 18

Tancred seeks Alexios' tents and the emperor is indignant

After Alexios understood the mind of this man who spurned money and
realized that he could not be bound in golden chains like the others, he
followed along because he did not know how to move him. And so he agreed
with [Tancred's] words. They joined right hands. But on the inside, the son of
the marquis was angry and his face burned angrily with a fierce light. After
celebrating the same rite that the other leaders had observed in making these
agreements, Tancred was invited to make a request from the king such that he
would receive no rebuff whatever his request. [Alexios] thought that he would
ask for gold, silver, gems, cloth and similar types of things that were needed
for travel or soothed a greedy soul. But this spurner of money, this soul as an
emulator of royal excellence, rejected these vulgar things and desired that
honor which the other leaders had turned aside as too burdensome. He said
only a piece of the imperial accoutrement would be pleasing to him. For the
king had a tent that was marvelous both by art and by nature so that it cast a
double spell on its viewers. It looked like a city with a turreted atrium. It
required 20 heavily burdened camels to carry. It could hold a multitude and
its apex soared above the others 'just as the cyprus is accustomed to soar over
the yielding roses'.[45]

This single gift seized the imagination of the magnanimous Guiscardian
and he marked it as an appropriate hall for himself. It was a useless burden at
present but hardly an ignoble sign for the future. When he learned of this,
Alexios grew violently angry at the one making the request just as once Delius
(Phoebus/Apollo) was vexed at Phaeton.[46] If his paternal piety had not held
him back, his hostile indignation would have grown savage. Phoebe groaned
over the danger to her son, and Alexios wondered at this sublime soul.[47]
Phoebe encouraged her son to desire healthier things. Alexios denied what
was desired and thundered: 'So, the son of the marquis compares himself to
me in seeking the regalian insignia? The common things are filthy in his eyes
and he desires nothing other than my palace, which is unique in the world.
What more can he ask except to take the diadem off my head and place it on
his own? But I think that he does not have enough space to hold his congress

---

[45] Vergil, *Eclogue*, 1.26. Anna Comnena also reports that Tancred asked for the
imperial tent. In her account, however, Tancred sought to have the tent filled with
gold. See *The Alexiad of the Princess Anna Comnena*, trans. Elizabeth A. S. Dawes
(London, 2003, first published 1928), 11.3, 275–6. It is very unlikely that Anna read
Ralph's account. It is therefore probable that this event took place.

[46] Cf. Ovid, *Metamorphoses*, 2.49. Phaeton was Phoebus' son by Clymene.

[47] Phoebe was a Titan, the daugher of the Sky and the Earth.

of clients nor can such a large military force fit within the walls of his dwellings. Thus, he seeks royal dwellings, immense in their dimensions, which are sufficient for such a magnificent lord. And if this request is met, where will the mules, mule drivers and vehicle suited to such a burden be found? And doubtlessly, if he did receive it, he would not have it otherwise than it followed after him as if by some sort of divine will. Let him recall that it was the skin of the lion which was the cause of sorrow for the dissimulating ass. Dressed in these skins in order to cause terror, it was fitting that he suffered the farmer's terrible wrath.[48] Warned by this example, let him not desire to terrify the ignorant under the shadow of my name for at the end he will be recognized as nothing more than Tancred. Let him be measured by his own merit and his own foot. Let him obtain his own tent and leave off any hope of gaining this one. And if he is still angry at this refusal, well I treat his anger like the dregs of wine, and his threats the same as his anger. Now, more and more, his stolid ambition reveals the mind of this man to me. While he was quiet, I thought he was a philosopher, since he has opened his mouth, it now appears that he deserves to be considered insane. So, whatever fraud, acuity, anger, or fury you have, son of a marquis, throw it at my head. I receive your anger and I do not perceive you as worthy of being either an enemy or a friend to me.'

Alexios said these things partly out of anger and partly from his astuteness. In part, he was covering over his fear and in part softening the fermenting of his atrocious bile. But Tancred, as if imitating a humorous passage, seized upon the last of these words and ever freely spoken with all responded: 'I deem you worthy of being my enemy, but not my friend.' They then parted and never met again.

Chapter 19

Tancred and Bohemond tear themselves from the emperor's hands

Tancred returned to the shore where his boat stood prepared. He had called upon fortune and she was present. He then crossed without delay since there was nothing less desirable to him than delay. Bohemond left a little later. He was expecting and almost fell into a royal trap. However, he was secretly warned and took flight away from the chains. Then the royal messenger followed after them summoning and recalling them. But having been delivered, extricated from their bonds, and having been immersed in the storms, they had no desire to be exposed again to these tempests. The

---

[48] Cf. Avianus, *Fabulae*, 5.

summoning of someone who is absent is a dirty deed when that person was spurned when earlier present. Hearing about the perfidy of the one who had summoned them, that is Herod, they would not return to the household of the highest king.[49] Turning back would be condemnable as they had already once experienced. But two other examples also held those who had turned to the light from going again into the shadows: the first of these concerned the chaos at Sodom, and the other was the wife of Orpheus (Eurydice).[50] Warned by these many examples, it seemed to them that they would avoid all of these torments so long as they avoided this one torturer.

Therefore, the Latin leaders, who had been afflicted by the long delay, ended the tedium and loaded their draft animals with the supplies necessary for themselves and their mounts. The intervening territory was sterile and offered no fertile areas for many days to those who passed through it, indeed no crops at all alleviated its desolation. Within the confines of this land, Solymannus,[51] the Turkish king, was planning to oppose those intending to cross so that the prepared would attack the ill informed, the well-supplied would attack the starving, the speedy would attack the burdened, and the strong would attack the weak. Thus, a decision was made by the faithful people, as if inspired by God, that they would carry a great supply of food through this uncultivated waste so that what was carried, in a manner of speaking, would carry its own bearers.

Chapter 20

The army of the Christians is divided into two

But when the penultimate day of their journey across this arid land passed, fortune turned its slippery favor from the supporters of Christ to the supporters of Mohamet, and dared too much against Tancred's troops. For it happened again, as they had become accustomed during their daily, or rather nightly, marches, that the road divided in two and the army of Christ was likewise divided into two sections. Many thought that this error was due to a decision, namely that a wide area might provide greater supplies to a widely

---

[49] Cf. Matthew 2:12, and the refusal of the Magi to return to Herod after receiving a warning in a dream.

[50] The first of these women was the wife of Lot who turned into a pillar of salt after looking back at the city of Sodom then being destroyed by God for its wickedness. Cf. Genesis 19:26. The second woman was Eurydice, the wife of Orpheus. Cf. Vergil, *Georgics*, 4.491.

[51] Kilij Arslan, the son of Suleiman, the emir of Iconium.

spaced people than a constricted area would to a tightly packed group. It so happened that the Norman count, Bohemond, and Tancred with their men were separated from the crowd as if with one common thought they sought to propagate the unique glory of their fatherland. But in a clear effort to commiserate with the misfortune which occurred and to limit anger, the other [leaders] asserted that the separation from those who went off was not voluntary or planned ahead but was rather accidental and unforeseen. This view is strongly supported by the following arguments: namely, that the aforementioned leaders did not leave behind the baggage belonging to the lesser folk, that they were pleased by the presence of foreign military forces alongside them, and that in the end they did not protect their own baggage which was far away.

Chapter 21

The battle lines of the Latins and barbarians rush to arms in a mutual attack

Therefore, when the banners of the Normans announced the threat of war to the Turks – for ardent Tancred, who followed his custom of going out ahead, achieved his end of being the first both to see and to be seen – both sides deployed their forces in such a manner that the river which flowed between the forces obligated the faster to bend back toward the slower. Afternoon began to merge into twilight as the battle lines of the Latins and barbarians began their mutual attack. The approaching night was spent half in rest and half in labor. The faithful were more prompt and around the first hour of the morning preceded the infidels to the banks of the aforementioned river where the Turks' less than zealous leader had established their first camp. At this point, the sharp cry of 'behold the enemy, behold the enemy' was raised repeatedly [among the Christians] and they charged. The force of [Muslim] archers was engaged, now pierced by spears, now killed by swords, it was engaged, I say, so that the lead group was carried to the middle and the group in the middle was forced to seek its own safety. When the Normans came on driving the enemy in flight before them, the Muslims took renewed strength from their own dense ranks so that those who recently had been the pursuers were now forced to take flight.

In the meantime the count of the Normans (Robert) and Bohemond organized two battle lines each one organizing his own, and they now gradually entered the fray with joy. The Turks were holding their position and the Christians were advancing against them. There was no scope for the use of bows and little for spears. Swords were being used everywhere. The Turks were defended by their countless multitude while our forces were defended by hauberks, shields and helmets. Much blood was shed on both sides, but more on the side of the barbarians. The carnage among them did not cease but just like the returning heads of the Hydra, where a few fell, countless others took their place.

Chapter 22

The Christians are forced to retreat. Count Robert of Normandy gives them fresh vigor

But the legion of the faithful suffered the same losses without having the same reinforcements. Thus, wounded while it struck, shaken while it resisted, and weakened while its ranks were thinned, the [legion] retreated. And what had never been taught anywhere before, was taught in that moment, namely, to flee. O miserable war, o pitiable flight, o loss in loss, o wound in wound. The impetus of the flight of the heavily armed mounted troops trod underfoot the slower moving foot soldiers, and the exceptionally dense forest of spears held by the foot soldiers first blocked and then ended the flight of the others. There was a terrible slaughter at the hands of the enemy since they shot arrows at the backs of the Christians. The latter also were struck by spears and skewered just as if on a spit over a fire. Neither side now took any care, those who were driving the enemy with their bows and those who were being driven on by their spurs. The latter sought refuge in their camp which was not of much solace, but the only one available.

There, at last, one who was of the royal blood of William (William the Conqueror of England), recalled to himself his lineage and the fact that he was a fighter. He uncovered his head and shouted 'Normandy' and then caught the attention of his colleague Bohemond who had followed him in flight with the following words: 'Ho Bohemond, why are we fleeing? Apulia is far away, Otranto is far away. Hope for the borders of any Latin land is far from us. We should make our stand here for we will have either the glorious punishment of the defeated or the victors' crown. I say that both of these chances are glorious, but the first is even more blessed than the latter because it will make us blessed that much more quickly. Therefore, go forward my young men, let us die and charge them under arms.'

After being admonished in this way, the remainder of the young men joined themselves to the leaders more prepared to die than to flee. They stood there ready like a lion that had been roused from a long slumber in its cave and waited in fury for the hunting spears as its anger gradually increased, disturbed by the barking, and signals, and clamor, and spears. And this anger did not belong to both sides but rather only to one of them at a time running back and forth between them. Thus, the more the anger of the lion grew, the more tepid the leader of the hunters became. In a similar manner, as the faithful people grew in strength, the infidels weakened. They no longer dared to attack those who feared nothing. Both sides rested, the one side, as was noted, remembering its boldness, the other side its fear.

Chapter 23

A great slaughter of the faithful

In the meantime, a messenger was sent to the part of the army that was ignorant of the battle in order to announce what had happened. The messenger was supposed to hurry away so that the army would hurry back. But the enemy also sent others, namely spearmen, to the struggle, men who were not seekers after salvation. This body of spearmen bypassed our mounted troops and attacked the lesser folk who were present in great numbers but lacked military ability. The latter, who had planted stakes behind the screen of the heavily armed mounted troops, thought that their walls would protect them from danger. But then, suddenly, the savage Turks rushed in on them first shooting with their bows and then attacking with swords. The Turks gained booty beyond their hopes and achieved victory without fighting a battle. The old men were killed and the young were carried off. Those in the middle age suffered the fate of those whom they most closely resembled in appearance. What happened most frequently, however, and most savagely was that the sword point made claims on those at the age of puberty. The great quantity of booty made the most savage brigand even more savage. When the hands of Briareus proved insufficient for rapine, he turned to slaughter and thus satisfied his voracious spirit.[52] Thus it happened that from such a great number only a few survived either wounded or in chains. Nor ever in all of the events of war that preceded or followed this one was so much Latin blood shed by gentile swords. What more can I say? Tired out from killing, but not yet satisfied in their rage, the victorious were followed into camp by the defeated. The latter were loaded down with their own baggage and that of their companions as well. This was a truly miserable sight for our heavily armed mounted troops, but not miserable enough to arouse their boldness. For they clung to their design of resisting the enemy if they attacked but otherwise remained content with what they held. Having stopped, they would not attack anyone else in the meantime.

---

[52] Briareus (Greek) was the hundred-armed giant also called Aegoeon.

Chapter 24

Tancred offers sharp resistance

But on the opposite side of camp, Tancred defeated the enemies who had climbed a little rise that divided the two forces. From here they were able to cause damage more easily and suffer it only with difficulty. After these enemies were dislodged, as I said, by a rapid assault, the brave man occupied the heights having attacked many and been joined by but a few. Bohemond had not wanted him to take this action and prohibited him from taking more than a few companions once he had begun. Bohemond wanted to keep the enemy army, which had spread around, from encircling ours as if in some kind of circus spectacle, and thus, having enclosed our force, threaten death on all sides. In this manner, the foresight of the Christian leaders denied permission to the burning spirits of the young men to go forth into battle lest the rashness of a few undermine the order of the whole force.

Chapter 25

Tancred's brother William also fights manfully. They kill the enemy

William, the son of the marquis, although he feared for his brother, had no concern for himself. He did not pay attention either to Bohemond's summons to fall back or to the strength of the large enemy force since he burned to join in his brother's audacity. Oh, how miserable and blessed he was in doing this thing, he who rushed into death so that he might cross into life. After having been driven from the hill, as was noted earlier, the mob retreated not so much from those whose swords they had already experienced but because of those whom they feared, incorrectly, would follow. Therefore, when the mob of enemy troops saw how many rather than whom they had fled, and compared the numbers, their spirit did not grow sharper, but rather a pain grew up around their labor, and shame accumulated about their pain. And so, after shooting their bows, the [Muslims] charged so that they could ravage the [Christians] more boldly with drawn swords. They did not consider this to be a battle but rather a punishment. This was not a struggle against enemies but rather the fulfilling of a sentence on those condemned for capital crimes.

But the numerically far inferior force set in opposition a truly formidable strength, and an audacious wall. Even if King Solymannus himself along with all of his forces had attacked them, they would not have broken. The battle commenced. The Christians shook their spears while the others, as was noted, unsheathed their swords. The former had coats of mail to protect their chests and added strength to their armor with shields. The latter had smaller crescent-shaped shields. The former fought from the heights downward while the latter fought in the opposite direction. A mixture of pain and shame encouraged the latter while the former, as if holding a watchtower, were urged on by as many stimuli as their eyes could see. For the first group, the place in which they were located, the soundness of their arms, and, indeed, their small numbers proved to be a help, while the great numbers in which the others had trusted proved to be an inconvenience. Thus, a spear cast at an advancing Turk meets him a spear's cast away. There is a similar strike and easy impact on the one who is about to fall which either pierces him or throws him down. And having been struck or cast down one man forces others into similar ruin as he rolls about. However, as happens in such a great multitude, when one fell there were soon many others and again still others to replace him. And thus it happened that those who in their fury and indignation advanced in contempt of the Christian soldiers, covered the ground with their losses before setting foot on the hill, while the small force of Christ was neither injured nor threatened. The points of their spears gave them great service and were aided by their swords and shields. But what could a sword do? It is in the nature of the sword, I say, to kill when close and to spare when far off, to penetrate when nearby and to threaten when far off. To conclude a discussion of its attributes in a few words, its length determines its capabilities. It can be unsheathed to threaten but cannot harm at a distance.

After the Turkish attack was broken on the bold battle lines, the Turks realized that audacity offered no safety and decided that they would no longer send strength against strength. Instead, they relied on their bows that they had set aside. If they had continued, as they had begun, to set foot against foot, hand against hand, and shield against shield, the death gathered unto this scene would still have struck this magnanimous man [William]. Only one piece of consolation would have been added, namely, that all of his fighting men would have had the same opportunity.

Chapter 26

William dies

But when they took up their bows again, the great flight of arrows did not spare those whom the swords had spared. It struck those whom the swords had not reached. Where the swords had not ascended, the arrows descended. What before had been such a heavy burden, armor, shields and helmets, now formed a most appreciated barrier which determined the boundaries of life and death. It is often the case that those who take off the burden of armor suffer as a result. The drawn bowstrings of the Turks inflicted wounds and hailed arrows. Our men withstood these attacks hoping for a storm to fly in from somewhere and scatter this enormous cloud of missiles. The ranks of their comrades were near, the enemy was everywhere, but there was no aid anywhere.

In the meantime, the wounded cried out. Here a man was struck in the hand, there in the eye, others were struck in the foot, and still others in the head. What misery, what suffering, what distress. The son of the marquis was a shield for the others, and William himself was struck along with the others. He felt the suffering of their wounds, and they suffered on account of his wounds until his death. His noble body fell. His friends picked it up and bore it back to the camp. The poor piece of ground, which had been the cause of the battle, was relinquished. What do you think, O Tancred, seeing such things? What groans were you making?[53] This man who was strengthened with three-fold bronze around his chest,[54] turned the hearts of others and softened them into womanly tears. Their mouths took up womanly cries. Fingers tore hair from their beards, their cheeks and their heads. Finally, they tore to pieces whatever bits of armor they had while the lightly armored men savaged whatever was left in a cruel betrayal of themselves.

Many of the faithful heroes were resolute in this lament and mourned for the son of the marquis. Nor did they mourn less for the tears of Tancred than they did for the death of William. It was at this time, moments after the Turks had recaptured the hill when behold,: The rising dust was a witness that the cohorts of the supporters of Christ were there.[55] The spirits of those who had been downcast were lifted up and those who had been elated were cast down. The cry rang out, 'God wills it', and our men shouted out this call laughing. Muttering, the enemy groaned alas, alas. And they were trembling, not so much because their hope had been taken away but because fear had been put into its place.

Chapter 27

Hugh the Great appears

Leading the reinforcements was the most noble descendant of kings, Hugh the Great, accompanied by almost 300 helms. He rushed toward the center of the enemy, not as someone who is prepared to fight but rather as one who follows those in retreat after a battle is over. Rapid, fearless and protected on all sides, he attacks, he strikes, he drives into

---

[53] Cf. Vergil, *Aeneid*, 4. 408–9, with respect to Dido, queen of Carthage.
[54] Horace, *Odes*, 1.3.9–10.
[55] Cf. Lucan, *De bello civili*, 6.247, 'the dust attested that Caesar's cohorts were present' (*caesareas pulvis testatur adesse cohortes*).

flight, he follows, he presses, he pushes, he shouts, he exults, he roars, he exclaims, he rages, he burns. King Solymannus sent an iron battle line against him. Huge in number, strength, menace and ferocity, its numbers exceed the stalks of grain in your foothills o Gargaran range.[56] Its strength is equal to the walls around mount Etna. Its ferocity and menace might conquer the whole world. It took pleasure in landing heavy blows and returning them. Here stood an enormous joyful cohort with huge numbers of spears and bows. There stood the count, great in name and in prowess. They were equal in attack but disparate in the numbers engaged in the charge. The [Franks] charge into battle. The [Muslims] stand opposed blocking the Gauls. Shields crash against shields and swords against swords. Part of the [enemy force] forms a circle from the right and part from the left. The [Turks] shoot rapidly from all sides. Bold Gaul is surrounded on all sides by enemy forces. The [Franks] cannot face any unless they face them all. Unwittingly, the [Franks] turn sometimes toward these enemies and sometimes toward others. They were like a boar that has been surrounded by a huge pack of dogs, first threatening one group with its tusks and then eviscerating others, now gnashing its teeth at those at the back, and now threatening those in front. Thus, the great leader and the young men under his command were eager and turned themselves about innumerable times. Whichever direction [Hugh] rushed, he killed as he came, he continued on leaving the dead enemy behind.

Chapter 28

Hugh drives off the Turks

When a new [enemy] battle line approached, the count was already covered in blood from the slaughter and he was worn out from the fighting. Now anger exaggerated the work and sweat of this fierce man. The [Turks] attacked from the front, the back, from the right and from the left. Not having been worn down, they gave no respite to those so burdened. Afterward, there was no way of establishing how large the innumerable host had been, but it was certainly more than the enemy had lost. The count, saddened by the heavy losses to his small command, signaled a retreat. This was, however, only the image of fear.

---

[56] Gargar is a town in south-eastern Anatolia approximately 40 miles south-east of Melitene and 180 miles north-east of Antioch. Ralph may have been using this town as a designation for the fertile foothill region along the Euphrates as it passed down out of the Taurus mountains.

The other signs were of victory, of one striking, casting down and driving off. His sword was at the backs of those fleeing and was cutting them in two. His horse was fiery and his right arm was blazing. Now [Hugh], who had been killing the enemy, retreated. The one who was fleeing death came upon the turned face and menacing aspect [of the count] and faced him without hope. Now, hoping that it would be safer to charge the unknown multitudes than again to undergo the blows experienced on the right, the count attacked the frightened [enemy], and they withstood his attack. [Hugh] retreated and attacked, being both a pursuer and the pursued.

Chapter 29

Count Robert of Flanders along with Hugh drives off the Turks

Robert of Flanders, who was feared for his spear and his sword, opposes them. He flies into battle in an unrestrained charge and thus lessened the delays and losses. Since he had been the last of them to draw breath, he burned to be the first to shed blood.[57] Blocking the path of flight, he became one of the pursuers. From this vantage point he saw the dense lines [of the enemy] bristling with bows. The threats were whizzing and bristling there. The Turks charged the count, and the count eagerly charged them in turn. And the foot soldiers from Flanders, their numbers equaled by their prowess, burned with an equal fire. They followed on foot toward the slaughter and din. The battle line of the [Turkish] archers was scattered and the bows were cast to the ground. The quivers were smashed and the bowstrings were trampled. Their small shields and the breastplates were as linen threads to the swords [of the Flemings]. They proved to be burdens rather than protection for the Turks bearing them.

Thus, the powerful count forced those [Turks] who had penetrated behind the Gauls to retreat again, and conversely forced the Gauls to turn toward the enemy. He led them back to cut down and to kill the forces of the enemy. At first, they had been without number, so that they could not be counted. The Turks paid them back in kind with not a few, but also not too many wounds. Since they were ignorant of iron spurs, their hopes of turning back all rested on the lash of the reins. But following the custom of their fathers, their bows also caused wounds even in flight. They acted, however, trembling with fear, so that the

---

[57] This would appear to be a comment on the age of Robert who was born in 1065.

arrows caused no damage. Indeed, their fear was so great that it passed to their innermost marrow. Pope! what fear the flame of Flanders caused.[58] When the indomitable count [Robert] dominated the enemy, and dispersed their dense formations, he cut apart the dispersed troops, overwhelmed the cut-off groups, and trod these overwhelmed men under his feet. He was joined by the great count Hugh. Nor did the slaughter cease until friendly troops rescued those in flight, by enclosing their units, and keeping out the pursuers. Again, there were new forces and fresh spirits. Eager hands joined together, along with other things appropriate to battle. Our people discovered all that had happened and, although already burdened by so much death, they willingly accepted the blows and returned them with even more vigor. You would say that Roland and Oliver had been reborn if you saw the raging of the counts, this one with a spear and that one with a sword.[59]

Chapter 30

Godfrey charges the enemy

Duke Godfrey was a man totally devoted to war and to God. He gave up nothing to Hector in fervor, in strength, in will or in spirit.[60] He excelled in arms and was happy. O what battle lines, what breastplates, what a long sword, how well armored on the left side. Behold, this was the duke's company! What snorting of horses, what growling of men, what glory of the Lotharingians! The duke pressed and pursued the Turkish battle line. But he was not aided by some wary skill or by the fittingness of the place. He was not aided by that art which drives even timid men against the brave. Rather, he drove the enemy force although they were aided by all of these, namely by skill, position and trickery.

---

[58] The word *papa* is used here as an exclamation.

[59] It should be noted that the earliest surviving manuscript of the *Song of Roland* (*c.*1120) is roughly contemporaneous with Ralph's composition of the *Gesta*. Concerning the dating of the Roland manuscript, see Gerard Brault, *The Song of Roland: An Analytical Edition*, 2 vols (University Park, 1981).

[60] Hector was the son of King Priam of Troy whom Achilles killed in single combat and dragged behind his chariot in disgrace.

Chapter 31

Godfrey is able to charge and follows after those fleeing. A nearby mountain aids the enemy

A rampart stood in the duke's path. The ground under him rose from the rampart to a mountain at its rear. It was to this place that the people who trusted more in tricks than in their bows took flight. The duke, ignorant of their fraud and foul trickery, thought that those who fled wished to use the rampart for battle.

He turned the face of battle against them and with a quick assault liberated the small hill that had previously held the enemy force. He then pressed on against those forced to flee over the plain to the mountain with great slaughter both among the enemy and among his own men. Indeed, this people, armed with tricks, transfixed equally the breastplates of the pursuers as well as those who were fleeing.[61] And unless a fast horseman pressed his assault with his spear, the more the [Turks] fled, the more they inflicted horrible wounds. But the result was that the flight of the Turks entailed victory for the Franks.

Once the cohort [of the enemy], reached the mountain, those who were not burdened with armor easily evaded the men who rushed after them who were so burdened. They shot with their easily bent bows, contemptuous of the spears being brandished in the distance. The duke, who was anxious to achieve his goal, raged at the foot of the mountain and then returned to the plain. If the mountain made the enemy uncomfortable, the empty fields and the rampart might encourage them to come back again. The enemy, taking pleasure in these events, descended, and again caused damage. They ran here and there always inflicting wounds, aided by their fast horses and by the protection of the nearby mountain. The duke pursuing again and again drew out many from the heart [of the force] and his sword repaid many while they were in retreat.

However, the mountain always diminished these deserved victories. It provided a place of safety for the defeated and blocked the banners of the victorious. It was as if a crowd of complaining birds flew around a hawk that was flying in an airy circle or was sitting on a branch, and filled the bushes with various cries. Then, as if by chance, an impudent crow offends the haughty bird by flying too close by, the latter now

---

[61] Although Ralph's text is cryptic here, it appears that he is making reference to the Turkish tactic of shooting their bows while fleeing. However, since the Muslim and Christian forces were intermixed to a certain extent, some of the arrows struck Turkish riders as well as their pursuers.

indignant and enraged attacks the aerial crowd with all of his strength. The former flees, seeking out his nest on trembling wings. Likewise, o thief, as your claws were outstretched toward your prey, the refuges enclosed within the rocks and tower held you fast. However, bearing back the feathers in your claw as signs of victory, you suffer in your fixed seat. Having spread your wings, opened your beak, flashed your eyes, and heaving in your chest, you lift up the feathered restraints of your escaped prey. Thus, anger greatly disturbed the duke while the Turks, who were driven from the plain had safe hiding places within the mountain.

Chapter 32

Hugh the Great aids the duke, and, along with Count Raymond, captures the mountain. The Turks are overcome by terror

But when Hugh the Great approached the battle on a different track, he easily climbed the mountain using a side path that was devoid of enemies. Soon, neither the ridges nor the steep path could restrain those who had been discovered. Rather, fast horses with loose reins bore the retreating Turks through the plains and rough regions as well. Count Raymond hurried first to the count (Hugh) and then to the duke (Godfrey). The enemy troops were fleeing and Raymond feared that none of the enemy would be left to fight against him and his men. His forces, the foot soldiers, horsemen and household troops provided this war leader and deployer of legions with such a large force, with such strength and with such a great number of banners that no one could believe that anyone was absent. And they were justified in believing that no one had been left behind. Therefore, fearing that he would not be worthy of being feared, he sought out battle with disordered lines in order to combat this fear. If a storm had carried the chains of Ida to the depths of the Sigean shore, everything near to Ida would have shaken.[62] Both the mountain and the valley might lie under Phoeban (Apollo's) ash. When you decrease the light, you seem to have more helmets and soldiers. This was the situation and this is how it played out – a similar attack, the same fear.

The crowds of the count's companions and their own military followings were there. When their roar struck the astonished ears of the Turks and the sight of them flashed in their eyes, the Turks feared that

---

[62] Cf. Ovid, *Metamorphoses*, book 13.

all of Europe had come leaving no duke, count, or king behind. At first
they stood wondering. But soon, as Raymond's front ranks turned
toward them, and came against them, and his sword drew close, then
the Arab no longer trusted in his javelin and the Turk no longer trusted
in his bow. Now, the horse no longer recognized its reins, nor did the
path recognize the horse, nor, in flight, the course. All that was left was
to flee in hope of safety. Therefore the Cilician headed for Tarsus, the
Choatrian for his forests, which touch the sky, the Syrian to Antioch,
the Phoenician to the walls of Sidon, the Jacobite to Artah, the Aleppan
to the Elamite towers.[63] Countless others set off without order and
without delay, each one seeking refuge in hiding places known to
them.[64]

Chapter 33

*After the enemy is dispersed, the leaders turn toward Antioch. Tancred's
boldness*

After this victory in which the enemy was dispersed and slaughtered, and
rediscovered victory had given them wealth and made them happy, the path
summoned back the solitary wanderer. But now that the road was safer, the
army was also more spread out. The commanders thought to take the units of
foot soldiers toward Antioch along the longer but easier road through the
cultivated plains. And so they put this plan into action. But Tancred chose to
follow the unfrequented ways of the woodlands, the difficulties of the
mountains, and the rivers of Cilicia, as these paths offered a more direct and
quicker route to the same city. O amazing fighter for whom labor is desirable,
war is safety, leisure is difficult, difficulties are matters of ease, and for whom
last of all nothing is sweet which was not the result of his own sweat. We are
amazed at this man who is never amazed. We fear for this man who never
fears.

Pope! Tancred, is this audacity not madness? You are bound for Antioch
and you are content to bring 100 men with breastplates. Your archers
number barely 200. You are fighting against Syria with all of its thousands?
You have too few. Increase your numbers! Your enemy is great and many
swords are against you. Your enemy arms more armies than you have men.

---

[63] This is a list of the peoples with whom the crusaders had contact in northern and
western Syria and in the Levant. The Choatrians were a people who lived near the
swamps of Maeotica along the Black Sea. Cf. Lucan, *De bello civili*, 3.246.

[64] The Christians obtained this victory in the Gorgoni valley near the city of
Dorylaeum on 1 July 1097.

The towns and cities wait for you like an enemy to ask for your protection. You will keep few of your command. They shall rise up, I say, five times the number of towns shall rise up so that it will take numerous defenders to hold them. Also, should you be called as a defender, you should not fail in your defense but rather should provide defenders for each group of people. The city of Antioch is especially well stocked with arms and protected by well-armed troops. It is well versed in war and arrogant in its triumphs. It has grown old in lordship and does not know how to be ruled. It is fitting to moderate the course of a headlong will and to use the advice of a certain wise man concerning restraint.

This leader and soldier, expert in what it means to be both a leader and a soldier, said: 'Before taking action it is appropriate to take stock. Once having done so, the task should be undertaken properly.'[65] It is clear even to the simple folk that it falls to the leader to plan and to the soldier to fight. But it often happens that the task of one falls to the other and vice versa. The glory of both sets you afire. But you are very incautious because you take pride in the lower of these when you would find glory more effectively in the higher. You burn to be called an intrepid soldier and in this you have ferocious prowess with the result that you might be called imprudent in your furor. And while you purchase this cheap trinket, you throw away your life, you lose the fruits of your labor, you earn jealousy and incur infamy. Therefore I beseech to you. Return to your position as leader. Take counsel, and when you have received counsel deploy your troops. For otherwise, when danger comes you will lack counsel. You ought to wish to go into battle having received counsel, not to go into battle without it.

Chapter 34

Tancred besieges Tarsus and prepares ambushes

Although similar and even more dire warnings struck Tancred's ears, he continued on in the manner of a deaf viper.[66] It was as if he excluded those speakers whom he thought would offer warnings. Instead, faster than the flames of heaven or a tigress who has recently given birth, he crossed Bythinia, and then passed through the Taurus mountains and the valley of

---

[65] Cf. Sallust, *De coniuratione Catilinae*, 1.14–15, 'For, before you begin, you should plan. And having planned, you should undertake the action in an appropriate manner' (*nam et prius quam incipias consulto et, ubi consuleris mature facto opus est*).

[66] Ralph may be referring here to Psalm 58:4: 'the deaf adder that stoppeth her ear, which will not hearken to the voice of the charmers'.

Butro.[67] The former were close to Beryte and the latter lay to the north. This was matter of indignation to the Turks, exultation to the Greeks, exhortation by the Armenians, and wonder to the entire world. For it happened that at this time the Turks ruled, the Greeks obeyed, and the Armenians protected their liberty in the difficult conditions provided by their mountains. But when Tancred caught sight of the city (Tarsus), while still at a distance, he marveled at the heights of the towers, the length of the walls, the prideful stature of the homes, and prepared to ascertain the military strength of the inhabitants.

When everything that could be checked ahead of time had been checked, he set a ruse. A troop of turcopole archers was sent out supported by some of our heavily armed mounted troops. They were instructed in which order and by which routes they were to go once the cattle [of the townspeople] had been let loose in the fields so that the enemy rushing after their prize did not discover the ambush before they were caught in it and had to pay the price. The plan was laid out and set in motion. The looters, who had been sent out, took flight and despoiled the area outside the walls. Once this had been done, they turned in simulated panic just as they had been ordered. The city roused whatever armed men and whatever strength it had and set them on their trail. They left very few men behind to guard the gates. The former charged and then [*the turcopoles retreated in feigned flight*]. Soon, those who had been in flight reached safety and those who pursued them found death. Those who had been in flight had victory and those who pursued them were defeated. [*When the turcopoles had reached the planned point, the heavily armed mounted troops under Tancred's command attack from their hidden positions. The force from the city then turned and fled.*][68] Tancred drew close to those who were retreating and struck them many times flying even more quickly after them [than his own men]. As fortune played its games, some evaded [Tancred's men] and some overcame them. Once the signal had been given with a mirror, the valley, which was filled with heavily armed men, poured out these forces from their hiding places. At first, [Tancred's men] began to shake their iron-tipped spears. Then a forest of oaks and ash rose up. Then the helmets and shields rushed forward in a similar manner. After them came the breastplates and finally the horses and men. The force rose up like the offspring of Cadmus.[69] When the madly raging Turks caught sight of them, as was their custom, they turned about and shot a huge torrent of arrows tipped with iron and backed with feathers.

---

[67] The journey through this valley leads to the gate of the Taurus mountains which is today called Gülek Bogaze.

[68] The italicized portion of the translation is our reconstruction of the lost text in this section.

[69] Cadmus sowed the teeth of a dragon, and warriors called Sparti rose from the earth.

Chapter 35

Tancred kills the enemy and drives them off

Since he had been counting on the large number of their men and the small
number of his own, when Tancred saw that the former had come out to battle
he drove into the middle of the fighting. He cut apart whoever faced him or
pierced him with his sword. Nor did his youthful followers lack faith. The
Turks could not resist them. They died first from chest wounds and soon from
those in the back. Some lacked shields. Many lacked protection for their
chests. All of them lacked time. They could not withstand the onrushing
helmets, shields and breastplates. The gate received those returning. But
although it had been spacious enough when they left, now it was too narrow
as the confused, terrified, mad and surrounded men rushed toward the edge
of the gate with the swords of the victors urging them on. If the wall guard
had not rained down a rocky hail and wrecked the wicker shield, the citizens
and the enemy would have arrived at the walls in one rush all together.[70]
Those on one side gained entrance. Those who were driven off passed by the
fallen bodies [of the enemy] and gave thanks to Christ. There was sadness
inside the walls and joy outside. Inside, hope had turned to fear. Outside,
there was no such transformation. Instead, hope grew. Then the day ended
and night rushed upon them, a time in which counsel was to be taken.

Chapter 36

Tancred attacks the city

Once the sun rose, Tancred hurried to break the gates, to fill in the ditches, to
set up the ladders and to scale the towers. He described the delays of the night
as being like a year. He had no sleep. And if anyone did sleep it was only for a
short time. But from the closing of the eye until the opening of the next day,
foreboding urged the Turks to take flight. Despairing of the enemy and of
their own citizens, the image of a long fight brought terror to the night. Nor
did the threat of Tancred recede at all. Rather, it clung to the eyes and the
minds of everyone. So, not waiting for the sun, they took flight into the

---

[70] The mention here of a wicker shield (*umbo cratis*), indicates that Ralph left out
part of the story, namely that Tancred had prepared siege equipment for an assault on
the walls. Wicker shields were normal equipment for protecting those attempting to
sap a wall or to protect soldiers advancing in order to assault a wall. It would seem
that Ralph expected the mention of a wicker shield to be sufficient for his audience to
understand what was happening.

shadows. Having experienced the sword they were more trusting of plans undertaken in secret. The first sign of their flight to the watching Greeks was a clamor from the walls.[71] [...][72] The night during which the besieged force fled had hardly passed when at dawn the city was opened to the besiegers. The local population came out as a liberated people in order to give thanks to their liberator. What a marvelous thing that freedom returned under enemy rule that had died under the rule of their fellow citizens.[73] O noble victor, from whom the conquered might ask for that which they had hardly hoped. Behold, man of the lineage of Guiscard, commanding but a few, you have prevailed over cities to spare the meek and defeat the proud.[74] And the more whom you defeat, the more whom you may spare.

Chapter 37

Tancred is frightened by Baldwin's unexpected arrival.[75] Baldwin's eulogy

After peace, quiet and freedom had been granted to the people of Tarsus and they in turn had marveled at the Franks, the latter returned to their camp. In the meantime, the sign of their victory, the banner of victory, flew high above on the tower. Then, suddenly, there was an amazing event horrible to both eyes and ears. A watchmen shouted that an armed force was coming out of the mountains and that the fields were now filled with armed men. Upon hearing the commotion, the son of the marquis grew excited and urged his heavily armed mounted troops to form into a battle line. And soon, once he had mounted, he was the first one out followed by his companions.

Like the son of the marquis, the desire of spreading his name had separated Baldwin from the bulk of the army, and by chance he had followed in the footsteps of [Tancred's] march. He was the third of Eustace's sons along with Duke Godfrey and Count Eustace from whose force of thousands he had

---

[71] Here we are dealing with a Greek population and a Turkish garrison that has escaped during the night.

[72] The text here is corrupt without hope of reconstruction based on other elements of the narrative. The surviving Latin fragments are as follows, *Sed Tancredus paratas insidias autumans, frementes jamque ... os post ... milites coercet, nemine minitante (?) ...*

[73] This passage indicates that the Christian population of Tarsus had been forced to serve against the crusaders so long as the Turkish garrison remained in the city.

[74] Vergil, *Aeneid*, 6.853, 'to spare those who have surrendered and to defeat in war those who are arrogant' (*parcere subiectis et debellare superbos*).

[75] Baldwin of Boulogne (*c.*1058–1118) was the younger brother of Godfrey of Bouillon. Baldwin became ruler of the city of Edessa in 1098. He ruled as king of Jerusalem 1100–1118.

taken many companions. Chief among them was Conan.[76] He had increased Baldwin's strength with Norman troops whose district he ruled under (Duke) Robert. Moreover, [Baldwin] was not lacking in youthful supporters. Since they were the most avid of the avid troops, they chose him as their leader. He was a man free with money, well-versed in warfare, humble in his language and great in his magnanimity. His physical appearance made him seem a leader from head to toe. 'Behold', you will say, 'whom nature has sculpted as a soldier with her own hand.'

But it is no wonder that he was adorned with such a wealth of riches at this time in his life when he entered life under the scepter of the French and died under the scepter of Jerusalem. Indeed, his bearing showed with ease his descent from Charlemagne and that fact that he was born divinely as one who was to take his seat on David's throne.[77] By law and by merit, he whose birth was illuminated by Charles and his death by David, surpassed Alexander. The sword of one whose birth and death were so illustrious should not grow blunt. His nobility illuminated them as if by a torch. He chose out from the great army those whom he recognized as his more fervent companions. They numbered 500 heavily armed mounted troops and 2000 foot soldiers. When they passed down from the mountains the son of the marquis saw our troops and believed that they were bringing aid. He had no sense that there was an ambush planned. So he told them about the battle and the victory on the previous day, mentioned the spoils, showed them what he had mentioned, and offered what he had showed. He then divided equally everything which [...] he had taken earlier without loss to those who came after him.[78]

Chapter 38

Baldwin's injustice toward Tancred

But the leader of the more secure force objected that it would be far safer if the shields and arms were distributed either individually or if all of the arms were given to fighting men from the stronger force, adding that the flight of the enemy resulted from their fear of those following behind rather than of the swords of those in front of them. Tancred had certainly fought against them, but clearly the result was due to Baldwin. And so his companion took what the son of the marquis barely gave just as Telamonius took the arms of

---

[76] Conan, the count of Montague.

[77] This is a reference to King David (*c*.1000 BC) whose capital was at Jerusalem.

[78] The ellipsis here marks a damaged portion of the text that we have not been able to reconstruct.

Pelidae which had been denied to him.[79] Tancred raged, and was furious, and was depressed that he had not taken these fleeces for himself, that this honey or rather this vein of gold which he had pulled from the depths of the earth would be seized by an ungrateful thief for his own treasury.[80] For what end did he gain from this miserable division? That which was pleasing when voluntary was now displeasing when forced. Even the title of his victory seemed to be transferred now that he was turned from a spontaneous sharer into a seemingly punished deliverer. What should he do? Should he fight. But the enemy was his fellow citizen. Should he attack? But the blood was Christian. Should he go into Tarsus? But being enclosed in a city was base. Should he leave Tarsus? But to go to fight alongside the barbarians against his brothers was to be an apostate. Therefore it was bad to be defeated but much worse to be victorious.[81]

He sat there looking for a road in a thousand byways and then scorning what he had conquered, he hurried to go to war,

> Just as you the sparrow hawk give way before the eagle and you panthers give way before the lion. Just as the lesser, although important, gives way to the greater.

The son of the marquis left bemoaning one thing, namely, that the servitude of the people of Tarsus rather than being alleviated by the arrival of the Latins had actually been made worse. He left, I say, to what people call greater deeds so that it not come to pass that people take flight at the mention of his name and impoverish this rich land.

Chapter 39

Nevertheless, messengers are sent to Tancred to discuss the handing over of the city[82]

Now that his fame spread before him at a more rapid pace nothing remained secret from the people of Adana regarding this innately great man: his strong

---

[79] Cf. Homer, *Iliad*, 7.181–312.

[80] Ralph is alluding to the verses attributed to Vergil, 'So, you do not bear wool for yourselves o sheep, so you do not make honey for yourselves o bees' (*sic vos non vobis vellera fertis oves. / Sic vos non vobis mellificatis apes*). This is a classic phrase for complaining about the plagiarism of one's works.

[81] Cf. Lucan, *De bello civili*, 7.706.

[82] In classical usage, *fetiales* were members of the Roman college of priests charged with sanctioning treaties that had been negotiated and demanding satisfaction from an enemy before war was declared. We have translated the word *fetiales* as messengers.

defense of the Christian name, how he defeated a multitude of unbelievers, his great mercy to those whom he had defeated and his harshness toward rebels. This conquered city sent messengers[83] to lead this man inside the city walls accompanied by hymns and instruments. For Christ, with compassion for his people, recently had lifted the yoke from their necks. Now, although their oppressors had been driven out, the leader of the Turks, a man or rather a dog, was still kept in chains. They believed that their anger could not be mollified nor their drunkenness be made merry until he was struck in the eyes with an arrow while on a Christian stake. Therefore, he who sees humility and recognizes the haughty from a long distance reserved judgment so that he would be judged with Tancred making the final decision.[84] Indeed, it was a divine matter: for no law is more just than that the artisans of death die by their own art.[85]

Chapter 40

The activity of Ursinus whose story is told here

At this time, the ruler of the city was Ursinus,[86] a follower of Christ and an Armenian. It was he, as noted above, who had sent messengers to summon the son of the marquis. Upon the arrival of this important guest, he went out personally and sweetened the path, offering his right hand and his faith, and promising not only the forces of those allied to him but also his own personal forces. He offered up the spoils of Mamistra, which was situated nearby and could be captured easily. Nor did he receive less worthy gifts in return. Indeed, the fruits grew a hundredfold from the seeds that had been cast. They went within the walls accompanied by the applause and singing of the entire population.

Then, when the horses had been given over to their blankets, hunger had been assuaged by banquets, and Bacchus had chased away all cares, Ursinus was asked about the current state of his city, how he was able to survive, and what means the citizens used to protect themselves surrounded by so many thousands of the enemy. He began, 'You see me,' he said, 'as a new inhabitant sent to restore the old liberty. For although the fields and the valleys served miserably for a long time subjected to Turkish domination, I was an inhabitant of the mountains. I was free, but I did not groan less at the

---

[83] The word fetiales is repeated here to designate a messenger.
[84] Cf. Psalm 138:6.
[85] Ovid, *Ars amatoria*, 1.655–6.
[86] Ursinus ruled the city of Adana.

servitude of the Christian people than those who actually suffered it. This endured for many years.

'But in the wake of numerous failed efforts one certain path of liberty became clear. The fields returned their crop, and the foliage of the earth, having suffered the sickle, was turned into hay. It was a daily chore to load this hay onto carts. In those days, the farms were cultivated by those who looked to you like nobles bristling and shining on their horses in their purple clothing – for a short time before [Tancred] had seen many men dressed in purple among the fleeing Turks. They were accustomed to lead their individual wagons back and forth constantly. Moreover, they were superior to their draft animals in one way only, namely, that their cattle were subject to control and they were subject to none. From this opportunity a suspicion arose, and from this suspicion a plan, and from this plan audacity, and from this audacity freedom. For while they [the Turks] were loading the wagons, out of sight, they [the Christians of Adana] thought that it would be possible to load them just as easily with men and arms and to hide the materials of war on the inside while covering the outside with peaceful goods. Once these arms had been carried inside the city, it would be easy to kill or drive off the Turks.

'As they were considering these plans, word came to me in the mountains where, as I said, I was living. As soon as I realized what was being considered, I was joyful and urged and warned them not to delay or withdraw from the grace of heaven which was driving them on. "You," I said, "quicken your return and make the wagons ready and I will provide fighting men to take with you." They carried out my orders and I fulfilled my promises. Without delay the hay wagons were filled with troops. For my part, I simulated a raid so that the garrison would be drawn to fight outside and would make victory easier for those attacking. Matters turned out just as they had been planned. For when they rushed out after me they brought the wagons carrying war but prudently clothed in peace and in hay inside the walls. Having entered inside the walls, the armed men threw off peace and fastened the bolts of the gate. They killed the guards and took their places. All of this was done in secret because the gate had secret places for the killing to take place. Then they rushed everywhere through the streets, in the palaces and in the towers. Woe to any Turk who was found with a bow or without, on foot or horseback, youth or old man. No one was spared, regardless of age, beauty or sex. All were laid low by the sword, both the humble and the great. The victor punished at one time the wounds which he had suffered from old and returned manifold death for his servitude.

'One of the Turks, however, was left alive. This was no one less than the prince of that evil people. He was bound in a very heavy neck collar and fetters. Then he gained an understanding of eternal torment through temporal pain. After the sword had left none of the infidel crowd untouched, the trumpeters ascended and filled the walls and the whole region with their happy sound. For I had given the order that once the slaughter had ended, they were to let us know by cheering.[87] So, when my alert ears gathered in the joyous towers I exclaimed, "My companions, let us turn about. I have heard the joyous news trumpeted, the city summons us back as citizens." Acting as if to capture booty, we had shown our backs to the enemy in a feigned retreat. But then we wheeled about toward the summoning trumpets and horns and boldly attacked those whom we had prudently been fleeing. They were amazed by this insolent audacity and delayed for a moment. Then they, in turn, turned their backs to us. We pursued them with more confidence as the city grew closer and closer. The enemy, who were ignorant of what had happened, thought that the calling trumpets, the thundering drums, and the bellowing town were the instruments of their own support. Thus, it happened that we enjoyed grace greater than we had hoped and the enemy suffered a punishment greater than they feared. This same sound, marvelous to hear, was a true guide for us and a false one for them. It brought both sides back, leading us and seducing them.

'They were pleased to be back in the vicinity of the suburb when they saw the Armenians upon the walls and realized that they had been misled by the false sound. What were they to do? Hope was gone from the walls and swords threatened them from the rear. It was not possible to remain outside nor to be received within. But there was also no place to flee and no place to fight. They all attempted to flee but not one of them was successful. For, confused by this unexpected and unanticipated event, they fled so that somehow they could evade their own footsteps and thereby live. But soon they returned to this path so that they would die. Thus, the profaners of God's church had eyes but they could not see. So too did their hands, bows, and swords all weaken in their proper use. By contrast, their sadness and our happy fortune increased our strength.

'But so that I not offend you with my prolixity, we attacked this confused and mindless crowd and our swords did not leave a single one alive. Moreover, the deaf sword did not hear the offers of money which were offered repeatedly for mercy. From this point on, *Allachibar*, which the infidels call out in prayer, was no longer heard in the city. It was replaced by the returning sounds of "Christ conquers, rules and commands".'[88] When Ursinus had finished, Tancred cried out 'thanks be to God'.

---

[87] It should be emphasized that this is the reported direct discourse of Ursinus and not Ralph's own observations.

[88] The Muslim phrase is Allah Akbar meaning God is great. The Christian chant 'Christus vincit, regnat, imperat', is an important element of the *Laudes Regiae* or hymns in praise of the Lord, which were sung at royal coronations in the West from the time of Charlemagne (crowned emperor on Christmas Day 800). Concerning the *Laudes Regiae*, see Ernst H. Kantorowicz, *Laudes Regiae: A Study in Liturgical Acclamations and Medieval Ruler Worship* (Berkeley, 1946).

Chapter 41

The townspeople gather around Tancred

They continued on as day turned into night and sleep carried off those burdened by daytime labor sending those thus carried off into tomorrow. But Phoebus (the sun) had not yet worn out the chariot horses of Venus (the morning star) when Mamistra learned that Tancred's glimmering helmets were coming to lay siege to the Mamistrians. But forewarned by this same Phoebus, the Turks, who had too long held this city, using it rather more for their rapaciousness than enjoying its delights, now found that to delay there was more delightful than it was safe. Thus, they gave up during the evening rather than face the strength of the conqueror of Tarsus in battle. Upon learning at the sun's rise [that the Turks had fled], the people went out to make a treaty with Tancred and to be secure in his wake in order that their necks might be worthy to bear his sweet yoke and light burden.[89] Having been freed from impious slavery, they viewed it as necessary to serve the one who had freed them. Given their meritorious behavior, they found it easy to ask for an alliance from one who did not send away empty-handed even those who had not merited anything from him. As a result, they bound themselves to each other, Tancred through the filial obedience of the city, and the city through the paternal rule of Tancred.

Chapter 42

Baldwin, who had established his camp outside the walls [of Mamistra], withdraws and seeks peace. He obtains both peace and trade from Tancred

In the meantime, burdened with spoils, lacking mercy, having abused its freedom, and enjoying its illicit gains, the army of Count Baldwin left Tarsus, thereby exchanging to his own disadvantage the thousands of Franks around Tarsus for hundreds. [. . .][90] [Baldwin's] officer carefully explained that Tel Bashir could be found along the right channel and that Edessa could be found along the left channel of the Euphrates whose headwaters were present in this region.[91] Neither place regarded the other as equal, either the town located in

---

[89] Cf. Matthew 11:30.

[90] The passage here is corrupt. The Latin reads as follows, '... *comitis injurias abominans ad maj ... quos levibus quibusdam viderat occupatos ...*'.

[91] Tel Bashir was a Muslim fortress and Edessa was a major Armenian city. The latter formed the nucleus for the crusader state of Edessa founded in 1098 by Baldwin of Boulogne.

the midst of nearer Syria or the city in the area of the Transeuphrates called Mesopotamia. Each possessed a great deal of rich land and prided itself on being able to call on the service of many towns and cities.

Since the messengers had frequently reported these matters to the one mentioned earlier (Baldwin) and he had repeated them to his followers, he left Tarsus. Now, having crossed with difficulty each of the rivers near to Adana and Mamistra, he established camp nearby to Tancred. He was indignant at having been kept away from the more rural courses of the channel because of the local habit of maintaining only those bridges nearby the city. Even so, there did not seem to be any way to cross them because Tancred had ordered [the locals] to capture anyone who approached them. For [Tancred] did not wish to call him [Baldwin] a brother who had driven him away as an enemy. Therefore, Count Baldwin established his camp outside the walls and sought peace from the city. Moreover, he did not seek to seize supplies by force or ask for them out of grace but rather through discussion and payment. For he knew that the mind of the man [Tancred] was upset by recent injury and that he, who had brought this injury about, was an object of hatred. Moreover, the city was well guarded with towers, had a large population, had a good supply of arms, and offered no hope to a thief through any weakness of its own.

Furthermore, Count Conan, who was mentioned above, was forced to take to his bed by a grave illness. Baldwin did not wish to proceed while leaving him behind, nor to bring him along in his condition. But Baldwin could not remain there if trade were denied to him. All of these concerns moved him to ask for peace. What a marvelous thing! Matters that were unknown to other princes were commonplaces for the son of the marquis. He who had been enraged by the losses, injuries and insults from three days earlier personally conceded the peace that was asked of him and announced it himself. Whether he was happy or angry he never wavered or was unwilling to take the correct path. To gain pardon from him it was only necessary to ask for it. Therefore, after he was asked, as was noted, to promise peace to Baldwin, Tancred responded that he would not deny trade as long as the merchants did not suffer from violence. Thus, they came and went and bought and sold, these from the city to the camp and those from the camp to the city. The heavily armed mixed with the lightly armed. Those who were afflicted with weakness outside the walls or whom the sun had burned were saved by the hope of a speedy recovery inside the shade and the walls. This pause lasted only a few days when a fire brought forth from the crafty ashes[92] began to issue flames. For just as trade was reestablished yesterday and the day before conflicts began to arise among the buyers and sellers about prices and the quality of the goods that were purchased.

---

[92] Cf. Horace, *Odes*, 2.1.8, 'you walk upon fires buried beneath treacherous ashes' (*tractas et incedis per ignes suppositos cineri doloso*).

Chapter 43

The peace is broken. Single combat

A camp follower in a food stall, it was from this that a conflict broke out that
eventually reached to the princes themselves. The one who had suffered the
injury thought it was worse because of his previous experience while the one who
had caused it feared the retaliation that was in the offing for him. Thus,
divergent views deluded both men while each one imputed a four-fold greater sin
to the other. The matter quickly came to swords and their arms took on a fury of
their own. The men from the camp, who were discovered within the walls, were
placed into custody if they were ill, or beaten with sticks if they were capable of
fighting. The common men were driven out while the nobles were placed in
chains. A similar fate befell the men of the town who were caught outside the
walls. The same thing happened among the heavily armed mounted troops
except that those who were outside assaulted the gates of the city while those
inside, seeking battle, opened the gates that were being attacked. At this point,
there was no obstacle between the two sides. A field of battle stood between them
with banners planted here and there. Finally, the leaders stood facing the men
arranged opposite them and each feared to commit himself to such a battle.

Baldwin, as was noted earlier, had a great many men and was superior in
numbers. Thus, he drew off a little distance so that he might entice the smaller
force to leave the shelter of the walls. Tancred had far fewer men. For this
reason, he armed the towers with missile weapons so that they could strike the
first blow and thus the greater descent of the javelins would support his
smaller numbers in the fight. The commanders trusted in and were divided by
such advantages and concerns so that each delayed an attack. Neither one
wished to be the first to attack but rather desired to be attacked by the other.
There were many reasons for this but the most important was that the first to
attack would bear the shame and would be seen to be more guilty. But as is
the military custom, during this delay, many young men from each side
participated in single combats. It would be possible to judge which side had
the more just cause from these acts if the attackers from one side fell and
those from the other prevailed. However, both sides had victories and both
sides losses and men from both sides fell and triumphed. It is unfitting to
know who bore his arms more justly.[93]

Among those who were engaged in these martial games was Richard of the
Principate.[94] He was not insignificant with respect either to his family or to

---

[93] Lucan, *De bello civili*, 1.126–7.

[94] Richard of the Principate, also known as Richard of Salerno, was a cousin of
Bohemond. He was made count of Edessa by Tancred for the period 1104–1108 while
the latter ruled the principality of Antioch.

his spirit and he urged on his men with his tongue and his spear. He was the son of Count William, the nephew of Guiscard, and having left Syracuse to his brother Tancred, followed his paternal uncle Bohemond and joined Tancred.[95] And while he was flying to and fro he passed by one man and defeated another when a spear pierced the unprepared man in the side and quickly transformed one who had been mounted into a foot soldier. What was he to do after he fell? He drew his sword and brandished it about. But then a crowd of the enemy rushed upon him since he had left behind the support of his fellows to come closer to the enemy. Alone and attacked by so many adversaries, he was captured, dragged, disarmed and placed into captivity. This same fate struck many on both sides who were degraded from their seats on horses to their feet. But, to those possessing greater wisdom, it seemed insane that those who had set out together against an enemy should turn on each other. It was necessary to strengthen their force against the barbarians rather than weaken an already weak group.

Chapter 44

Peace is renewed

Conscientiously thinking a great deal along these lines, the wise men exchanged war for peace. But the son of the marquis, who had suffered from these injuries, was difficult to persuade, turning a deaf ear except for when the return of Richard, the kinsman of his uncle, softened his will just as his capture had enraged him. Thus, the same man was both the cause of hatred and the cause of peace. Likewise, Conan, the count mentioned above who lay sick in the city, told his companions that they should have peace. Everyone returned to his own side, the heroes in exchange for heroes, the horsemen for horsemen and the foot soldiers for foot soldiers. Losses and gains ended up just as they had begun, unchanged so that it is with merit that the common complaint could be raised that 'he who had, had, and he who lost, lost'. Nor did [the leaders] remain together any longer. Baldwin left to conquer and Tancred remained to enjoy what he had acquired.

This delay was not a lazy one nor did he, to whom even a brief period of quiet was a long period of laziness, delay for long. Therefore, after delaying for a short period, he set out to meet the Syrians. He hoped to capture Cilicia and hoped even more to capture Syria. However, before he left, he punished

---

[95] The first Tancred in this sentence is the brother of Richard of the Principate and is not be confused with Ralph's hero.

that foul Turk whom he had incarcerated at Adana and gave laws to the people of Mamistra, laws which were more paternal than princely in nature.

After carrying out these tasks, he climbed the mountains which lay between Iskenderun and the little town of Gaston.[96] This path was difficult but it was also the most direct route toward the Syrians. When he had scaled the highest of the peaks, he decided with both his eyes and his spirit to cross the hills and plains of Antioch, the paths and unpopulated areas, the swamps and the dry regions. Thus, he crossed the entire plain in which stood the rivers, towns and cities of Sephchet, Spitachchet, Dommith, Commi, Suweidijeh (Seutunijeh) and Artah.[97]

Chapter 45

Tancred arrives at Artah. He frees Baldwin who was surrounded by Antiochenes. Artah is attacked by the enemy

When he arrived at Artah, he found Count Baldwin, who had happily driven out the Turks from the city but was now unhappily besieged by the Antiochenes. When the latter caught sight of the son of the marquis approaching, they packed up part of their baggage and then departed abandoning the rest [of their goods]. It was thought that the approach of this one man presaged all of the leaders of a large army, so that he carried with him both trembling and fear. However, even he had left part of his force in Cilicia so that only 50 men remained of each unit of 100. But the renowned news of the truth announced the one son of the marquis as if he were manifold soldiers. This new guest arrived at Artah, but his recompense in hospitality was far less than the magnitude of his deeds. He was prohibited from entering and was only allowed to remain in those areas outside the walls. It was supposed that this external defense would protect the city and keep the narrow spaces within from renewing quarrels. It was certainly the case that the underlying causes of the recent dispute had not yet disappeared. Whatever the real cause, one side was enclosed within adamantine walls and Tancred was placed in danger.

Antioch learned of the increased strength of the Latins. Having tested it and learned about it, the [Antiochenes] fled and announced the size of the force, so that the weak [Anitochene] force could be strengthened in turn and their small numbers could be increased. Antioch thus sent a second force to

---

[96] This is near the mountain of Amanum which later would belong to the Templars. Gaston later became the site of a major Templar fortress.

[97] We have not been able to identify the modern names of Sepchet, Spitachchet, and Dommith.

be overcome, and it would have been the seventh force to meet this fate if they had sent seven. Not wishing to give up any type of aid, and having already put equal faith in themselves and their arms, the Antiochenes now prepared ruses. They hid during the night in the shadows of what commonly are called the bushes of Saint Palladius. Then, when the sun had risen, they sent five horsemen to threaten Artah. In the meantime, the means of war remained hidden in the branches and boughs. Once having been sent out, they did not delay but rather offered threats to Artah.

At this point, the flocks guarded the shepherds as much as the shepherds guarded the flocks. Both the former and the latter were dragged off and no one escaped from the captors. The city watch gave warning and the shepherds and swineherds pleaded at the gate. Their common complaint was that they had suffered from the coming of the Franks against the Turks. Their suffering was even greater because they had hoped to obtain freedom through the protection of these strangers. When Tancred heard this he hurried out and saw that the city was surrounded by battle. But, once he had seen the state of affairs outside, he realized that the bravery of those out in the open depended on others still in hiding, and that the boldness they showed was more that of others than their own. In order to obtain evidence for this view, he sent out three turcopoles. If the enemy retreated, they were afraid and alone. If they fought, they had hope of reinforcements. But not only did the five not retreat at the sight of their attackers, they themselves went onto the attack. Thus, it became even more clear to Tancred that others were in hiding so he prepared for battle, deployed his troops in battle lines and advanced.

Chapter 46

Mars favors the Turks

The enemy force, which was armed with bows and was monstrous in size, spurned the shadows once it caught sight of us and hurried out into the open. It was ashamed to hide since it opposed ten and more bows to each of our spearmen. Thus, the Turks joined battle with the Latins, the inhabitants, who knew the area well, against the pilgrims who were ignorant of the people and places. In the first exchange, the lances were vigorous, piercing and casting down. But soon, weakened by such a great burden, they were no longer able to penetrate fully the shields, as well as the chest and stomach armor. A bursting pack saddle weakened one horse, a short spear cut down another, and a Turkish sword laid low still another so that a man brandishing a javelin might be thought of as a foot soldier armed with a club rather than a heavily armed mounted soldier armed with a spear. The bows, despite being much less expensive gave a much richer count of wounds. Bows always shoot and

frequently cause wounds. Arrows are never cast away and bowmen suffer
injury themselves only when it is too late. They are useful up close, far away,
in front, and in the rear. Even when they are turned from their proper
purpose, they rarely are permitted to disappoint those using them. This was a
matter of consolation to one side and a misfortune to the other. At the same
time that the leaders Baldwin and Tancred were working together they were
still divided. Discomfited in this manner, they were driven to a position
beneath the walls. The Turks, for their part, set up camp in front of the city
and continued their night's vigil during the day.

Chapter 47

Artah is handed over to Baldwin

The next day shone brightly, since, when the enemy returned to Antioch, fear
departed. Then, the son of the marquis was ordered to leave. As always,
having no faith in his fellow rulers,[98] he was summoned from the outer wall,
which is called the barbican, and expelled. The son of Eustace (Baldwin)
handed over control of Artah to that Baldwin under whose rule Edessa
flourished for some time. Then he, along with his remaining officers Airard
and Conan, set off for Edessa. Tancred was aware, because the path of war is
the way of man, that there was nothing safer than being in battle. So, he
occupied the nearby mountains and attacked large units with his small force.
The barbarians in this hill country were roused by such a great name. Some
fled and others waited to meet him. Many of them were unafraid. A shared
faith bound some of them to the Franks. Fanatical error separated the
remainder. Therefore, those who knew Christ received the Christians who
arrived. Fear, complemented by flight, persuaded those who did not know his
name or who spurned it to leave the towns of Apamea (Biredschik), and
Hersen.

   Now, having changed his place of residence, Tancred was happier as an
exile than as a guest in the city (Artah) since he did not experience any loss,
attacks or chains. For even though the enemy, in its accustomed manner, was
preparing ambushes and hiding its preparations for war in the bushes,
[Tancred] showed off his booty of mules, mule drivers, wagons and wagon
drivers in a sophisticated spectacle. The draft animals groaned burdened by
hay that covered them like blankets and pressed on as if ignorant of the
danger although aware of it. [But later on], just as they caught sight of the
river (Nahr-Belnias), which waters the fields of the town called Belnias, they

---

[98] Cf. Lucan, *De bello civili*, 1.92.

were themselves captured and carried off when some of their allies hurried off and left them in order to gain booty. Alas, why did you carry off booty when you were soon to be taken as booty? Why do you kill, bind and torture when soon you will be tortured, bound and killed? Hardly had they left the gates when they were set upon by ambushers whom, in the end, they were able to defeat.

Chapter 48

Antioch is besieged and the site is described

After besieging the city (Artah) and blocking their (the Latins') return, the Turks either killed or enslaved those Latins who had set out to follow them. Heaven then showed mercy to those afflicted by the siege so that the Antiochene besiegers [of Artah] gave way before the Franks hurrying to besiege Antioch. This venerable army of kings passed by cities and neighboring towns, as well as the Orontes river which flowed here, and then fixed camp outside the walls of long-desired Antioch.[99] Twin mountains, one in the south-south-west and the other in the north constricted the sides of this middle plain [where Antioch lies]. The sea touched the plain from the west. The mountains grow broader the further east one moves from the sea. The Damascene Orontes flowing south washed this mountain. As it wound its sinuous path to the sea through the plain, it lay between the mountains but closer to the southern side. At this point, however, it was bending into the shadow of the mountain so that there was nothing in the middle except for a footpath. It was here, where the slope begins to descend into the narrows, that the city was situated. The rivers and mountains ran along its flanks. The city was even joined to the flank of the mountain, although it was inhospitable, with walls reaching up to its summit and a citadel built there as well. The city also descended with the river and ran along with it over its middle portion. At its western edge, however, it withdrew a short distance from the river. In the east, the distance was greater. In this region of the city, a stagnant marsh strengthened the double walls. The sponginess of the ground made the fortification stronger than the hardest of rocks. Only the front of the city, exposed to the rising sun, offered a means of approach in this middle area, that is at the lower gate. The upper gate could not be reached although the ascent toward the broken rock seemed accessible to human eyes.

---

[99] The Orontes River is also called the Farfar, as in Ralph's account, and the Barbar.

Chapter 49

The order of the besiegers

A hill nearby but opposite from this place held Bohemond's standards. This rocky area extended all the way down to the road which issued from the gate, and, in fact, rose up to a small hill nearby the gate. It was here that Tancred established his camp, closer to the city than the others, that is about a missile shot away.[100] Behind him were the counts, the Normans and those who were in his company, and then the count of Flanders who was between him and Tancred. On the other side were the men of Blois, the men of Boulogne, Albemarle, and Mons, the men of Saint-Pol, and those serving Hugh the Great. All of these men were obligated to the Norman count because of gifts he had given them and some even through homage. Between them and the river were the camps of the heroes in the order I set them down on this page: Duke Godfrey, (Adhemar) the bishop of Le Puy and Count Raymond.[101]

This first positioning of the camps along one edge, besieged a single quarter of the city while leaving the others free. This first site was convenient as it was located near the plain whereas the other parts of the city were protected by impeding rivers, ravines or mountains. But as day after day passed, sometimes the requirements brought on by enemy attacks forced them to change positions and sometimes it was fulfilling their own desire to attack that did so. Indeed, the rock on which Bohemond had established his camp, although it was difficult to approach, was seen by the Turks to offer an opportunity to descend from their mountain and attack with bows. Once they had carried out their mission of death, they sought refuge again in the mountains with their light arms. The men following them, heavily burdened as they were [with arms and armor], could not find any way of making the ascent. In order to resist these attacks, the little hill above Bohemond's rock was girded with a wall and handed over to Hugh the Great's men to defend.

But the two northern gates open to both sides of the river continued to pour out Turks to the loss of our army. By attacking the lower of these two gates, Duke Godfrey succeeded in blocking their exit. But he was grieved by the loss of Marquis Garnier in the first attack.[102] Count Raymond took on the task of blocking the further gate through which the Turks were

---

[100] This reference would appear to refer to missiles shot by engines rather than bows. Ralph mentions below that when the Turks wished to attack the crusader encampments with their bows they had to descend the mountain.

[101] Adhemar, bishop of Le Puy, was assigned by Pope Urban II in 1095 to serve as the spiritual leader of the crusade in his place. During the crusade, Adhemar played a crucial role in maintaining peace among the crusade leaders.

[102] This man may have been related to Eustace Garnier who served as regent of Jerusalem in 1123.

accustomed to cross the nearby bridge. This spacious area across the river was empty of camps and therefore afforded considerable area in which the Turks could maneuver. Thus, a bridge constructed of floating material was placed in the river. An upper layer of hurdles weighed down on its interwoven beams, all of which rested atop a subordinate layer of boats. This continuation of the banks in service of crossing the channel permitted the count to cross and to block egress from the gate noted above.

The actual site also aided the besieger as well as providing a useful point from which to strengthen the siege. The ground here rose up in a small hill at whose crown sat a stone temple which, in the vernacular, is called a *muhammariam*.[103] This place suggested itself to the count as an opportune spot because it was set across from but near to the river gate. The count [Raymond] therefore supplied what was lacking in fortifying his camp, namely, a ditch which ran the circuit. It offered twofold protection: first through the depth of the ditch and second through the steepness of the berm raised above it. A wall was then raised over this berm which was humble in itself but proud in the audacity of its defenders. The more the Turks were constrained, the less able they were to do damage. Indeed, it was certainly the case that their ability to wander was curtailed. On occasion, however, the gate remained an effective means of going out to kill and still presented a difficulty for the prosecution of the siege.

Chapter 50

The difficulty of the siege

The intermediate constraints of the mountain and river made the siege difficult as these same impediments denied access to the ford on the one hand and to descent on the other. The ignorant foreigners were excluded while the knowledgeable inhabitants were able to cross. Furthermore, looking down on the road which led to the port, they frequently shed Christian blood.[104] It was only possible to go from the army to the port or from the port to the army with an armed force and not always even then. Indeed, this single gate made up for all the other exits which had been blocked. Tancred discovered a remedy for this evil as later events would demonstrate. Since he was closer to the walls, he was the first to face the raging Turks. As a result, he passed his days fasting under the sun and his nights in vigil under the dew. He alone had experienced all the events of this war, but in a measured manner up to this

---

[103] Ralph is referring here to a mosque.
[104] This is the port of Saint Simeon.

point. The enemy [in the city], who had been driven off by the great efforts of this man, now stopped their attacks and were content with their towers and hiding places.

But Tancred's brash audacity turned from this subdued eastern region to the unconquered western areas. There, in the course of a battle against the enemy, he said that he had found a wall and a fortress, albeit only at the beginning stages of construction, that he could use as a base. O love of praise, o boldness, o temerity! In other cases I would say that you Tancred were being strong, but here you are rash. In other cases, I would say you were constant, but here stubborn. In other cases, the appropriateness of the place, or the hope of aid, or compelling necessity or some other trace of prudence would excuse you. Here, however, everything argues for your rashness. The age of the run-down wall, the strength of the brigands, the closeness of the enemy, the distance of your friends and other matters such as the fact that the Orontes separates you from any aid that might come from the other side all make this clear. What if, heaven forbid, you fell to Turkish arms? You would pass cooked into the belly of the enemy before your capture reached the ears of your friends. You remain, you fight, you besiege, you protect one gate and batter another. Now you attack and then are attacked in turn. All of the West, however great it might be, fights in the East. You alone with your few fellow soldiers rejoice in fighting in the West. But you are strengthened thus, that the small fortification that I mentioned does not permit many inside but rather has the capacity to hold only a few.

Chapter 51

Tancred kills 700 Turks while sallying forth to capture booty

But let me go back to the beginning. For at first, Tancred sought to carry out his plans in secret so that he could fool the people of the city who were accustomed to go out every day to gather fodder. Thus, he came to his enclosure at night. But for some reason of which I am unaware, the [people of the city] were suspicious. So, on that first day they sent out only a few people to gather fodder so that in this manner they could find out if there were any new ambushes. When they saw this, our men hid themselves and not a single one went out. The [Antiochenes] thus returned safely inside the walls without being disturbed by any armed attack. They went out in a similar manner the next day although in slightly greater numbers and somewhat closer to the fort. The previous day, which had seen those gathering fodder go out and return in safety, had made them more confident. At this point, Tancred was hardly able to hold back his lions when they caught sight of the sheep who were so close by. He said, 'hold for just this short day my brave men. Tomorrow, unless I am mistaken, a much richer prize will fall into our net'.

Thus, he foresaw and thus it happened. Now, because of the two days of trials and shortfalls over the previous two days, on the third day they went out feeling safer but also compelled to do so. In addition, because they already had gathered fodder in the nearer fields, concerned up to that point by the possible presence of the Franks, the many people going out now crossed near to the Franks. Then, bursting forth from his concealment, Tancred rushed forward and demonstrated how prudence and audacity can be combined. He charged into their midst and devoured them all with the mouth of his sword. Their guts were scorched even more sharply because of the three-day thirst which his sword had endured while sitting among these goblets.

Lest this account be too long, after about 700 [of the Turks] had been killed, Tancred sent 70 heads taken from the dead men to the bishop of Le Puy, a tenth of his triumph.[105] The bishop experienced a two-fold joy at this gift, first because of the victory of his friend, and second because of the honor and glory he received in the granting of such a gift. Thus, in turn, he repaid the victor with the same number of marks that he had received for the necks of the murderers. At this time, Tancred owed a great deal of money to his fellow soldiers and had nothing in his coffers. Therefore, this money, received with great joy and exultation, soon freed the leader from his debt. The distribution of the money also relieved the needs of these soldiers. But, it happened by chance that a messenger, one not sent by the bishop, arrived [at Tancred's camp] before the man whom the bishop had sent. When he heard the news, [Tancred] distributed what he did not yet have. He soon enriched others while going back into debt himself. He told himself in his heart that, 'my soldiers are my treasure. It causes me no concern that they are provided for when I am in need so long as I command men for whom provision has been made. They load their pouches with silver, I load them with cares, arms, sweat, tremors, hail and rain'. He gently supported those worn out by fighting during the day and vigils at night by taking on their turn at watch when this was merited by wounds or by illness. His respect for his own lordship never gave way to laziness. Rather, he always took his turn, and not only that, but as was noted above, he also took the turns of others.

---

[105] This reference to one-tenth of the heads would seem to be a play on the tithe required of all Christians to support their local parish churches.

Chapter 52

Tancred skewers three Turks in single combat

While he often acted in this manner, it happened once that he set out to patrol 'accompanied only by Achates'.[106] Having set aside his hauberk and his helmet, he rode out girded with only a sword. The boy held a spear and a shield. Three armed Turks were also on patrol having left the gate from Antioch. Both sides were ignorant of the presence of the other because the short distance that divided the city from the camp was strewn with bushes, little hills and valleys that were useful for setting ambushes. But once the two were found, the three rushed upon them ignorant of whom the were attacking. But, o pitiable men, fly, fly, I say. Castor's Cyllarus, Achilles' spear, Meleager's right, Tyndeus' bravery, Hercules' threefold [club] and Ajax's sevenfold [bull's hide shield] all arm this one fighting man.[107] It was superfluous to arouse him as he charged armed into all of them. It would be cautious to flee, foolish to wait and insane to attack. Therefore, since he who waits unwillingly, acts likewise in killing,[108] rush in swiftly, so that you might fall as quickly as possible. Fall immediately so that the son of the marquis might live for eternity.

Upon seeing this mad charge, Tancred took up his spear and transfixed, as is normal, the leading man. A shield and hauberk usually offer protection. But this is when they are set against another attacker. Tancred did not permit any hauberk to be faithful or allow it not to fail. His attack transformed a helmet into a turban, a shield into a cloak and a hauberk into a shirt. He struck wood as if it were flax, steel as if it were hemp, and a blade as if it were wool. When the Turk in the middle saw the death of the first one he slowed down so that he could be aided by the last one. O unlucky one, how you once envied the head start of the faster and now you prefer the blessed delay of the slower. But this is all in vain. For both the fast and the slow will fall to one right hand. Indeed, the one (Tancred) attacks both cutting to pieces the man facing him and stopping the other in his tracks with a thrust to his back.

But what amazes me, indeed, that about which I am not able to be amazed enough is that this man (Tancred), the precious purchaser of praise, sealed the mouth of his armsbearer with an order of silence. I do not know whether it

---

[106] Vergil, *Aeneid*, 1.312. Achates was Aeneas' faithful arms bearer.

[107] Cyllarus was Castor's horse. Cf. Vergil, *Georgics*, 3.89. Meleager was one of the hunters of the Calydonian boar. Tyndeus was the son of Aeneas and Periboa. Cf. Vergil, *Aeneid*, 6.479.

[108] Cf. Horace, *Ars poetica*, 467, 'he who saves a man, who does not wish to be saved, does the same thing as if he had killed him' (*invitum qui servat, idem facit occidenti*).

was shame, or religion, or fear of being believed which was the cause. If it were shame, what could anyone do at any time to be honored if this one considers it a matter of shame to have killed three armed men in one attack? If it is a matter of religion, they say that it is a monstrous thing for fish to appear under a plow. But I say that it is more unnatural still for a man so desirous of praise to flee it. And finally, this most famous fighter, having overcome so many difficulties, and made it through so many rough spots, and survived so many battles, would easily be believed. This is especially true since the area around the battle contains weapons that could serve as witnesses. But most of all, there is nothing trusted more than his word. If the cause of the silence remains hidden, the effect of the deaths became known. But it became known long after the event when the sworn armsbearer completed the fixed period of silence.

Chapter 53

The patience of the Christians during this long and hard siege

Time summons me, after a delay, to return to the siege so that those who poured out so much sweat might receive their small reward. During a delay of almost eight months many men in the army had undertaken many difficult tasks, and this was true most of all of the great men. However, they all, the highest, those in the middle and the lowest, suffered badly, from hunger, from the movement of the earth, from floods, from various terrors of the sky, and now from the attacks of the outpouring sky and from military assaults. They also witnessed many prodigies and visions. Many saw these privately, but some shone forth from heaven for all to see. I will describe each of them (the leaders) by their order, manner and dignity. In the meantime, Tancred will be silent for too long, for just as I am a scorner of silence, he too is unworthy of it.

But in order for our ship to come to port, I must pass through the tempests of a great sea. For who would presume [to pass over in silence] the amazing strength of Godfrey whose drawn sword turned one Turk into two, whose lower half rode into the city and whose other half swam jumping into the river? Who might not worthily admire Raymond's lonely resistance against the attacks of Antioch, sometimes manfully repelling attacks on the ditches and sometimes attacks against the walls, or that he once attacked the bridge without any help from the army that was too far away? Surely, Robert of Flanders's spear deserves its own writer? While he enriched Antioch every day with dead, each day the count was himself impoverished through the loss of a horse. And, although the love of praise concealed this loss, sometimes this leader would have been left without a horse at all if he had not gone as a beggar through the streets. An open basin was carried from inn to inn where those with pity, including the keeper of a tavern, provided the count with a horse, albeit a meager one.

But, what has our time seen to be compared with this, namely, that around 200 men, poorly armed, mostly mounted on donkeys and worn out, drove off 15 000 armed and robust horsemen? This victory was accorded to the count of Blois,[109] who was the leader in conjunction with Godfrey and Bohemond. Seven hundred and more heads were taken from this fight and carried toward Antioch to serve as a spectacle, a demonstration of mourning. Each head was fixed on a stake with about half a foot separating their eyes. How much glory do you think this brought to the sword of Blois?

But, as I said, the hundred-fold path of these matters again calls me back lest remaining as a wanderer in each of these byways, I deviate from the path on which I began. Normandy and Flanders celebrated their Roberts. The remainder of the West celebrated their leaders. One son of a marquis is enough for me although I am not adequate or complete in my treatment of him. Forgive me, o Gaul, rich in writers! It is proper for me to spend my time with the Antiochene prince. Through the present *Gesta* I as a debtor will rather easily pay off my creditor. But, lest my silence fail to repay with a reward in any manner those matters worthy of merit, I will try to limit this lengthy text, so that posterity will be able to explicate my writing in a more prolix style.

Chapter 54

The heavy burdens of the besiegers

Therefore, the city was besieged by three winds, the south wind did not blow over any besieger. There was no water or space on their side. These discomforts were comforting to the men of the city, keeping out the besiegers and keeping the besieged safe. Whenever a Frank went out to seek supplies or returned having found them, there were ambushes and harsh attacks on those who had been traveling. This whole people, so many thousands of them from so many different nations, lacked large numbers of cattle and great quantities of grain. Syria, Cilicia, Rhodes, exceptionally rich Cyprus, certain islands, and certain kingdoms aided the army. But this amounted to very little even though Chios, Samos, Crete, Mitelene and innumerable other islands of lesser

---

[109] Ralph gives far more positive attention to Stephen of Blois than any of the other major crusade chroniclers from the late eleventh and early twelfth centuries.

fame were joined in this effort. Emperor Alexios' herald was also there urging people to bring grain by land and by sea.[110]

The siege began in the winter and, during its course, the winter brought horrors down on everyone. There were floods of water, sometimes in sudden downpours, and sometimes in continuous streams. There was great movement of both the heaven and earth so that it appeared that the two elements had been joined together with the one rising up and the other coming down. But what about the storms, what shall I say about the raging of the winds? While they were blowing, neither tent nor hut could stand. Indeed, it was hardly possible for the palace and the tower to survive. The nobility endured this through God alongside the poor. The winter spared neither. But it was much harsher for nobles in as much as the peasant is tougher than the noble, as a toiler is compared to one who is accustomed to luxury.

Hunger accompanied all of these tempests, and death accompanied hunger. Death, the comfort of battles, having free rein, was present before people and horses. It was the rare stable in camp, which had one horse in ten remaining with the other nine taken off by hunger. Rust seized hold of all of the iron and steel weapons. Shields lost their nails and leather coverings. Very few spears and stools made of wood remained whole, and many of these had been repaired. No one's wooden goods were tidy and many people had none at all. Bows lacked their sinews and arrows were bereft of their shafts. Everywhere there was want, calamity and desolation.

Chapter 55

The marvelous faith of the Christians

The situation was exceptionally difficult and sad when suddenly their burdens were heaped up with still more burdens. As the Ram succeeded the Pisces, as winter passed into spring, the plants in this period gave renewed strength for the horses of the Medes and Persians to go to war. The Turks were now present in unexpectedly large numbers and were prepared for war. They were nearby and close enough so that on the same day they could enter the city or attack the camp before speeding rumor outpaced them and reported the situation to the Christians. In its customary manner, rumor expanded and made still greater things out of already weighty matters.

Thus, the Latin leaders were roused to prepare to fight. Although this was a difficult task, it was as if a distaste for life made it possible to think about

---

[110] This acknowledgment of Byzantine aid in obtaining supplies during the siege of Antioch is rare among Western crusade historians.

rushing toward death. For, from this great multitude, from the great number of heavily armed mounted fighting men, who had besieged the city, hardly 200 could be summoned to set out mounted. And furthermore, a sizable portion of these had to ride asses in place of horses. It happened that our men, fearing nothing of this kind, had sent the horses far off where there was fodder. Therefore, this small force set out to fight against 15 000, about whom they had learned from their scouts. What boldness! This should be discussed for all time. In this group were the leaders Godfrey, Bohemond and Stephen of Blois. When they came to the bridge, which is wrongly called the Iron Bridge in the vernacular because of the Orontes river, they saw the enemy off in the distance.[111] But not remaining there as if afraid, they crossed in order to cause fear. Bohemond was in the lead, then followed Godfrey, with Stephen in reserve.

Chapter 56

The few attack the enemy and put them to flight

There was a small hill just across the bridge on the plain. Our men waited near it. The Turks crossed the plain which was very wide. They caught sight of our men from a long way off and wondered by what faith such a small group had crossed. This passage, which was more a matter of carefulness than boldness, struck great fear among the enemies so that the small number of our men grew in their minds into a great multitude. The Turks stopped when they drew near. They feared that the hill, mentioned above, which showed a few men, hid many. The supporters of Christ simulated this by attaching banners to their spears, affixing one to each, as if the hill hid as many units as there were banners. And soon, waiting no longer, our men raised their lances and broke up the enemy force with the type of charge one might expect of a falcon attacking a crowd of coots (river/marsh birds). Dust rose up, arms rang, hooves stomped, shields clanged, eyes were blinded, ears were deafened, and they overwhelmed the hearts of their enemies since the latter feared as many thousands of Franks would charge from hiding as there were banners which they could see. It is marvelous to tell and hard to believe. But that great multitude turned in retreat. Very few on the Christian side were lost, the most important of these was Conan, count of Brittany, who, once his spirit was inflamed, dared to charge out front against the Persian army with just one companion.[112]

---

[111] The local name for the river was the Farfar, which may have suggested *ferrum* (iron) to Ralph. It is not clear that the name of the bridge actually was derived from the name of the river.

[112] Conan, also called Brito, was the son of Count Geoffrey of Lamballe.

Long afterward, his grave was pointed out to me along the road near the bridge. It had been decorated, as much as is permitted by the piety of his people, with a stone and a cross. But the Franks, who had seized victory, only pursued the enemy for a short while. They were held back by the small number and sluggishness of their horses, both brought about by hunger. As a sign of their victory, they brought back 700 heads from the dead troops. First, however, the count and his fellows in martyrdom were buried, just as the situation required. And, if I remember correctly, these deeds were done on that day when Christians are accustomed to look after their bellies and indulge studiously in the eating of meat before turning the next day to ashes.[113]

Chapter 57

The homeland of the author of this history. Hunger in the city

The following night brought a horrible redness to the sky positioned so that those in the west could see it. They shouted, 'the East fights'. I myself saw this same sign while in my father's home at Caen where I spent my youth. I had not yet seen anything of note, not even Rome, and Antioch was then just a name to me. Many people marveled at this vision, and they all said with one voice that it indicated war and blood. But when our victorious men returned they fixed the heads they had taken on stakes and then placed these stakes in a row in the earth before the walls in sight of the enemy. One of the heads was found which was quite remarkable having a distance of half a foot between its eyes. Those who fixed it on a stake shouted out to the citizens looking down from the walls, 'behold your hope, behold your threats, behold the strength called up against the Franks, we are reserving this same payment for you. You are shut in, the chance for flight has been removed, your grain is eaten, hunger has come, aid has been removed, everything is against you'.

When they had seen and heard what the Franks did and said, the people of the city were afraid. They did not open the gate, as they had done earlier, rather they languished in hunger and lamented in their fear. They passed the whole spring in this state of calamity eking out their lack of bread in the manner of beasts with the produce of spring, that is with leafy branches and plants. Then Cassian, this was the name of the commander of the besieged city, issued an edict and sent out men who were to see it enforced.[114] Whoever

---

[113] The Franks won this victory on Tuesday, in the month of February 1098, that is, on Shrove (Fat) Tuesday before the beginning of Lent. The ashes refer here to ashes worn on the forehead on Ash Wednesday.

[114] Yaghi-siyan, the commander of Antioch.

of the citizens was found to have grain was to divide it, sending half to the court and keeping half for himself to sustain his life insofar as this was possible. When they heard the news, the citizens were upset but accepted it nevertheless. They divided their grain, giving this part to the court and keeping the other portion to sustain their lives. The use to which it was put lessened the loss to those deprived, however, especially since the supplies were intended to support the garrison.

Chapter 58

Many leaders leave the siege

In the meantime, the count of Blois (Stephen) and the Norman count (Robert) left camp, exhausted by the miserable circumstances, and went respectively to Cilicia and Latakia. The count of Blois went to Tarsus to repair his health. The Norman count went in hope of commanding the English. At this time, the English held Latakia, having been sent to guard it by the emperor.[115] An army was moving on the borders of this area and attempting to strike in force. In face of this threat, the English called the aforementioned count, an action which was both faithful and prudent. It was a matter of faith because they placed themselves in the hands of a man who was loyal to their lord (Alexios). It was a matter of prudence because they had left the Norman yoke and now subordinated themselves to it again. They had experienced both faithfulness and the gifts from this people and easily returned whence they had left. Therefore, the Norman count entered Latakia and spent his time in slumber and idleness. This was not entirely useless, however, because he found substantial supplies there and gave them out generously to those who were in need.

Cyprus, abounding in wine, grain and great numbers of cattle, supplied Latakia and its needy Christian hinterland as if it were a foster sister. For this city was the only one on the Syrian shore which was both Christian and loyal to Alexios. But this did not excuse his idleness, and the count was summoned to camp once and then again in vain. It was only on the third occasion, now under threat of anathema, that he returned unwillingly. The traveler had a more difficult journey than he should have had in light of Latakia's responsibility to provide him with aid.

---

[115] The Byzantine emperors had a unit in the official list of the army called the Varangians made of up Danes and English.

Chapter 59

The deployment of the commanders conducting the siege

The other leaders occupied the nearby towns, and there was, therefore, a better opportunity to bring aid easily. Sedium, which was a large, populous town, rich in wine, fell to the duke (Godfrey).[116] The count of Flanders held the nearby valley where the towns of Belnias, Bathemolin, Corsehel, Barsoldan, as well as many others were located.[117] Thus, up to the present day, this valley is called the valley of the count, and Sedium is called the city of the duke. Hamah and Hirem served Tancred along with many other productive [towns] near to the camp. He was the first of all to arrive, as I mentioned above, and was thus the precursor. The effect of his early arrival confirms the common expression that 'he who sees first is the first fed'. For when hunger struck, this man, who lived in opulence, never excluded any of his household from his table. He also took in and supported many excluded by the others. The valley of Doueir supported Bohemond. It deserved the name which it had been given because it held a position of glory among the other valleys, having an abundance of fruits, vines, trees and water. Thus, indeed, it deserved the name Daphne, meaning delightful, which it had been called of old by the Greeks.[118] It was close to Antioch in the south south-west and required a great protector who could provide for the hunger of the citizens from its great stores of food. The other leaders held other towns whose names have been forgotten over the intervening long period. However, time has not forgotten that the towns of Rubea (Riha), Arqah and Besmedin served Count Raymond.

Chapter 60

Great hunger in the army

Thus, the leaders occupied the province. But others of lesser fame, just like the great men, were afflicted with great want. Since there was no way to leave and no way to remain, death and hunger, like twin misfortunes with no middle ground, struck down the people. Both the long delay and the great

---

[116] We have not been able to identify the modern name of Sedium.

[117] We have not been able to identify the modern names of Bathemolin, Corsehel, and Barsoldan.

[118] Daphne was a famous grove and sanctuary dedicated to Apollo outside the walls of Antioch. During the Roman period, the gardens and running water at Daphne were regarded by the citizens of Antioch as a pleasant retreat from the city.

number of people increased the hunger. But a day did not go by when reports
of the deaths of those having gone out to obtain supplies did not terrify the
ears of the besiegers. The leaders, now this one and now that one, brought aid
to the foragers. Sometimes, however, the leaders themselves required aid. For
the southern gate, mentioned above, was always open for ambushes and
never ceased to pour out troops who watched the narrow places on the roads
and then rushed upon the surprised foragers.

But now an even heavier problem, that is hunger, weighed down and sent
the army wandering to and fro just like swarms of bees contemptuous of
death. For what does hunger not spurn? To what lengths will it not impel?
Whom will it permit to remain in a state of shame? This was the reason why
Guy the Red and William the Carpenter fled.[119] These were not obscure men,
but rather important men among the paladins of the king of France. While
they were preparing to leave, Bohemond, who was there, said, 'And in seeking
safety are you giving no thought to this common labor? You are nobles and
the path is clear. Your tents shall remain here and will be set aside as a public
latrine to the eternal shame of your name and of your family.' They thus left
secure in their infamy as the stimulus of hunger condemned them to infamy.
They followed Count Stephen who, as noted above, sought rest in Cilicia.
These men who shared a common generation and common manner of life, all
hated labor and sought after pleasure. They were fighters. In between wars,
however, they were accustomed to luxury.

Chapter 61

The customs of the men of Provence

This people has lofty eyes, a ferocious spirit, is prompt to take up arms, more
profligate than others but more slothful in gathering wealth. The Provençals
are as different from [the Franks] in their customs, their will, their manner of
worship and their food as a hen is to a duck. They are frugal in their manner
of life, more careful in investigating matters and more apt to work hard. But,
that I not hide the truth, they are less warlike. They reject ornamentation of
the body, which they say is a vile thing and is to be left to women. But they
take pains in the ornamentation of their horses and mules. Their zeal in this
time of hunger aided them more than many peoples who were more eager to
fight. When there was a dearth of bread, they endured, content with roots.
They did not spurn husks and they took up long iron tools with which they

---

[119] Guy the Red, called Trussellus, was the seneschal or the steward of the king of
France. William the Carpenter was viscount of Melun and Gâtinais and a relative of
Hugh the Great.

found grain in the bowels of the earth. Thus, boys still sing that 'Franks go to war and Provençals to food.'

There was one thing that they did out of greed which was shameful. They sold dog meat to others as if it were hare and mule meat as if it were goat. And, if it were possible for them to reach a fat horse when no one was watching, they would give it a wound in its guts from the back or through its rectum, and the animal would die. This was a source of amazement to everyone who was ignorant of the fraud. For they saw a fat, quick, robust and frolicsome animal. They never found any traces of wounds and the cause of death was hidden. The observers were terrified by this unnatural situation and shouted, 'Let us keep our distance, the spirit of a demon has afflicted this beast.' After the observers had spoken, those knowledgeable about the death approached as if they did not know. Upon being prohibited from touching the animal they said, 'we would rather die in eating this food than from fasting'. Those who suffered the loss had pity on those who had caused it, while the latter repaid them with a laugh. Then, this people approached the cadaver like a flock of crows and each one took away whatever portion had been cut off either for his own stomach or to market.

Chapter 62

Cassian's harshness toward an Armenian

Now Christ, recognizing and taking pity on his supporters, led these happy people to end their agony. He opened up shade and the city to those consumed by the rays of the sun in this manner. Among those whose grain Cassian had divided in half was a rich Armenian who had rejected the teachings of Christ and followed the errors of the gentiles. He had a large family and enough grain to feed them. However, as the famine grew worse, this was reported to Cassian, and he had this last part, which had been left earlier for their pitiable existence, divided again. Before, there was a general seizure from homes and families. This individual seizure seemed much harder to bear as if an injury had been superimposed on loss.

Having been deprived of the means of supporting life, he was mournful and out of his mind. He kissed the prince's feet and begged him for the support that had been taken from his children now left in want. Who would not be moved by this flood of tears and cries reaching up to heaven? 'Please, my children can no longer be called my beloved guaranties for the future, they are now my dire wounds. Your hunger consumes mine, your heart penetrates mine, I cannot feel my hunger. What good does it do me to feed with delicate foods those to whom bread fit only for useless slaves is denied? It would be better for a father's misery to see them slaughtered rather than afflicted by starvation. It would be better for them to be struck by spears, scorched by lightning, or drowned in the sea than I see what my soul abhors, namely, that they die in this manner set out by you. My only solace is that I will die first and that the sword or noose will free me from seeing you. Be merciful citizens, intercede for the innocent, for I shall surely die punished as a guilty man while my family is not yet tortured by the torment of famine.'

Chapter 63

The city is betrayed

Having pitifully but uselessly poured out these laments, he was spurned, ridiculed and sent away. From the beginning of the siege, the custody of one of the towers had been entrusted to him. It was located in a western corner of the city situated on the mountain far away from the [Christian] army. Cassian had entrusted the nearby lower tower to the brother [of the Armenian] so that it could be said that the two sisters were entrusted to two brothers.[120] This was not done incautiously or casually. Guards, who had been Christians were placed prudently far away from the Christians. This was the plan, this is what was done.

But when the first brother was rebuffed and saw that he had subjected himself to affronts, and that no one interceded for him and no one showed him any mercy, he looked to his own salvation. He would avenge his injuries by betraying the whole city. So, when the sentries were asleep, he looked down from the wall joined to his tower and let down a rope on which he and two of his children descended. Tired out by a long walk, he finally reached Bohemond.

The people of the East considered him among all of the others to be a sort of prince among princes. Since the time he had fought alongside Robert Guiscard, Bohemond's fame, glorious from many battles, had terrified peoples. From that beginning, he had become celebrated in Asia and was now considered to be the lord of all of those here. When the Armenian was ordered to explain why he had come, he agreed to betray an entrance to the city, and set the most opportune day, hour and place for them to come. Soon, after leaving his sons behind with the besiegers, he returned alone to the rope. However, with anger, boldness, hope and fear, as his companions and goads, he easily climbed back up.

---

[120] The two towers commanded by the two brothers were known colloquially as the two sisters.

Chapter 64

Bohemond gives the news to the bishop of Le Puy. The bishop of Le Puy's
sermon to the magnates

Bohemond, who had never before been roused by an equal feeling of joy,
went to the bishop of Le Puy, the man whom the pope had sent to lead the
army in his own place, and told him his secret in confidence. The bishop
promised to keep this matter quiet and to strive to keep it a secret. He
therefore immediately summoned the leaders of the army and those who were
important among the people, and once they had been gathered, addressed
them in this manner:

'Brothers, the present labor has been long and heavy, and it would burden
us even more and for longer if God's eyes were not looking down upon us.
We built siege engines, but the bog blocked them. We undermined the walls
but were repulsed. We fight, but this matter has ceased to be profitable. But
there is only one thing to fear, that is this battle which they say will be even
greater and in which [the enemy] will be even more numerous. The enemy
numbered 15 000, they are now approaching 400 000. The strength of the
enemy has not ceased to grow and ours has not ceased to diminish. Consider
the strength of this city, where it is located, that ravines make it impervious
on three sides and on the fourth lies the river and the swamp. Its circuit of
walls has no equal anywhere in the world. Fountains flow inside and those
who have passed a year since the threats brought by our arrival are able to
gather sufficient quantities of other supplies necessary for life. O Antioch,
that you had never existed or that we had never come upon you. Our path is
to Jerusalem. What is Antioch to us? What if we retreated from here, if we left
having been driven off? Then nothing was accomplished and there is nothing
left for which to hope. I say, if we abandon this place, it will not abandon us.
It will be our constant companion. Indeed, I say truly that it will be our
adversary blocking the roads, attacking us from the rear and the front. It will
give hope of resistance to others whereas its capture will throw all the others
into terror.

'O walls, that you had never arisen! Would that you had remained far from
our eyes and ears. But let us deliberate o leaders. Let us confer, let us propose
some prize for bravery. I hope that we will excite the hearts of our men once
they have heard of the greatest of the prizes. Consider what Saul did and we
will take examples from antiquity. There was no one among the Hebrews who
would go against Goliath until the promise of the king's daughter and the
liberty of his father's house roused David.[121] Many say among themselves

---

[121] 1 Samuel 18:25.

and even openly, "for whom do I labor? For what reason do I suffer? Why have I taken these wounds? Shall I give my life as a prize to Antioch? Some ingrate, I do not know who, is in command. Far be it from me to beg so that any other ingrate can mock my tears." Therefore act, so that it is not the ambition of rule which moves you but rather the completion of this journey we have undertaken. It would be better that this city fall as a prize to one, if it is by his ability that the city receives us, than the lack of this prize weaken our strength by setting forth the excuses that you have heard. My mind cannot conceive of anything that could be considered better, more efficacious, and more excellent. By your discretion, o leaders, if I have left something out, add it, if I have said too much, remove it. If what I have said is wrong, change it. If it is good, agree to it.'

Chapter 65

The command of the city is granted to the one who succeeded in gaining entry to it

The entire council was in favor. First the leaders, and then those who followed the leaders, each according to his rank, gave his assent. No one was opposed. Everyone agreed that the city should go to him, whoever that might be, who gained entry. Then Bohemond spoke saying, 'a promise which is bound by an oath is as good as completed just as if the future were to pass in some way into the present and hope were to pass into joy. But what are words worth which have been freed from this bond? Whoever was able to get rich from a promise?[122] If you wish this matter to be fixed, bind yourselves in an oath to what you have promised.'

There was no delay, there were no retractions. They swore just as they had been called on to do. If he had asked them to swear on even greater matters, they would not have refused to do so because of their hope of aid. Thus, even more certain and aroused, Bohemond set out his plan to some of the leaders, and showed everyone more openly how to prepare for the attack. He promised them a ready plan with certain hope of success. Then, when each had bid farewell to the other, they returned to their own areas and began to prepare ropes. But [Bohemond], alone among all those rushing about, intended to seize the prize. He rushed, he thought, he made ready for the arrival of the coming night which seemed slower to him than to someone waiting for a mistress or for the workday to end.

---

[122] Ovid, *Ars amatoria*, 1.444.

Chapter 66

The city is betrayed

And when night fell, while everything was kept silent, Bohemond moved out toward the tower that had been promised to him, not, however, without a great deal of sweat. The rough terrain precluded the use of horses. Nevertheless, Bohemond sent out a messenger who scouted and looked over the situation to see if everything was safe along the approach to the walls. When he had left [Bohemond's camp], the blessed betrayer had provided this signal saying 'when you come, my lord, send your messenger to the foot of my tower. I will keep a zealous watch on the wall. If everything is well, I shall drop one stone and then another. If there is danger, one stone will indicate this.'

The scout, who had been sent out to find out how matters stood, was immediately seen as he approached the tower. Once having been recognized, he received the signal that all was well. He then returned and reported what he had heard. Therefore, just as he had begun, Bohemond came to the wall and found a rope hanging outside. He bound himself in the rope and the Armenian drew him up. And when he had made a strong enough knot, the young birds, with armored bodies and girded with swords, flew along the ropes. The first of these was Govel of Chartres. Just as an eagle summons its young to fly and flutters over them, this noble man, who from his youth had eaten and drunk nothing other than praise, did not wish to be praised in order to live, but sought to live for the sake of praise. At first, they were silent while their small numbers had reason to be fearful of the multitude of their enemies. But as the numbers of those inside the city increased, the spirits [of the attackers] banished fear and transformed those, who had the appearance of eagles during their ascent, into lions.

Chapter 67

The slaughter of the people of the city

The attackers ran to the gates and whoever got in their way died. The first one who met their swords, the one into whose tower they first charged, was the brother of the man who had let them enter. His brother had left him uninformed fearing that if he knew what was going to happen, he would prepare a trap for him and the men with him. Thus, when he and his fellow guards were suddenly cut down by the sword, a shout rose up which reached the other towers. Some of the guards succeeded in running away. As for the rest, the towers became their tombs and guarded those buried within just as they once had been guarded by them. Our men came down to the gates. The gate in the west was opened up by Bohemond after he removed the bolts. The other gate, in the north, was opened up by Raymond. Bohemond had climbed to his gate through inaccessible paths. Raymond had besieged his gate for a long time. And when he heard the tumult, he wasted no time in arriving there.

Their greatest concern and fear was that the city would rush against those of our men who had entered, that the gates would be held, and aid would be kept out. But Christ cast a merciful eye over his people. So, while they arrived, the enemy fled. Once the guards had abandoned their gates it was easy to enter. Those outside, safely out in the open, used rams to achieve entry. Night had aided the Christians. Now, as dawn broke, the day was envious of the night's joy. As the sun rose, the Christians rushed into the palace, battered the captured city, and tore up the hiding places. They seized whatever gold, small children, women, young girls and anything else they found. Whoever offered resistance was killed and whoever surrendered was saved. But the people of the city, at least those who were prompt in fleeing and left everything behind, made it to the mountain.[123] But the father did not wait for the wounded son nor did the son await the aged father.[124]

Chapter 68

Cassian, the prince of Antioch, seeks his safety in flight

The citadel situated at the top of the mountain received many of them but many whom the Christians swords had met and turned this way were excluded from the citadel. Some of them rushed to their deaths. Others climbed the inner staircases up to the walls, which offered safety outside. For some this meant death and others a new chance of life. As was noted above, this side of the city was not besieged and thus offered these people a means of escape. Indeed, this area of separation from the city seemed valuable in their efforts to flee. Prince Cassian himself managed to escape, although he was wounded in the head by a sword, in the back by a spear and in the leg by an arrow. Night, the dawn, his spurs and his horse enabled him to come near the town of Rubea (Riha). Here, having given up his horse and lying in the shadows, he hid himself under a bush hoping that the coming day would bring a helpful traveler, or at the least that the coming of night would offer him shadows for his escape. Pitiable in this hope, and as I said, wounded, he sat there in great thirst, with his ears perked up and his eyes fixed on the road.

---

[123] This is a reference to the citadel that stood at the highest point of the city.

[124] Cf. Vergil, *Aeneid*, 2.650–71 where Aeneas did not abandon his father Anchises but rather carried him to safety from Troy on his own back.

He lay hiding there like a little hare that finds safety in the thorns after being taken from the jaws of puppies.

O glory of the world! Who is more unlucky than he? Yesterday, he was the prince of Antioch, the lord of Syria and Phoenicia, the terror of Assyria, the most powerful of all the eastern kings, second only to the sultan who rules the kingdom of Persia. But while this miserable man suffered these burdens, his thirst grew worse, and tortured his guts. Then, he caught sight of a farmer carrying an amphora filled with water. He made himself known to him, approached, and drank. When the farmer caught sight of his state, and considered his face, he was amazed at both his condition and his wounds. He said, 'Alas my prince, whom have you allowed to do such a thing, whose boldness has grown so strong against you?'[125] He recognized him because the eyes of the subject are always turned toward royal majesty. And he was therefore amazed since he was ignorant of recent events.

Chapter 69

Cassian is killed by the farmer

Then Cassian, placing his trust in the one who had shown compassion for his sorry position, feared at the same time that if he showed his distrust by dissimulating, then the latter would in turn take the role of an enemy because of this mistrust. He said, 'Antioch is lost. The Franks hold it. I, as you see, barely reached this hole in the ground with three wounds. But I beg you, do not make this known. If it is possible, I will flee at dusk. If I escape, you can expect the greatest possible reward.' The common man follows fortune. When she smiles, you have innumerable friends. When she cries, they all rush off leaving the cask dry down to the dregs, unwilling to bear the burden equally.

The farmer, astounded by such a rapid fall, was beside himself. He shook inwardly, stupefied, as he considered what ought to be done at such a crucial moment. He considered the wounds that had moved him to pity and he thought about two things, the ease of carrying out this task, and the benefits of doing so. If he killed him, there would be an immediate reward from the royal clothing, and the horse, and the gratefulness of the Franks. But the friendship of Christ, whose enemy he would kill, was to be preferred even over these. Moreover, there would be immortal praise for the killing of such a prince, a factor which has driven many mortals to their deaths. But these thoughts were foreign to the mind of the farmer, who had no noble feelings. Thus, he considered what would be useful. He saw someone who was

---

[125] Cf. *Aeneid*, 6.502.

exhausted, bloodied, half dead, alone and unarmed. He decided it would be easy to extinguish what remained of his life. What more is there to say. Unmindful of honesty, and having set aside piety, the servant beat the lord with a raised club, and scattered his brains, preferring the spoils taken in this manner to big promises.

Chapter 70

Tancred complains that he had not known about this expedition

In the meantime, Tancred, who was ignorant of what had happened, in his customary manner was keeping watch far from the city on the roads that often provided a means of exit and return to its inhabitants. When he had found out what was happening from the people whom he had captured during their flight, he groaned, 'alas to me, alas. I am the only one to suffer in the midst of such ineffable joy. What shame that some labored while I slept, that some scouted while I snored. O Bohemond, Bohemond, you shared your plans with others but kept them secret from me. O kinsman of my blood, you would act thus to your kinsman? You made sure I would be absent when you know I would not have failed to take a leading role in such an action were I present. You know that if I had been there, I would have been the first to rush the wall, the first to clasp the rope, the first to go over the top and the first to kill. You cast a jealous eye on my glory although strength, age and perhaps even purpose deny this to you. Lucky is he, whoever he is, who offered up the first fruits of glory to our Lord God. But let us move out, my comrades. We missed the first wave but we shall at least follow after. For he who made you paupers and robbed me of glory shall not take away this opportunity. The One who fixes the hearts of all men and who understands their actions will Himself judge and provide vindication.'

Having spoken in this manner, he arrived at Antioch and found joy. He who had wept with the mourners now felt joy with those rejoicing. Common happiness drove private sadness from this noble heart. It happened, however, that some private joy was added to the common feeling because that part of his force, which he left behind to guard the camp, entered the city with Bohemond after they heard the trumpets blowing. In the absence of their lord, they readied a distinguished palace for him. And now all of the rulers had entered with the exception of the count of Blois who had been shamefully excluded whether by the just anger of heaven or by the jealousy of fortune.

Chapter 71

A miraculous event

It happened that at this time there was an unexpected event, without precedent, such that neither the past nor the present could remember a prodigy of this type having come before or after. Having been summoned to dinner by Bohemond, the counts sat together with him, the count of Flanders on his right and the count of Boulogne (Eustace) on his left. There were a great many people in the palace at this time, some sleeping and others working, so that there were a great number there when the leaders came together to eat. Food made them quiet. But drink, as was said once by a wise man, made them talkative.[126] After dinner, Bohemond brandished a knife in his right hand. Alluding to this, the count of Flanders said, 'What is this brandishing for? I see it as a clear sign of disquiet, but this is not a time for care, it is a time of joy not one of concern.'

'Indeed,' responded Bohemond, 'my dear count, this is something else. Your presence does not make me concerned. I am preparing a game while I brandish this knife. This candle here, its size surpasses that of the others – and a candle larger than the others was burning in the stick in front of them – and I shall cut it in two with a single cut.'

This seemed silly to the counts and there did not appear to be any way to respond. Therefore, the count of Flanders said, 'Do what you have boasted my prince and I shall give you my jerkin as a mark of your strength. But if you fail, you shall not fail to give me your own.'

They agreed and soon Bohemond, having drawn his sword, cut the candle. Slicing from the right side, he easily separated off a section so that one candle was turned into two. What was remarkable was that it remained burning. The upper part which fell off continued to burn and the lower part which remained standing burst into flames on its own without a single hand bringing a flame to bear. Those standing around were stupefied, and even the one who had performed the deed was taken aback by what happened.

News of the event spread among the people and they rushed in from every hall and office. They were mystified as well and could not satisfy their curiosity simply by watching.[127] They were standing there watching in amazement when the light which had burned so suddenly also suddenly went out. This was an augury of sadness. If the wax and the flame had managed to remain in their close union and had perished together, then a long lineage and succession would have been promised that would last to the end of time. But,

---

[126] Cf. Horace, *Epistolae*, 1.19.
[127] Vergil, *Aeneid*, 8.265.

because this little fire, which had burned, instead disappeared the soothsayers promised hope of future offspring but their quick end as well.

> Should the fates show such a thing to the lands,
> they will not permit them to endure for long.[128]

The Mantuan (Vergil) added further things that we saw come to pass in the death of Bohemond the Younger.[129] The novelty of the prodigy kept the count from losing the jerkin he had pledged to the contest. But now riches and poverty surrounded the prince and the count, respectively. Furthermore, not only was the count freed from paying what he owed, he was even loaded down with many gifts.

Chapter 72

Once the city is captured, the Christians are besieged by an innumerable force of infidels

That day was a day of joy, but the next day was bitter. Kerbhoga, the general of the king of the Persians, was there with 400 000 mounted troops.[130] He besieged the city and threatened death and slavery to those inside. When he heard the news, rather than considering the recent victory, the count of Blois hurried his flight so that he could avoid joining his fellow commanders now condemned to death. Therefore, he returned toward Greece and met at Cuthai, a city in Lycia, with Emperor Alexios who was hurrying to the aid of the Franks with 100 000 Greeks.[131] With him were Guy, the brother of Bohemond, and certain other Frankish nobles who commanded about 10 000 armed men.

When the emperor heard the rumor from Stephen concerning the besieged Franks and the besieging Persians, this account at first made him want to press on to provide aid. But he gave this up after being discouraged by the one who ought to have urged him on. Responding to a question about the number of Persians, Stephen responded, saying, 'If, my lord, your army were given to them as a meal, it would not suffice to provide each of them with more than a meager serving.' The emperor, who was terrified by this news, fled back to Greece and devastated with fire the towns, countryside and

---

[128] Vergil, *Aeneid*, 6.370.

[129] Bohemond the Younger, who eventually came to rule Antioch, died fighting in Cilicia in 1130.

[130] Kerbhoga was the ruler of Mosul in what is today northern Iraq.

[131] Lycia is a region of central Anatolia.

houses along his path. He even brought the people along with him so that they could not provide aid to the enemy following after him. Guy wished to bring aid to the besieged supporters of Christ, and was barely prevented from doing so even after being deprived of Greek support. But he was kept from going after the emperor recalled him.

Chapter 73

The besieged are afflicted by dire hunger

In the meantime, the Franks besieged by the hostile force, were shut within the walls, suffered from the arrows of the Persians, and were tortured by hunger. The last was a hard thing, but their hope was stronger still. There was no rest for the suffering. Here the mountain rained arrows, there, they came from the plain.[132] The wall and the water shut them in. The mountain offered nothing to them. The mountain passage provided access to the enemy.

Therefore, the day brought war and so did the shade of the night. The Turks held the heights and the Latins defended the depths. Innumerable arrows stood against a few spears. The struggle was uneven: numbers, strength, location, arms. They were all unequal, and all of these favored the Turks, all except the morale of the Franks. With the support of their spirits, they drove away all sadness. With the support of their high morale, they overcame all of the other disadvantages. They discussed by what means they could turn aside this enemy effort and thus offer gentle sleep to their own eyes.

Chapter 74

They resist and build ramparts

They readied hewn stone, rocks, plumb lines, and craftsmen, ropes, baggage, and mattocks. Once everything was prepared, they built at night. This was a good thing because the work hated the day. Work took place at night. The arrows returned during the day. Their spears stood opposed to the [Turks]. When the spears were present, the work went up. When the spears retreated, the work ceased. Thus, in the midst

---

[132] The reference to arrows from the mountain concerns the Turks who were ensconced in the citadel at the top of the city.

of changing fortune, a wall was built that stood as a barrier to the Turks descending from the heights. When it was necessary to collect wood for a fire, they had to go a distance of 16 flights of an arrow to do so, and the yoked animals became soaked with sweat. None went without obtaining some arrows for his quiver. Therefore, the [Christians] gained some measure of sleep, but it was hardly ever quiet. Parthian arrows struck at the Franks now in earnest.

Now they turned to other cares in another battle. Altogether, our people faced tears, anxiety, labor wounds, hunger, cares, cold and heat. But they were able to be happy having seized sleep from the night. In this place, it was the bread to soothe empty stomachs.

Chapter 75

While they are sleeping, the enemy attacks

While the people were snoring, the walls were bereft of guards. For, as it is commonly said, he serves badly who snores well. The guard in charge of protecting the palaces to which they had retreated shouted through the streets, 'rise, rise, I beg you. The enemy is here, he has climbed the tower, he now holds the city. Why are you still resting quietly? Hurry and save yourselves.' While he shouted, people rose to his cries just as if Ismarus and Rhodes, burdened by Thracian rocks, had been ordered to rise.[133] Having been summoned by these same cries, the commanders ordered that the homes, which served as hiding places, be burned. Once the buildings were alight, the walls would have guards.

Chapter 76

Robert burned the city so that the troops would appear

Robert the Fleming was summoned to carry out this task. The diligent man personally called out those who were lazy and slow to undertake their duty. The following plan was decided upon, lest the great perish while the small folk engage in idleness. Robert devastated the city with fire and he saved the walls while he served the townspeople. If you remember correctly, Provence had sent forth those who were lazy in the

---

[133] This comment would seem to indicate that they moved slowly. Cf. Vergil, *Eclogue*, 6.30.

shadows, but whom the addition of flames gave speed. This people was at the lower end of the mountain but not at its foot. The people in the area around the base of the mountain had the largest houses because once [Antioch's] gates had been opened, the division by lot was conducted among the first to enter. It was pleasing in this first instance for them to choose the largest courtyards. The palace of the prince here fell to Raymond. Part of his people rested here quietly while another part was acting arrogantly. But when Vulcan consumed their lofty buildings, they roused themselves.[134] Those who had been dilatory repented of having indulged in rest. They rushed to the walls to put large protective shields into place. Some of them had woven mats. Thus, the closeness of loss saved the walls. The loss was lessened by losses. The common evil gave way to individual [problems]. It confirmed the saying that 'sorrow is the medicine for sorrow'.

Chapter 77

The fire consumes the churches and the palaces

Alas, once the fire got started it grew and grew. The medicine went too far. After homes had been devoured by the killing fire, the churches were burned. These were churches whose sight had astounded Greek painters, Arab goldsmiths, as well as both Irish and English sculptors. What marvelous material this decor had covered! There was the line of columns made from the stone of Paros.[135] The form of the pavement was like that of the transparent sea, like a crystal. The fragrant building materials of Choatrae were from the cedars of Lebanon and the beams were taken from sky scraping forests. The marble was from Atlas, the glass from Tyre, the gold from Cyprus, and the iron from England. Each kingdom strove to send its treasures. And although the Antiochene furnace cooked bricks, they say that the temples were roofed in lead sent from Amathonta (in Cyprus). One was consecrated to the mother of God and the other to James, although it is not clear whether this was the one who was killed with a sword or the one who

[134] Roman god of fire with his forge located in Mount Etna.
[135] Parian stone refers to a famous type of marble which is mentioned in the Book of Esther 1:6.

was thrown from the roof of the church attached to a beam.[136] These were the precious works, the beautiful monuments that were consumed by the flames.

Chapter 78

Although the walls are saved, the enemy nevertheless attacks

But now that the walls had been protected in such a great struggle, the enemy advanced hoping to fool the guards. The night served as a guard against ambushes. Light spurns what it knows it ought to fear. [The Turks] who looked down on the lower areas from their rocky heights saw everything openly, who was snoring, who was on guard, which areas lacked protection, and which benefited from the presence of a guard. During the night, the Germans guarded the walls which face south-east and they spent the day in sleep. The Turks often noticed this as they looked down from the heights and decided to attack them at this point. They, therefore, prepared ladders and advanced secretly toward this point on the wall. They proceeded furtively without meeting any opposition. The pitiable guards, who were lying there as if dead, were roused from their sleep.

Many bows and swords now climbed into the towers. Such a situation had not been seen on the wall for some time. The alarm was given, the city shook, and finally the people went into action. The crowd [of Christians] was stupefied at seeing the Turks running so close to them. Some of them drew their swords, and others fled in shock. Those who drew their swords went on the attack while those who fled were attacked. The supporters of Christ advanced toward the walls that were held by the Persians. Lucky was [the Turk] who had a ladder or a rope available. Unlucky was he who had neither. He leapt from the high walls brave in the face of stone but timid and fleeing in the face of drawn swords. Finally, the Germans, having been roused, surged forward and charged. The crowd of Latins, shameful as it is to say, but as the Greeks themselves testified, went through the streets shouting, 'Germans are shit.'

---

[136] The two saints named James, mentioned here, were Saint James the Great who was beheaded by Herod Agrippa (Acts 12:2) and Saint James the Lesser who is supposed to have been martyred by being thrown from the roof of the temple in Jerusalem.

Chapter 79

Increasing hunger forced certain of the besieged nobles to leave the city

Nor did fortune now cease to lacerate Christ or Christ's supporters. Fortune's efforts were overcome during the assault. After Fortune's attack within the walls failed, she prepared a descent and exit for herself. But she gave up none of her intentions. She attacked now from the right and now from the left, and said, 'if I am not able [to divert] those above, I shall arouse Acheron'.[137] The supporters of Christ, suffering during the difficult days and harsh nights, suffered also from hunger, crueler than any enemy. It afflicted them, lacerated them, consumed them, vexed them, and assailed them. Yesterday was harsh. Now is even harsher. Tomorrow and the next day will be harsher still as the food disappears. In the face of such want and such daily difficulties, and the lack of hope that aid would come, some of the troops considered the idea of flight. This was a worthy, noble group inclined toward battle that, up to this time, had enjoyed praise for its worthiness. These were William and his brothers Albert and Ivo, all three having the family name Maisnil. There was also Ralph of Fontenella from the Tourraine. Alas and shame, it was Normandy who sent forth the brothers. Everywhere the Normans had victory and were the glory of the world. This people was victorious over the English, the Sicilians, the Greeks, the Campanians and Apulians. The people of Maine, Calabria, Africa and Japix served them. Oh that shame should come from such a lineage![138]

They had spoken of their concerns to many others so that many able companions had joined with them. But God and His Arnulf summoned those who were preparing to leave and recalled them from this shameful state.[139] But the youth, forgetful of God, their homeland, and of themselves persisted in this shameful path that was the author of such ignominy and thus could not be called back by any argument. In their minds, it would be a good result of this plan and something worthy of note if, with all their fellows having been killed, they saved themselves from the enemy. Therefore, they lowered ropes, and having lowered and secured them, they climbed down from the wall during the night, and fled through the night. This nocturnal flight was discovered when the

---

[137] Cf. Vergil, *Aeneid*, 7.312. The Acheron was one of five rivers that is traditionally thought to flow through Hades and into the Styx.

[138] We have been unable to identify Japix.

[139] This is Arnulf of Chocques, who had been Ralph's teacher at Caen.

sun rose. Soon, an edict was issued that no one was to dare to remove the ropes that stood as a monument of their shame to posterity.

Chapter 80

The besieged eat deadly foods

Where the wind and the fan strike the dross, what remains is pure grain. Gold, after being tested in fire, is purged of its impurities. This unterrified people, constant but struck by hunger, misery and lack of sleep, runs to the works of death in the hope of gaining life. They ate poisonous food, including Celtic nard, hemlock, hellebore, sorrel, darnel and cockle. These suffering people died while eating in order to live. Whatever old soles of shoes there were and whatever leather they found left somewhere was thrown into a cooking pot and softened by flames and water. From this, they made meals, and lucky was he to whom fate gave such things. Those upon whom fate looked with jealousy were given over to illness and death. Pressed by these bad conditions, and accustomed to the good life, the noble offspring of dukes, counts and kings were hedged in by the walls in a manner that had never happened before and has not happened since. They feared hunger, and had barely enough water to serve as their nectar. Here there was dysentery and there a fever brought on by a plague. There was no solace, and death was everywhere you looked.

Chapter 81

Through Peter the Hermit's embassy, they seek single combat from the Persians[140]

They searched, considered, examined, circled about, and went in circles, by what means, by what reason or art, death could be turned aside and fleeing life be called back. They passed day and night in open discussion.

---

[140] Peter the Hermit is an exceptionally enigmatic figure. He preached the crusade in the territories of the king of France in 1095–96 and led a large group of pilgrims in what scholars have come to term the People's Crusade. After several setbacks in Byzantine territory, Peter the Hermit's group was dispatched by the imperial government to the coast of Asia Minor and ordered to stay there until the main crusading armies arrived. Peter the Hermit lost control over the people he had led and this group of pilgrims was utterly defeated in battle by the Turkish ruler of western

Once a decision had been made, they decided to send legates to the Persian satrap whose name was Kerbhoga. I say, they sent five men among whom was Peter the Hermit.

Peter's skin was dark and his spirit was tough. His feet were bare, he was short, and his face was thin. His horse looked like a small ass and had the harness appropriate to a small ass. A threadbare tunic covered him in the manner of a hermit. He was dressed in this manner when he approached the berobed tyrant.

Seeing his clothing, his face, and soon other things as well, the Persians were pleased and hoped that this wretch would cast himself before the feet of the prince so that he would twist himself over, bending at the knee, thereby coming forward as the man who would announce peace.

But it did not happen this way, impious ones, it did not happen. Rather, like powder which the wind blows away, so too you were rejected. Thus, Peter rose up, standing upright and said: 'The nobility of Gaul, the pilgrims of Christ, seek the holy sepulcher, and fear nothing since they hold this city. Peter, leader of the apostles commands the troops here.[141] He favors this place with his support and is happy to have his fellow servants nearby. You entered within the boundaries of Peter's people and you blockade the supporters of Christ with your siege. In the name of Christ, and of Peter, I order that you leave these borders and quickly. And if you seek justice, if the Persian kingdom seeks something equitable, something correct, let them run, arm and gather together ten or six or even three from your side and an equal number from among Christ's supporters shall meet them. The people that has victory shall claim Antioch as its own. The people who is defeated, shall depart Antioch. And if these weighty terms are displeasing to you, listen to what follows. What we propose may be even more burdensome. When tomorrow the morning sun shines forth, have no doubt, rather know that the battle will be taken to you. These are the words that the Latin people have commanded are to be said to you.'

Anatolia, Kilij Arslan. Peter the Hermit escaped this debacle and continued to have an important role during the remainder of the crusade up to and after the capture of Jerusalem.

[141] The church at Antioch is considered, in Christian tradition, to have been founded by Peter the Apostle.

Chapter 82

The response of the Persians

While Peter was speaking amidst the Persians, the crowd of commanders laughed and then the common people did so as well. They mocked the poor man who spoke as if he were clothed in expensive robes. Then, the highest leader responded arrogantly, 'this migrant people despoiling the kingdom of the Persians offends the god Mohamet, to whom alone the sultan ranks second. You have been sent to search and plunder. I have found my booty. They are enclosed within walls that I shall break down. I will give your bodies to the teeth of dogs and lions. Send back these, my words, to your Latins. For what do I care about Peter or Christ? What is Peter or Christ to me? Neither one matters to me. They make me laugh, both of them make me laugh'.

After listening to these breathless threats, Peter returned to his comrades and narrated the leader's savagery in the order that he had spoken. Then, the bold hearts of Gaul girded themselves for war. But their bones were consumed by hunger, without any meat.

Chapter 83

The faithful consider an attack

They gathered in an open area beneath the wall nearby the gate that opens to the north bordering the bridge and the river. It was from this point that this sacred people advanced. They established who would go first against the enemy and who following next after the first rank would carry the banners. Then the remainder organized themselves into the order of battle, in which places the pikemen were to stand, and where the spearmen were to be, and the archers as well. They also organized where the horsemen and foot soldiers should stand and whether they were to charge or stand and meet the enemy. Once they had all been organized in their lines, the sun rose and the time for battle arrived.

[Earlier] the north wind blew and a third of the night remained, when Arnulf's man, after a fast dash, pounded at the hall with his hand at the same time that he called out 'rise up, act, get up quickly. For what sign or polar star are you waiting? Behold, victory shines in the sky. Look at the stars. O Arnulf, those that had been following now are in the lead, while those that had been in the lead are now falling behind. Rise up, gather the leaders, and gather them for battle. If there is some danger, I am a hostage to it, ready to be burned or crucified along with my wife, both of my parents and my son.' For both of his parents, his wife, and his son were with him.[142]

This man had been instructed from childhood about the order of the stars, what they portend, how a comet alters kingdoms or a frozen old man threatens fire and rain, how the savage lion brings fire from Phaeton's chariot, how too much excitement by sword bearing Orion is a sign of war, and finally what was threatened by the present configuration of the stars.[143] A most learned man had instructed many in this art, including Arnulf. He had shown Arnulf that the twin stars of war show how all things have come about. The first showed the fate of Christ's supporters and the latter the fate of the Turks. They were now running in a different order. The first one was the joy of the Franks and the second showed the end for the Turks.

Chapter 84

They attack the enemy

Therefore, when the sharp ears and eyes of Arnulf had perceived the signs of the stars, as he had learned from the tongue and fingers of his master, he hurriedly rushed to the commanders and roused them to arms. He informed them that fate had turned from its course because all of the new good things had transferred from the old. In the meantime, night had given way to daylight. Therefore, after opening the gates, the starving people marched out girded for war. Now it is necessary, o restoring spirit, to bring strength to the one summoning you. Instruct the poet thirsting for you, who is in the first line, who is in the second, and how the remainder are arranged.

Chapter 85

The order of the leaders in the attack on the enemy

The first was Hugh the Great who led the Franks from the city. He shone brilliantly before his troops in his brilliantly noble manner. Next followed the banners of the Norman Robert. Both of these men were the highest counts and they alone were the offspring of kings. Hugh's

---

[142] This line is found in the manuscript written between the lines in another hand.
[143] Both Leo (Lion) and Orion are constellations.

family was the greater, Robert was superior in other ways. It was not without reason that they deserved the leading positions in this battle. Godfrey came third, leading out a multitude in his force. These included Lotharingians and Germans with the Lotharingians. Fourth in the order of battle was Tancred. He was exceptional in the use of arms but his force was not large. Fifth in the order and superior for his strength and the size of his force shone the precious banner of the son of Guiscard. The banner was partly made of material and in part in the shape of the cross.[144]

Raymond followed in the sixth place with a lot of noise. He was here not so that he could join his comrades in battle against the Turks but rather to support those fighting with his aid. He was to keep watch in all directions and send his troops to those about to be crushed once the young men had been killed. He was there to be the strength of the battle, a wall, rather than taking part in the attack. The count of Flanders was left to govern the city. He commanded the gates and crowned the walls with his armed men. The walls were covered by men with javelins, bows, clubs, spears, swords and fiery brands. Robert often dispatched additional troops to the new works (which faced the citadel). He acted wherever there were threats or fears of an attack, so that no break would admit the enemy. Now he gave orders with a leader's voice, now he killed with a soldier's sword. He was a barrier to the Turks descending [from the citadel]. He alone defended the great fortress that served as their great defender.

Chapter 86

Terror strikes the Persians

It is well known that the satrap of the Persians was playing chess as the first standard-bearer raised up the banner of Gaul. When news came that the Franks had marched out to battle, the prince took no action and continued to play the game as before. He did not stir even when it was announced that the banners of Count Robert the Great were announced as approaching.[145] What arrogance! When the third rank came forward there was great activity. Finally, [Kerbhoga] summoned

---

[144] Cross banners had long served an important role in the religious iconography of Christian armies. On this point, see David S. Bachrach, *Religion and the Conduct of War* (Woodbridge, 2003), 9, 40–42 and 92–5.

[145] This is a nickname for Robert Curthose.

captives from our people, for he held certain of our people as prisoners, and he asked whose banners these were and what they signified.

He heard what they signified and to whom they belonged. 'This one belongs to Robert, this one to Godfrey, that one to Hugh. This is the nobility, the great strength defending the city. Well, now you will fight or you will deny knowing how to fight.' While they were speaking, the standards of Tancred and Bohemond appeared as did those of the reserve force under Raymond. When Kerbhoga saw the Christians fully armed and deploying rapidly for battle, he grew frightened. Then suddenly, after summoning a translator, he offered to the Christians the same conditions that they had offered to him earlier, but which he had refused. Now they were refused again. Then, without delay, his men prepared their quivers and bows, the Assyrians, Persians, Parthians, Libyans, Elamites, Phoenicians, Arabs, Indians, Syrians, Medes, along with a host of others nations whom, for the sake of relieving tedium, we will not record by name.

Chapter 87

On the same topic

The Christian troops crossed between the mountains. There was a great rage among the Turks, as if there were 100 000 attackers. The Turks threw javelins from behind the Christians like a hunter trying to block off a deer in the hunt. Bohemond opposed them like a bronze wall. He turned his back to his companions and his face toward the enemy. As a result, this battle for God was bifurcated and appeared to have two faces like a dragon in a picture with two heads. Here and there a man poured out his blood for the blood of Christ. The outpouring of blood from the dead enemies made satisfaction in turn. Behold the steadfastness, behold the constancy of martyrdom. Athletes of Christ, glory of the entire world, take vengeance with your right hands, you few against a hundredfold enemy. Use your swords, let this ground, now choked with weeds, this field, this remaining fruit, support you in years to come.

On the other side of the battle, Bohemond was alone and without hope of human aid. He was placing his hope in the power of heaven. Trusting in his men and supported by Christ's aid, he attacked the gentiles, the cross, that noble sign leading the way. This sign of signs gleamed, a horror for the enemy, the hope of the soldiers of Christ, a wall, a glory, a splendor. A heavily armed mounted solider, who was not last in the crowd, but rather an exceptionally tough, brave, and the high-spirited pupil of martial Bohemond, as well as his nephew, carried the said sign. This was Robert, son of Gerard, famous throughout the world.[146]

With both his hand and his tongue, that is his mind and body, he was inclined toward the service of Christ and most inclined in service as a brother to his brother and thus to his association with Bohemond. Again and again he crossed the Turkish lines, urging on his comrades and insulting the charging enemy.

Robert was in among the Turks and Bohemond was at his side. The former remained among the enemy, and the latter did not give his place either.

Chapter 88

The terrified Turks flee

At the sight of the cross, the Persians lost their sight. They trembled, shook, and shuddered at its brilliance. No spear thrower or archer could perform his duty. 'Ha ha', was transformed into 'but but', and then 'alas alas'. Thus, they showed themselves to be cattle while the Franks were zealous lions. The former preferred flight to death while the latter preferred praise to life. Since the enemy could not reclimb the mountain, they fled down along the river. The victors were there and never stopped cutting them down until the two lines of battle came upon the positions of their fellow soldiers. The defeated [Turks] met those about to be defeated, and the victorious [Christians] came upon the holy ones about to have victory.

Now the battle no longer took place on two fronts. Now victory was more certain. One side gained hope while fear burdened the weapons of the other side. The course of the battle now persuaded some to fight and others to flee. The number of people here was great, exceeding the sands of the shore. But, the scarcity of horses limited the pressure that the Latins could place on the retreat and proved an obstacle to the supporters of Christ. This was an advantage for the Turks. They conceived of a cunning plan. But craft and trickery is nothing against Christ without whom there is nothing, no act at all.

---

[146] Robert, the son of Gerard, was Bohemond's constable.

Chapter 89

Battle on two fronts

The East Wind came to battle from the kingdom of Nabatea in support
of the Persians who were its neighbors. It overcame horses, bows and
quivers. It hurled back spears against those who cast them. Attacks
were turned back on the attackers. The Frankish sword was hardly able
to stand against the javelins of the East Wind. The now languid West
Wind lazed in its Aeolian grotto.[147] It had been a faithful companion to
the Franks all the way from Cadiz through the Pyrenean snows, and the
impassable paths, and the Alps, through the straits, and the Gulf of
Sidra, through Scylla, and Charybdis. It now betrayed them. The West
Wind gives no aid while Francia fights in the East. Recognizing this, the
Persians, since they could not fight with arms, turned to flames.

They tried to overwhelm the eyes of Christ's supporters with smoke
and darkness as if it were night. They burned reeds, and sedges, twigs,
and whatever else the East Wind could set alight. With a furious
purpose, the East Wind sent clouds of smoke from thistles, and the
remaining thickets, and from the bucklethorns, against the opposing
phalanxes [of the Christians]. Behold, the sunny day is transformed into
pitch-black shadows. It weakens the strong and comforts the weak
crowd. Swords fight in the shadows and arrows in the light. The moles
go into battle against the lynxes. Thus, the outcome of the battle wavers
in face of the furies of the East. How often has the West Wind delayed
after being summoned! Rush to our aid o West Wind, rise up sluggish
one, the East Wind rages on behalf of the Turks, rise up on our behalf.

Chapter 90

The Christians triumph

During this uproar, God took pity on the afflicted and opened his
treasuries. He sent forth the favorable North-west Wind which struck
the East wind and forced the defeated one to return to its vaults. Freed
from its western prison, the North Wind tormented the eyes of the
Turks with their own smoke. The North Wind did not delay in fulfilling
its orders, shaking and tearing loose everything which blocked its flight.
Now it entered into battle, but not with arms and men. It struck with

---

[147] This is in Asia Minor north of Ionia.

such force that it terrified the horses and blew away tents. The mountain, valley, fields and woods shuddered and trembled. Behold East Wind, you flee and you are overcome by your own smoke. Their own fraud redounded upon your Persians as if by the law of equity. Then, while the eyes of the Turks were closed and those of the Franks were open, the battle took place and suddenly the situation was reversed so that he who had been close to victory was defeated and he who was losing now conquers. The former fled, and the latter put him to flight. Baal (Islam) rushed about, while Alpha (Christ) overwhelms.

The fast horses of the Persians were both lazy and spirited. They were slow, skinny, anxious and sick when fighting against the Franks. But they easily fled not being able to stand boldly in place. The enemy was innumerable, our side had barely 600. Once the Persians were in danger, those who were looking on but not yet in battle now took flight. He who was fast or seized a fast horse was like fire. Once he escaped, he fled and rushed about lost and on pathless ways. But those who had slow horses or were slow afoot were either cut down or made into slaves and sold into servitude. The Christians recalled that in the midst of death, they found the shoe sole of a youth, which could be used to repel sun or rain when used as a covering. The West then carried on and the East pitied those who were carried off. The remaining works, the bowls, the drinking cups, tables, water pots, tripods, litters, bath tubs, cauldrons, pots, barrels, tents, cloaks, shirts, all of them of pure gold or ornamented with gold, belonged to the victor. The people became rich after their poverty. At first, they sat around and avidly devoured Turkish delicacies and game which had been prepared for the satrap. Then there was contention among them concerning the captured purple [cloth].[148]

Chapter 91

Tancred followed the defeated foe and inflicted an amazing slaughter among them

Tancred's prowess ate and drank praise. Desirous of nothing other than fame,[149] like a pauper who spurns wealth, like a faster who spurns food, like a laborer who spurns rest, he found a path between two branches of the Orontes where it is was divided into two. There was no place more

[148] The Christian victory was on 28 June 1098.
[149] Cf. Horace, *Ars poetica*, 324.

appropriate for him to be. With but a few armed companions, he pursued a multitude. He became intermixed with the Parthians, Persians, Indians and the men from all of the peoples who supported Mohamet. He was a panther among the sheep. The Guiscardian slaughtered them. He urged on his horse with his spurs and with his reins. He offered encouragement to his men with terrifying shouts and every type of effort. His rapidly moving battle line crashed into the armed foe. In order to avoid death, Turks goaded and lacerated their heavily burdened mounts on their necks and their useless rumps.

Nor did it take long for them to be thrown from their horses. They threw aside their bows and quivers and fled. Tancred soaked the green earth with their blood. Tancred filled ditches with heaps of the dying. Many died of wounds and many without wounds. While fearing wounds, the crowd avoided them. Some of the enemy rushed off willingly after giving up their reins and saddles. They climbed under thornbushes hoping to hide there. Horses eviscerated some of them with their hooves. Meanwhile, death caught others who had rushed off on foot. Their feet failed some, when either their courage or spirit gave out. The greatest number thought to save themselves in the river. But having entered the river alive, they perished from the waves that they hoped would aid them. A horse and rider entered onto a small hill that could be seen above the water. As they approached the bank, the mud sucked both it and him down. Therefore, those equipped with quivers, breastplates and armor went down to hell while the others trembled. Pluto himself feared to be found. His wife was both afraid and fled.[150] But fate offered shallows to some of the Turks. Some of them emerged from the water, some were submerged within it. But even those who did try to escape in this manner did not succeed.

Tancred followed them, knowing the shallows just like shallows of the Lyncestrian River, which he had crossed.[151] He approached them over the rough and unfamiliar ground fresh and eager when the fortress of Harenc rose up before him. This place was well fortified by nature and by artifice. It had no fear of the Turkish bows that were ranged in swarms against it. This tower was supported throughout by a strong military force. Now it opened its gates, which had been closed for a long time. A crowd of young men rushed out to the approaching lord. Looking on he cried, 'Provide me with new horses.' Thus, all at once, he found arms, men and horses all together.

---

[150] Pluto is the lord of Hades.

[151] The Lyncestrian River flows through Macedonia. Cf. Ovid, *Metamorphoses*, 15.329.

Chapter 92

Concerning the same matter

The grassy plain over the Artah beneath the walls of Hama and El-Hammam was surrounded by the divided course of the river. In the past it had excluded travelers and was the reason why people had to make a roundabout circuit. A double bridge separated this unfavorable area from the mountain. A gate opposite this rough terrain admitted the traveler. Thinking itself safe, the Persian force was now deployed between the two bridges. The men acted as if they had now received a respite from flight after a long period of weariness. Worn out, they thought that they had evaded battle. Then Tancred was there and with him horses, arms and men.

Battle was renewed. When they saw each other, those who pursued cried out 'oh joy', while the fleeing Turks sighed out 'alas' amongst themselves. The slaughter beneath the walls of Antioch had been great. The slaughter here was greater still when the fresh force was committed to battle. Here and there were laments from the wounds dealt to both sides. Here and there was laughter, but this was not a shared reaction. One side laughed mightily and the other side wept. The swiftly fleeing Turks wept while the battle-seeking Normans laughed. The Normans cut them down and the Turks died. The approach of the Norman spears and the narrow width of the two bridges kept [the Turks] from flight. Terror, the labor of their flight, and their weakened strength kept them from defending themselves. Blood came pouring from numerous wounds. The Persians had almost as many wounds as they had limbs. Whatever they tried turned to misery. Battle offered no consolation to flight nor did flight offer consolation to battle. The Turks tried both and had no joy from the outcome of either. Thus, they perished like a flock of sheep to which a lion and a panther had attached themselves.

Chapter 93

The stronghold of Artah surrenders

Flight and the waves saved only a few from this vast crowd of the enemy. While some were cut down, the Christians continued their pursuit to kill still more. The stronghold (Artah) had remained in Turkish hands up to now, and was well prepared for war. As I said, it had remained impregnable up to this point almost as if this were a divine work rather than the work of man. Neptune's Pergamon and

Apollo's Troy, whichever one you choose, was as much inferior to this place as all other places are to them.[152] The young defenders, however, terrified by the death of their companions, having no confidence in themselves, and equally impoverished of hope, exhausted all avenues of escape and thoughts of delay. Therefore, having weighed the option of delay in the balance, they decided to depart. They said that they wanted nothing to do with the Franks nor with the arms of heaven following the defeat of the Turks by divine power.

Certain of Raymond's people [who had been captured], forced either by a dire hunger or captivated by a false desire, had given up Christ and become the followers of Mohamet. The same walls held both these men transformed into Turks and the Turks themselves. The former were asked who was the leader of the supporters of Christ, and who was more trustworthy, to whom they might hand over the stronghold and themselves, and with whom they would be safe. The captives encouraged them to trust Raymond. 'He is the more trustworthy count,' they said, 'and the strongest.' 'There is no reason to fear if you commit yourselves to him.' Why delay any longer? It is proper to conclude this matter in a few words. They accepted this, summoned the Christians, opened the gates, left the stronghold, and the Christians entered.

Chapter 94

The words of the dying bishop of Le Puy to the army

In the meantime, the bishop of Le Puy died (1 August 1098) and having been carried within the basilica of nurturing Peter (at Antioch), he was laid to rest. But the dying bishop summoned others to him and spoke in the following manner in order to have his role recorded and to show the path of salvation. 'While God still illuminates me, o brothers, I shall not give up working zealously on your behalf. Solicitously, I have cultivated, taught, warned and urged you on like a mother with her nursling. I have torn away what was fatal and spread the seeds of life. I have taken care and performed the tasks assigned to me. Now I am being taken away, now the end of my life is here. Pope Urban assigned me to you to be a preacher of doctrine. And so now I hand over this man to you in this capacity.' He presents Arnulf who was second to no

---

[152] Neptune and Apollo were credited in the ancient world with helping to build the walls of Pergamon and Troy, respectively.

one in this task. 'Here,' he said, 'is my dear son in whom I have faith. Turn your ears to him. You, my son, be mindful of the warnings of your father. Spread the seeds of divine proofs widely. Return the seed freely which you received for free. Call back the sinners and praise those with a crown who are acting correctly. Carry out your task, and show yourself to be a minister of Christ. Carry out the duties assigned to you with zeal and honesty. Let no one use gifts to turn you in an unjust direction. And that I might speak briefly in my brief bit of life, be modest, sober, prudent, humble, pious and quiet.'

Chapter 95

His epitaph

Thus, he warned, and a short time later he crossed to Him whom his mind, his strength and his voice cherished, that is to Jesus. He was a man of great merit, and a man worthy of honor in any place. A man worthy of this inscription here, if not of a greater one. 'Here lies buried the most brilliant follower of Moses in doctrine, zeal, habit and office. Moses was the leader of his people and this one was the leader of his people. Both were leaders of Christ, and both were born in heaven. Both pursued justice and doctrine. Both were the voice of God and his mediator with his people. It is recalled that the land of Canaan was the reason for Moses' journey. So too was the land of Canaan the reason for his journey. Moses was granted the ability to see but not to reach this land.[153] This one also was not allowed to reach it, and was almost given to see it. Long fasts reconciled Moses to God. God consecrated this one through long hunger as well. God himself chose Moses, and Pope Urban chose this one, but he was following God's command, and thus God sent both of them.'

Chapter 96

Tancred, along with the counts of Normandy and Provence, besieges Marra

After the city (Antioch) was captured, the victors became rich and the defeated were killed. The first group was raised from humility to the stars and the others became submerged in Hell because of their luxury and drunkenness. Bohemond, who had taken over the principality of Antioch,

---

[153] Cf. Deuteronomy 34:1–4.

remained to rule there. Tancred, renewed the interrupted labor of his journey. He experienced cold, heat, hunger and thirst in the mountains, valleys, fields and towns. Tempe-Thessala spurned its own loveliness. Hama spurned its Heliconia, Harence its greens, Barysan its vines, and Hersen its fields of corn. In addition to these a huge number of other towns each preferred the works of others to their own. But the son of the marquis, another Julius (Caesar), believing that nothing had been done if there still remained something to do,[154] remembered that Jerusalem was the reason for his journey and that he had set out on his pilgrimage to go through Antioch, not for the sake of Antioch. Therefore, he joined with the counts of Normandy and Provence who also sought battle. He went with them to the populous and rich town of Marra (November 1098).[155]

The people of Marra had prepared. It is not known whether they did so because they had been frightened by the capture of Antioch, or because of the great number of Franks who had participated in the siege there, or because they had been warned about Antioch through reports from fellow members of their tribes. Perhaps warned by all of these means, they filled their city and stripped the countryside bare, leaving nothing for the army which was about to besiege them. Indeed, they even blocked the wells of water outside the walls thinking that the lack of water might repel the advance of their enemies. But the supporters of Christ, who, having taken the cross, never gave up and who had handed their bodies over to prayer for the sake of God, rejoiced once the city was surrounded as if they had been invited to a banquet. Some set up siege engines while others protected those who were setting them up. Some struck the walls using stone throwers while others carried on their shoulders the stones used to shake the walls.[156]

You can see some running agilely in hope of obtaining grain and others groaning under their burden as they return. Some restored the wells to their earlier use while others were engaged in the construction of new ones. Many were hoping for something from the cataracts of heaven and prepared containers to hold water from the sky. Looking down on their desires was the One who alone considered their labor and pain. He did not abandon those who placed their faith in Him. The rain sent from heaven was sufficient for everyone. Indeed, the rain that followed was too much and those who had demanded the rains before now asked that they stop. Those who had worked on holding pools lamented that their work had been for naught.

---

[154] Lucan, *De bello civili*, 2.657.

[155] Ralph uses the word *comes* here to describe Robert although the latter is a *dux*.

[156] This is a reference to the men carrying stone ammunition to the siege engines.

Chapter 97

A horrible famine in the camps of the faithful

This flood brought with it terrible hunger as all of the grain brought into camp rotted. No more was brought in from anywhere and victory was delayed. The bread floated away and hunger increased. It is shameful to report what I heard and what I learned from the authors of this shame. For I heard that they said that they were forced by the lack of food to begin to eat human flesh. Adults from among the gentiles were put into the cooking pot and their youth were fixed on spits and roasted.[157] In devouring them, the Christians looked like wild beasts, like dogs roasting men. They threatened at the end that they would eat the limbs of their own if foreign ones were lacking unless the capture of the city or the bringing in of foreign grain lessened their starvation.

Chapter 98

Discord between Tancred and Raymond

While these things were going on, a quarrel broke out between Tancred's men and those of Raymond and soon escalated from the men to their lords. Tancred was barely able to curb his emotions and to keep himself from soothing his anger with the slaughter of the Provençals, since reason forbade that he shed the blood of Christians. It was better that he turned to the arts of Guiscard, which had made the latter glorious throughout the world. He came to Antioch without delay where the guardians of the citadel were ignorant of this discord. Passing along the way, he instructed his soldiers how they should hold their swords secretly and depressed. Then, covered with cloaks, he as well as his companions approached the citadel and called to the guard. The doors were opened and they who simulated peace were admitted peacefully. They entered one after the other. When their number was sufficient for battle, all at once they all uncovered their arms, intentions and swords. Raymond's soldiers were ejected and sent back to him but not without bruises.[158]

---

[157] It seems unlikely that Ralph is recording here an actual case of cannibalism. It is far more likely that the discussion of cannibalism here is meant to indicate the extreme difficulties in which the crusaders found themselves.

[158] Ralph is referring here to the original division of the city of Antioch following the defeat of Kerbhoga in which Bohemond received the city but Raymond of Toulouse seized the citadel for himself and refused to surrender it.

Thus, Tancred took vengeance in the manner in which he was able, the more astute over the more powerful. He also restored the detached head to the body, that is, he returned Troy to Bohemond's Illium. For up to this point, whenever Bohemond looked at the citadel it seemed to him as if he had been mutilated. He said about himself that he was not a prince but rather named Raymond as his colleague in the principality of Antioch. This annoyance tortured his dreams and kept him awake. In truth, his hatred at Raymond's control of the citadel and his pleasure at his own control over the city crashed into one another in this frontier between the citadel and the rest of the city. After Bohemond's position improved he became more involved. He joined Tancred as the latter returned to Marra bringing with him a large force. Both of them had been upset by Raymond and now they prepared themselves magnificently against the arms of the enemy.[159]

Chapter 99

The origin of the discord

At this point it is fitting to return to the cause of this hatred which was so widespread that we marvel less at the rush of a raging river. While Antioch was still resisting the princes of Gaul, trouble arose between Bohemond's men and those of Raymond. Men from both sides were sent out to forage for grain. They found supplies but at the same time they found conflict as well. The cereal was divided by battle, and both sides, having been frightened, inflicted wounds. Both groups then returned home with their wounds. The leaders were upset by the blood that they saw on their own men. Since, in a similar case, the emotions of the wounded men had burned for revenge, the commanders ordered that this fire be kept covered in camp. But they fanned the flames into a storm outside. Their men happily went along with this and it was difficult to maintain the prohibitions against fighting in camp. Therefore, when a larger group from one side met a smaller group from the other that was burdened with supplies, they set aside their own loads of supplies and attacked them with a storm of blows. Thus, the side with more strength enjoyed the spoils. The weaker side, after being despoiled, lamented that their labor had been for others rather than for themselves. Sometimes men fought alongside their fellows who spoke the same language. Sometimes men were beaten because of the language that they spoke although innocent of any part in the conflict. The men of Narbonne, Auvergne, Gascony, and all of the

---

[159] Ralph leaves the ambiguous impression that the enemy is both the city of Marra and Raymond of Toulouse.

people of Provence were on one side. The remainder of Gaul, and especially
the Normans, were with the men of Apulia. The Bretons, Swabians, Huns,
Ruthenians and others protected those whom they heard speaking their
language outside the walls.[160]

Chapter 100

Discussion of the Holy Lance

Sedition did not only flow out of the city (Antioch), it flowed toward it as
well. While the besieged people was troubled by the hunger, noted above, a
shrewd speaker of lies named Peter came forth from among Raymond's
people and preached that the salvation of the people had been revealed to him
in the following manner. He said, 'Saint Andrew the Apostle appeared to me
and imparted this order to my ears: "rise up and announce to the suffering
people that a consolation has been granted to them from heaven. The lance,
which pierced the side of the Lord, having been found will be granted to
them. It is in the basilica of Saint Peter under the earth. You shall lift up the
stone in this place (and he showed the place), and there by digging you will
find the announced piece of iron. When the horror of war falls, set this against
your enemies, and under this you will have victory."

'Having woken, I thought that I had been deluded in my sleep. I did not
discuss my vision, and would have remained silent forever if I had not been
warned a second and a third time. The quiet of the second night was again
holding me when the same apostle said again what he had said earlier,
lamenting but in an angry whisper. He said: "why do you keep silent about
me in contempt? Why do you alone delay the salvation of many? The people
shouted to the Lord, and were heard. But up to now, your negligence makes it
as if He had neglected them. Hurry, therefore, and correct this as fast as you
can so that you might live."

'Disturbed by these [words], when I rose from sleep, I was now more
certain and more concerned, doubting whether I should keep this quiet or let
it be known. I spent the entire day and half the night worried by these cares,
praying and fasting, and asking God to give a third sign, if the first two had
been from Him. Twice the rooster acclaimed the morning when suddenly at
the third call, sleep claimed my wearied strength. Without delay, he who had
come the first and second times, came now a third time more terrible and
imperious than before. He said: "get up ignorant sheep, mute dog, delayer of

---

[160] Ralph's reference to Huns in this context most likely means Hungarians, that is,
Magyars.

salvation, retarder of victory, cause of loss to the citizens, comfort for the enemy. You have been afraid to go where there is no fear and where there is you do not fear." The threats and arguments were the same as before.

'Overcome with fear, my spirit dragged itself from these threats and from sleep. My body alternated between tremors and sweat as if one side burned in fire and the other were stiff with ice. It is by these steps that I came to teach what I have learned. You, fathers and brothers, should not be slow in learning the truth of this matter. It is for me to name the place and for you to dig.'

When news of this event reached Raymond's ears he held an assembly and then had Peter summoned to the basilica. When asked about the location, Peter indicated that it was under the altar, just as he had arranged it. He urged them to dig. Then, so that his words would have weight, he composed his face. They dug. But nothing appeared. For the upturned earth could not return what had never been placed in or been accepted by it. But Peter had secreted the iron point from an Arab spear that he had found by chance. He had picked this up as the means of carrying out his trickery. It was rough, worn, old, and dissimilar in form and size to what we use. He felt that because of the novel shape of the spearhead, people would believe his story. Peter therefore seized the moment for his deception. Picking up a hoe, he jumped into the ditch and turned toward a corner. While digging he said, 'here it is, here lies that for which we have been searching'. Then he showed it. Then adding more and more blows, he struck the lance which he had fraudulently placed in the ditch. This trickery was aided by the shadow, the shadow by the crowd of people, and the crowd by the narrowness of the place.

Chapter 101

On the same matter

When the one piece of iron was struck by the other it clinked. Then, having raised up the lance, the fomenter of this fraud filled the ears of the simple folk in this manner: 'behold, behold, what heaven promised, what the earth conserved, what the apostle revealed, and what the prayers of the penitent people demanded'. Hardly was this done when they carried it outside and followed the lance with hymns and songs. They gave gifts and covered it with gold and precious cloaks. Raymond, and those who favored him, agreed. The simplicity of the others was served through simple gifts. They gave them earnestly before the victory, and with even greater zeal after it.[161] It was as if

---

[161] This is a reference to the crusaders' victory over the army of Kerbhoga beneath the walls of Antioch during which the Holy Lance was carried in the Christian vanguard.

glory was ascribed to the lance that had been carried as a trophy in battle, just as the shouts of the Provençals demanded. Thus, Raymond's wealth grew, his spirit was raised up, and his army grew haughty. Certain of the leaders whom he had enticed either with gifts or with services now supported him.

Chapter 102

Bohemond suspects that the lance is a fake[162]

But Bohemond, who was not an imprudent man, considered the way matters had turned out. Who was this dreamer who had involved the people in such goings on? Which place had he pointed out to the diggers before he jumped in, dug, and made a discovery. Bohemond at once understood that this was an empty and false discovery and that the discoverer had acted falsely with false claims. He said, 'it is a pretty comment that Saint Andrew appeared to a man whom I hear frequents the drinking stalls, scurries about in market places, is a friend to loafers and has a reputation for nonsense. Surely, the saint chose a fitting person with whom to share the secrets of heaven. For is not the place in which this account is fashioned enough to make clear that it is a deception? If a Christian had carried off [the iron] why did he not find a hiding place in a nearby altar? If it were a gentile or a Jew, why inside the walls of a church? Why underneath the altar? What if it were neither of these two, but rather fate which should be invoked, who has found among the historians that Pilate ever came to Antioch? For we know that the lance belonged to a soldier, and that this was one of Pilate's soldiers.

But what follows is even better. I heard that this discoverer jumped in after the diggers had labored in vain, and it was granted to one man to find in the shadows what had been denied to many in the open. What unsophisticated silliness. What buffoonish credulity. How easy it is to overcome credulity of this type. Let a person merely be honest, then the vicinity to the cross strengthens the claim of the place. Does the most recent fraud of this man not make this clear? If he had walked purely and simply in the path of God, if he had trusted in the apostle to act as his advocate, he would not have to depend on the testimony of his own discovery, but would have deserved other support. For what shall I respond to this outrage that our victory, which rose from and descended from our Father's light, was owed to his piece of iron as the Provençals claim. The greedy count and his boorish crowd may claim this. However, we conquered and will conquer in the name of the Lord our God

---

[162] In this section, Ralph is returning to events that occurred earlier, during Kerbhoga's siege of the crusader army at Antioch.

and of Jesus Christ.' Bohemond, and with him the counts of Normandy, Flanders, Arnulf the bishop's vicar and Tancred, discerned the subtleties of what had happened.

Chapter 103

Bohemond displeases Raymond

Therefore Raymond, who had been wounded by the darts of Bohemond's arguments, considered this insult with a thousand arts and in a thousand ways and came up with a means of separating himself from the Guiscardian's charges without delay. He said, 'Either I will die or I will have vengeance. If an open course does not present itself, then there is a hidden course. Where there is no lance, there is a dagger. Who asks whether it was trickery or virtue in war?

'The defense of the city is mine, as is the citadel on the mountain, the royal palace and the forum. The bridge and the gates open to me. The lance is mine and my forces are large. What remains except that I obtain the principality once Bohemond is dead?' Considering these and other matters a great deal, one notion sat before all the rest, namely to create sedition among the people so that it would pour out from foot to head. So quarrels would break out in the marketplace, a clamor would rise up to disturb the people, and the leaders would each provide aid to their own men. Then, all of the arrows and javelins would be pointed at Bohemond. While Raymond prepared these ambushes like a lion in his cave, God did not wish to keep this iniquity silent. So He made it known to Arnulf and through him to Bohemond. Thus, having eluded this fraud, the soul of this man (Bohemond), who was saved from death, provided a great deal of help to those who had set out for Jerusalem and to those who would in the future. The anger of the two men came from this period and was the tinder for their hatred.

Chapter 104

Marra is captured

But the siege calls me back as a neglected field summons a reaper, and in returning I collect the arrows that have been shot. The [crusaders] undermined [the walls of] Marra which was now surrounded by troops. Arrows flew over Marra, stones struck the walls, and mines made them tremble. There was noise everywhere and assaults. Everywhere there were blows. The townsmen gave back equal to what they received. Their stone throwers reverberated. From far off they shot javelins and from up close they dropped plowshares and marble statues.[163] They caused many wounds and suffered many as well. Some died as others lived, some sickened while others remained strong, some weakened while others remained tough. It was the aim of the townsmen to disrupt the siege, which had begun and was only half completed, and to bring an end to this great labor. They strove to overcome glory, and to overcome fortune through their patience. But just as it happens with the ever-increasing blows of a hammer on an anvil, or strikes on the threshing floor, the walls were overcome by an inexhaustible supply of stones. The tower crumbled, the wall collapsed, the bastions fell away. Thus, both the ruins and the walls offered and raised up a path.

There was sorrow for the supporters of Mohamet and joy for the supporters of Christ. Certainly all things now prospered for one side and everything, even their hopes, turned against the other. However, even when the way was open, there was no delay in finding a defender. The city rose up to resist. They placed whatever strength they had to oppose those coming in. But while the struggle went on, one side grew stronger and the other weaker. This side was fervent and that side saw its defense weaken. The shields of the Christians rang less and less now when but a short time earlier they had almost drooped under a hail of stones. Therefore, the attackers placed the ladders against the wall. A climber topped the tower and jumped into the captured city. When this sound was heard and he was seen running back and forth, the morale of the defenders was broken (11 December 1098). Their feet sought refuge in the shadows and they hoped to live by throwing down their arms. But, once the city was captured, some of our men spent their time killing while others sought riches. Some sought out victims and others seized booty. With this victory in hand, it was possible to remember more joyfully the achievements of their harsh labors. And I, who was once a hunter, have seen a crowd of hunters joyful and yet worn thin from exhaustion of a labor that lasted from the last hour of the previous night to the third hour of the following day.[164]

---

[163] This curious reference may be to the Roman statuary that adorned the city during the late empire.

[164] It is possible that Ralph is speaking here of himself, but this seems unlikely given the canonical prohibitions against hunting by priests.

Chapter 105

Arqah is besieged

The supporters of Christ had become accustomed to rise up from the vale of tears to the lofty mountain of joy.[165] Their successes encouraged them to remain steadfast under the favor of divine power. They attacked the town of Arqah.[166] Their effort was not unequal to what was expended at Marra but the outcome was different. A small hill rose up at the edge of the plain which stretches south by south-west from the Lebanon mountains. The sea lies to the west about 20 stades (2 miles/3 kilometers) away. A river runs past its base and flows to the sea from its source. The area subject to Jerusalem lies to its left and the area subject to Antioch lies to its right. It is the best-known boundary between Tortosa and Tripoli.[167] It is fortified by both human efforts and by nature so that it offers a difficult path to an attacking force. However, the supporters of Christ, who had now experienced many battles, had seen that everything gave way before their strength. So they besieged Arqah. Part of the force crossed the river so that they could block egress from the gate. Part remained on this side of the river in order to obtain supplies more easily from the towns of Crak and Raphanie (Rafineh) and others in this area. Tancred was first among those who crossed the river. He was exultant that he had merited to enter the kingdom of his desire. An old stone bridge connected the sections of the army so that it was easy to transfer men back and forth across the river. Where there were walls, they were encircled by our troops. Where there were fortified points, these were encircled by our strong points. Where there were gentiles, they were encircled by Christians. According to common practice, the leaders built catapults to deal with the walls. Each leader had his own. The Norman count had one, Raymond had a second, and Tancred a third, for Bohemond, once Marra had been captured, returned to Antioch. Duke Godfrey and the count of Flanders were wintering there as well. War had summoned Hugh the Great back to Cilicia. He had suffered a wound to his leg and was carried to Tarsus for treatment. He was later buried there.[168] Thus, the work of the siege fell to the three leaders named above. They fought continuously and were resisted. While this battle was in progress, an important event occurred, and it would be foolish to pass over it because to recall it is both useful and fitting.

---

[165] This is a play on words for Mont Joi and the biblical vale of tears.

[166] The Franks attacked this town on Monday, 14 February 1099.

[167] Evidently, Arqah marked the usual extent of the territorial claims of Tortosa to the north and Tripoli to the south,

[168] Hugh returned to the West and did not participate in the capture of Jerusalem. He later returned to the East on the crusade of 1101 and died at Tarsus in 1102.

Chapter 106

Anselm's miraculous vision of his approaching death

In this army there was a noble hero, whose name was fashioned by his
honesty, by his family, by his virtues, and by Ribemont, his inheritance,
which was famous for the exceptional soldiers that it produced. His name,
Anselm, was known in the court of the king of France and even in the three
parts of Gaul.[169] When, at midday, he took his customary rest, Anselm saw a
vision. When he awoke, he reported his vision to a wise man, that is to the
Arnulf whom I mentioned earlier. He said, 'it seemed to me in my dream that
I was standing above the vaults of heaven. Here I saw a lofty palace all of
which exceeded greatly what is normal, in size, height, material, form,
strength and ornamentation. Its base was of marble adorned by ivory and
silver. The remainder of the structure was of gold and precious stones. An
innumerable group of people was walking through its gates and each person
seemed fit to be in such a building. They were exceptionally attractive, noble
and ornate. They sparkled with noble grace. When I looked more closely so
that I could admire them, I realized that certain of the figures were known to
me, that they had been companions in our military undertaking.

'Then, with my heart and soul gaping and panting for some path to open
up so that I might descend to them, a man, who had died while serving with
us – and here he recalled the name, and the place, and the day on which the
man had died – came up to me and said, "Do you not recognize this
multitude of Saints Anselm?" Hardly, I said, for no signs remain by which
they could be recognized unless in some way we might recognize a 50 year old
who departed from us as a seven year old. Then he said, "these are the
pilgrims to Jerusalem, who set out on the path of God in which you now
labor. They have left behind worldly matters and have merited eternal
crowns. Lest you become jealous, you also will come to join us in the near
future. You have fought the good fight and have finished your journey." Then
sleep and this vision cast me out stupefied. May your wisdom, o lord, console
me.'

Then Arnulf eased the fear from his mind with consoling words. But he
warned him to confess his sins, to accept penance, and after this to receive the
Eucharist. When he had attended to these matters, Anselm was to pay the
wages he owed to his civilian staff and to his troops. Then, the brave man
mounted and made a circuit of the walls with a unit of his heavily armed

---

[169] Anselm had formerly been in the service of Archbishop Manassas of Rheims and
several of his letters to the archbishop have survived. They are printed in Heinrich
Hagenmeyer, *Die Kreuzzugsbriefe aus den Jahren 1088–1100* (repr. Hildesheim, 1973),
144–5 and 160. The reference to the three parts of Gaul goes back to Caesar.

mounted troops as was customary for the nobles. Then, suddenly, a stone was dropped unexpectedly from a tower. It struck Anselm and scattered his brains. And so, his men took up his fallen form and carried back the body with tears whence it had come with joy. His soul ascended to its promised beatitude.

Chapter 107

The townsmen of Arqah offer sharp resistance

After this illustrious man was buried, as was fitting, the aforementioned Arnulf was ordered to return to Antioch since our army was having no success in the siege. He was to disturb the rest of Godfrey and Robert of Flanders who were delaying there, and announce to them that forces were being sent by Damascus to aid Arqah. Since Arnulf was always prepared to act for the public good, he willingly undertook this mission using a small boat. Because of the enemy naval forces at Tortosa, Maraclea, Valania, Jabala, he took a roundabout path finally reaching Latakia. From there, he went with a few companions through many dangers to reach Antioch. Once he arrived, he told the leaders the reasons for his journey and urged them to rouse themselves because a war was threatening and their absence would preclude the possibility of a positive result.

After Arnulf made his report, the Frankish troops urged on their leaders, and the latter were no less moved by Arnulf's news. Since there was very little time for preparation, they quickly gathered up their weapons before beginning the journey to Arqah. When the army was summoned from the areas around Antioch, all local fighting stopped. [Back at Arqah], the enemy was content to remain on the defensive and did not launch any attacks. By contrast, our men constantly strove to take the city, but made no progress. Arrows, javelins, stones and all manner of things flew between the two sides. Nature favored this place, and the Christians achieved nothing. Many people realized, from their own experience, that sometimes rest can bring victory when labor has been undertaken in vain. Therefore, the besiegers discussed the matter among themselves and agreed to wait so that hunger might torture the townsmen. The major reason for this advice was the great quantity of supplies outside and the fact that hunger was threatening those on the inside.

Chapter 108

The fraud concerning the lance is discovered in a trial by fire

While they set aside their arms and put aside military operations in this period of rest, the question was raised about investigating the discovery of the lance mentioned above. For a schism was disturbing the people with some praising what had been done and others condemning it while neither side was completely sure. The leaders decided that the one who was the initiator of this error should be the one to settle the quarrel. He would demonstrate the trustworthiness of this dubious matter with a trial by fire. Thus, after Peter was summoned before the council, they decided that he would go nine steps in the midst of burning logs. By means of this examination, the truth of the discovery would be proved by his unhurt state while its falseness would be proved by his burns. He was ordered to undertake a three-day fast that would serve as a period of quiet in which to pray and keep vigil. And so, this is what happened. But, soon after, on the day after the fast ended, there was another assembly. The logs burned in a double row. Peter, who was wearing nothing but a tunic and trousers, passed through the burning logs and fell down at the exit after being burned. He died the following day. When the people saw what happened, they decided that they had been fooled by his clever words and regretted having erred. Thus, it was confirmed that Peter had been a disciple of Simon Magus.[170]

Chapter 109

On the same matter

But Raymond and his Provençal accomplices stubbornly defended Peter and claimed that he was a saint. They threatened Arnulf as if he were the perpetrator of a fraud for having uncovered this fraud. Finally the Provençals sent a group of armed men to deal with Arnulf and they would have launched a surprise attack on his dwelling if he had not been warned and hurried to the count of Normandy (Robert) whom he had served in a soldierly manner. The count was feasting with the count of Flanders and they were both reclining at dinner. But when they had heard the reason why Arnulf had hurried there,

---

[170] In Christian tradition, Simon Magus became a follower of Jesus in a selfish effort to gain magical power for himself. His name became synonymous with efforts to purchase ecclesiastical office – the sin of simony. Cf. Raymond of Aguilers, *Historia Francorum qui ceperunt Iherusalem*, trans. John Hugh Hill and Laurita L. Hill (Philadelphia, 1968), 100–103.

they summoned him into their presence. Both of the counts then left dinner and sent a force of armed men to confront the Provençal troops. When the latter heard the sound of the approaching Normans, they grew frightened and hid their plan by pretending to be looking for something else. They saved themselves with this ruse, but not only did they take up their arms in vain, they also did so in an evil cause. They would have regretted their action, if fear had not chased them off.

Chapter 110

A suggestion is made to create a golden image of the Savior

After the author of this fraud, Peter, suffered the punishment which he deserved, a new assembly was convened in order to provide a new source of consolation for the army following the discovery of the fraud. The people proposed that an image of the savior be molded from the purest gold on the model of the Israelite tabernacle so that they would spend as much on their devotion in this age as the Israelites had in their own. Moreover, the assembly did not pass over in silence the fact that there had been a delay in acknowledging their frequent victories over the enemy. It was stressed that God must be thanked for protecting them from danger and that supplication had to be made so that God would continue to do so in the future.

Arnulf was the instigator of this exhortation and he turned his listeners in whatever direction he desired. The bishop of Marturana, who was not much better educated than the common folk and hardly well read, stood by his side in order to extend his right hand over the people in blessing once the sermon was over.[171] The task of having the image created was left to these two. The rest of the people were to give donations.

This great work was finished in a very short period of time. If it had not been carried out with urgent zeal, a formless mass would have been carried on to Jerusalem because the third month of siege [of Arqah] had passed into the fourth and the leaders were regretting the delay and also ashamed that they had waited so long at such a small town.

---

[171] The bishop of Marturana, also named Arnulf, was a close friend of Arnulf of Chocques, and was the first to suggest that the latter be elected as the patriarch of Jerusalem.

Chapter 111

The army proceeds to Jerusalem

Once they gave up this useless siege, they crossed happily to the gates of the cities of Tripoli, Djubail, Beirut, Sidon, Tyre, Acre, Haifa and Caesarea. They boldly demanded great quantities of money and supplies from these places and supplies and money were immediately handed over and paid out. All of these cities, each protected by high towers, blocked the pilgrims' route from north to south along the seacoast. But when the Christians left the shore behind and arrived at Ramle, Tancred broke camp before dawn and marched out before his fellow commanders. When he arrived at Jerusalem, he circled the walls but only after he freed Bethlehem from the enemy.[172] This besieged city had sent a messenger to him the previous day to ask for help. Getting his first view of Jerusalem from a distance, Tancred greeted her, placed his knees on the ground, fixed his eyes on the city, his heart on heaven, and this is the image of his salvation placed into poetic meter:

> Greetings Jerusalem, glory of the world in whom our salvation, the passion of Christ, was made sport of to the shame of the Jews. With the heaven and the sun alone as witnesses, the nourisher was extinguished by the enemy of the human race. He brought those who were free from evil back from hell.[173]
>
> You suffered on the cross and were buried in the sepulcher. You are light propagated from the divine light of God, penetrating the inferno and then coming back. You submerge under the waters of the river Styx those who seduced Adam.
>
> But soon he taught that he had been reborn and had risen on the third day. And after these things he ascended to the heavenly temples, where the brilliant clouds received him. When the people of the Galilee saw him He heard, 'thus he goes as if he seeks the stars'.
>
> You know these things o sacred mountain named after olives.[174] You are a witness to these things, farewell to a view of the king. Greetings also to royal Zion,[175] upon whom the disciples chant Kyrie eleison[176]

---

[172] Bethlehem was the first of the sites closely associated with the life of Jesus to be captured by the crusaders.

[173] This refers to Christ's descent into Hell, his freeing of the righteous dead held captive by the Devil since the time of Adam, and their deliverance to Heaven. Cf. I Peter 3 18–20.

[174] Here Ralph is referring to the Mount of Olives.

[175] Here Ralph is referring to Mount Zion.

[176] The *Kyrie eleison* (Lord have mercy on us) is the only part of the liturgy of the Latin Mass that was always sung in Greek during the Middle Ages.

with great passion so that it sounds as if a storm had been sent down from heaven. Suddenly you are replete, renewing spirit. Terror and fire are coming in tongues.

Greetings, star of the sea, door of heaven. The sole mother of the father, daughter of your son.[177] You remain an eternal virgin, after, during, and before the birth, knowledgeable of no fault. O river in its circuit, banks, fountain, glade, city, cottage, mountain, valley, farewell.

Chapter 112

All alone, Tancred observes the city from the Mount of Olives

After he had fixed his banners near the Tower of David and had given the order to establish camp, he climbed the mountain where he had learned that Christ, the son of God, had gone to meet his Father. Tancred went alone without a companion or an armsbearer. Whether this was rashness or whether it was a new type of siege is unclear. Tancred's soldiers besieged the west and Tancred the east. A few besieged one part and one besieged the other. On one side there was a military force without its commander and on the other there was a commander without his military force. Neither one was confident of getting help from anybody else. For the closer he went to the place [Mount of Olives], the further he was from the aid of the Franks. He was far to the west of his encamped men. The army that was following behind was even further off to the east. Tancred was therefore his own mounted troops, his own foot soldiers, and his own standard bearer.

He fixed his gaze on the city from the Mount of Olives with only the valley of Josaphat dividing them. He watched the scurrying people, the fortified towers, the roused garrison, the men rushing to arms, the women to tears, the priests turned to their prayers, the streets ringing with cries, crashing, clanging and neighing. He was amazed by the bronze dome of the temples of the Lord, at the unusual length of Solomon's temple, and at the circle of the spacious arcade, as if it were another city within the city.[178] He turned his eyes frequently toward Calvary and the church of the Lord's Sepulcher.[179]

---

[177] According to the editors of the *Recueil* edition, this short verse is crossed out in the manuscript. Put in its place in a different hand is *Partus plasma, tuae filia prolis.* These epithets are standard poetical forms of greeting for Mary, the mother of Jesus.

[178] The crusaders confused the Dome of the Rock, a mosque, with the Jewish temple. The Dome of the Rock was built on the temple mount where both Solomon's and Herod's temples had stood. The latter was destroyed by Titus in AD 70 during his sack of Jerusalem. The only remaining part of the Jewish temple is the western wall.

[179] In this period, the rock of Calvary, the place of the crucifixion, was believed to be enclosed in the Church of the Holy Sepulcher, which was also Jesus' tomb.

Although what he was seeing was far off in the distance, he was high up and these places were visible from this height. He longed for and desired these things. He was willing to give up this life for the light if he might be permitted to kiss the base of Calvary whose summit he observed.

Chapter 113

A hermit meets Tancred

As it happened, while he was setting out to discover these things, a learned hermit, who lived on this mountain, gave him good information about the location of Caiphas' headquarters, where Judas hanged himself, the Gold and Beautiful gates, where James was cast off the precipice, where Stephen was cast to be stoned, and many other matters of this sort.[180] Then they asked each other about their religious allegiance, fatherland, family and name. Tancred responded that he was a Christian, a Norman, of the family of Guiscard, and Tancred. When the other heard that he was a Guiscardian, he was amazed and looking at him more carefully said, 'Are you of the blood of the duke at whose threats all of Greece trembled, from whom Alexios fled in battle, at whose siege Durazzo surrendered, whose rule stretched all the way to Bardar in Bulgaria? You are not speaking to one who is ignorant. For I will never forget this ravager of my homeland. This one was once my enemy. But now that you have been sent, the injuries done to me are cancelled. He lives in you, this terrifier of peoples' lives, the vigor of the audacious uncle, the new signs bring me back to the earlier ones. I was confused at first by this enemy, this stranger, who spurned company, wandering about trusting so much in his arms and in his horse. I was hoping that companions would follow or that military forces had preceded him. But ignorance was the cause of my amazement, an ignorance which you have lifted from me. Now, you are new to me and I have become aware of you out of ignorance. From being one who was rash, you are now strong, from being an old enemy, you have become a brother. Now, I will not be amazed if you do amazing things, I will be amazed if you do not. It is not fitting for one from this family to tread the common road of man. But beware, take care my son, behold the enemy.'

---

[180] Caiphas was the High Priest at the time of Jesus. Concerning the casting out of Stephen see Acts 7:54–60.

Chapter 114

Alone Tancred cuts down the soldiers rushing from the city

Behold, soldiers poured out from the gates. They sent out five men to climb up and attack him in the valley of Josaphat. They came toward him with great confidence, five against one, but each one a leader surpassing his companions. They all hurried so that they passed each other, and each one passed the others so as to gain the spoils. But the Guiscardian, after saying farewell, ended his conversation. He turned his mouth, spirit, step and his spear to the attack. He sent the soul of the first one he found climbing the mountain to Hell and his body crashing to the ground. In the second case, a horse condemned to death saved the rider. This rider, I say, found fortune in misfortune because as his face hit the ground, his chest was protected. Thus, an unexpected ruin proceeded that which was expected. This was more upsetting to the one who was going to cut him down than to the one who fell, if this situation can be described as hateful to the latter at all. For although it was useful to both men, saving the effort of one and the life of the other, this utility nevertheless was condemned because the will of both was impeded. The third one then attacked and I would call him fortunate as well, even if the one lying on the ground bemoaned the fact of his being on the ground. But he was himself guilty of making himself unfit to carry out his desire because he delayed charging into his ruinous attack and then rushed in both harder and more incompetently.

Two of them now remained unharmed but Parca, was displeased, and snipped the threads of their lives.[181] Their threads began to be snipped away while coming forth but soon were whole again when they were in retreat. Tancred's lion like roar drove the astonished men to flee back to the gate. Just as sometimes when it happens that lambs seek the sheepfold where the bars lock out the wild animal, an even more intense hunger drove the beast against those now protected.[182] The victorious Tancred, who had been driven from the walls, was not moved at all by the spoils that had been left behind, by the freely running horses, the richly ornate armor or the arms, shining with gold, of those who had cast them aside. He returned to console his men who had become desolate in his absence and now groaned in their desolation. In the meantime, numerous troops, burning with youthful vigor, had arrived to provide aid. Also present were those of delicate and rough age and even those of the softer sex. Those who were infirm equaled those who were strong in their single devotion to joining the conflict.

---

[181] Parca is one of the three Fates whose task it was to mark the death of mortals by snipping the threads of their lives.
[182] Cf. Vergil, *Aeneid*, 2.355.

Chapter 115

Description of the city

At this point, it is appropriate to enjoy for a short while a description of this holy city. Since it is not possible to nourish the eyes because of the distance, may the [material] transmitted by hand and absorbed by the ears at least nourish the soul.[183] The circuit of this holy place is a quadrangle and large inside. The eastern frontage and the northern wall are straight while the other front and wall are curved since broken ground intervenes there at the middle point. The southern front slopes down toward Galilee, and this is what it is normally called. The [western wall] looks upon the square-shaped Tower of David. The valley of Josaphat touches on its eastern side and separates it from the Mount of Olives.[184] This latter site is situated over a valley and rises above all of the surrounding area. Here are the gardens of Gethsemane, the rushing Cedron, the courtyard of the palace of God, the sepulcher of the queen of heaven, the place where the proto-martyr Stephen was stoned, and where the intensity of the Lord's Prayer was demonstrated by his bloody sweat.[185] But, that I might follow my description in order, there are two pyramids there. The upper one is round and is from King Josaphat. The lower one is square and is said to belong to Jacob. Inside are the wells of Syloe and Jacob.[186] All around on both sides of the valley are numerous hermitical foundations. Similarly, the valley separates Mount Zion from Aceldema leaving from the valley of Josaphat near the well mentioned above.[187] It heads up in a circle to the Tower of David.[188] A little mountain in the western corner of the city, which presents one of its sides to this wall, descends here. It is a little higher on the right side. But on the left side it is almost at the same height as the nearby ground. Here it is attached to the valley of Josaphat and provides a good place to establish camp.

---

[183] Cf. Horace, *Ars poetica*, 180.

[184] The valley of Josaphat is named after King Josaphat, the fourth king of Judah after the separation of the northern ten tribes into the kingdom of Israel. The valley was named after the king following his victory over a coalition of enemies including Moab, Ammon and Edom.

[185] Cf. Luke 22:44. The Cedron is a ravine that lies below the eastern wall of Jerusalem. The sepulcher of the Queen of Heaven is the church of Our Lady of Josaphat where Mary, the mother of Jesus, was thought to have been buried.

[186] The Syloe valley lies between the Mount of Olives and Mount Zion.

[187] Alcadema was the potter's field where Judas, who betrayed Jesus, hanged himself. Cf. Matthew 27:3–10.

[188] The Tower of David was the citadel of Jerusalem.

Chapter 116

The disposition of the army

The counts of Normandy and Flanders established their siege opposite the
gate which was called, at that time, the gate of Saint Stephen. Tancred was
established to their right. If you consider his position from the east, it was a
little bit lower down. However, if you consider it from the west and the rise of
the ground, it is a bit higher. The aforementioned corner [Tower of David] fell
to him to attack and, following its capture, it was called the Tower of
Tancred. The camp of the duke (Godfrey) sat in the shade of the valley and
touched on Tancred's camp at its highest point. Mount Zion benefited from
the presence of Count Raymond who was separated from the city by nothing
more than a low-lying wall. The section that is now a suburb of the city was
part of the old city, or rather was the city. It used to have what is now
Jerusalem as its suburb. Three gates were besieged by the Christians. Two
were confronted directly and one, which is the western gate, from the side.
The valley that it dominated kept it free from attack while the others, which
bordered on this valley, offered opportunities to attackers. But the valley of
Josaphat remained empty, freed both by its location and by the limited size of
the besieging force. This part of the city was defended without fear, by a deep
valley, a difficult ravine, and by an impregnable wall.

Chapter 117

Bohemond and other leaders are absent

But the army, now outside, was worn down by battles and disease, and was
especially weakened by the absence of the Gallic counts, Stephen and Hugh,
and of Prince Bohemond. The army did not have sufficient strength to attack
the lower wall nor to attempt to encircle the city, protected by towers, in the
east and the west. They were arrayed along two walls, both of them at about
their midway point. The people of Christ roused themselves even more so that
a smaller number might attack a greater force since it was clear that the
enemy was growing stronger and that their forces were growing weaker. The
heat of the month of June (1099) was tormenting those in the camps with
thirst. Those inside were well fed, had shade, quiet, leisure and sleep. Those
outside suffered from hunger, the sun, labor, battles and vigils.

Chapter 118

Siege engines are deployed

Although they longed for rest, they worked diligently on machines that they could use to assault the walls at dawn on the day before the Sabbath. For the monk of the tower (the hermit), whom I mentioned earlier, had indicated, according to Tancred, that the assault should take place on that day. But after searching the area all around, there was no meadow, palace or tower which could provide wood for building ladders. Memphis (Egypt), that new victor, had expelled Damascus (the Turks), its old conqueror, from Jerusalem.[189] The recent Egyptian expedition of that year had left nothing untouched whether dry or green. However, secret shadows hid some beams which could not fool Tancred's usual careful effort. Therefore, once these were removed and carried out, they were sufficient to build one ladder. It was thought at this time that this ended all of their need since the day fixed for taking up arms had arrived. Grave difficulties, both immediate concerns and future problems, faced them from both sides. The more pressing difficulty was that they had but a brief two-day period in which to find material for the ladders. The longer-term problem came if they launched their attack after this day, rather than on the day set for the attack, since they would then annul the oracle given by the monk.[190] Because of these problems, there was only a single ladder. But the attackers were grateful to have this one. Thus, the ladder was set against the wall studded with towers that stood to the left of Tancred's camp. The ladder was set up about a third of the way along the wall. And now that it was standing tall, the ladder argued, as if from its excessive length,[191] 'since I expected that I would not have any comrades, I shall not wait until I have them'.

---

[189] Shortly before the march of the crusaders south from Antioch, the Egyptians had captured Jerusalem from the garrison that had been installed there by Damascus.

[190] This is a reference to Tancred's conversation with the hermit on the Mount of Olives.

[191] Cf. Horace, *Ars poetica*, 97, who also uses the word sesquipedalia to indicate something of excessive length. The word literally means a foot and a half or half a yard.

Chapter 119

An assault on the wall

The proximity of his camp, the discovery of the wood, and the construction of the ladder, all give the leadership of climbing the wall to Tancred, who was near, who was the discoverer, and who had carried out the task of construction. The misfortune of having only a single ladder might have turned aside another, but this fierce spirit claimed such a great opportunity for praise for himself. Thus, knowing nothing of delay, he pressed on in the first stages of the climb, and shook with eagerness holding his sword in his right hand. But the mass of his troops and the nobles were opposed and reluctant. They hindered the efforts begun by this man who demonstrated the majesty of his family, the dignity of his name, and grace of his merits, and his hope of increasing them. Those who were clinging to his left side, disarmed his right.

After [Tancred] had been called back from this duty, a young man came forward. He was worthy of rejoicing if fate favored him and even worthier of being mourned if fate cast a jealous eye upon him. He was seen as lucky by every class from lowest to highest. But he was unlucky in this final task. For as he reached the top of the wall with his left hand, the sword of an adversary fell upon him. He who had climbed up quickly using both hands was hardly able to climb back down bereft of his sword and hand. The one was gone completely and the other almost entirely. This man, who was the driver of Tancred's wagon, was carried into camp to be cared for. If they had held him back, he would have fallen in these great deeds of bravery.[192]

But in order that his name not remain in silence and that worthy favor reward the audacity of this soldier,

> the name of the young man was Raimbaud and he was from the land of France. His family name was Cretons and he was a noble from Chartres. Strong and honest, these are great things, although

he was carried back wounded. No one suggested that it would be a useful thing to take his place since they feared the swords of the defenders, a thousand against the one of the attacker. For the whole enemy force had gathered at that spot leaving the remainder of the city, as if sleeping, since the circuit was empty on the outside. Seeing that their efforts had been in vain

---

[192] Cf. Ovid, *Metamorphoses*, 2. 328, 'Here Phaeton lies in his father's (Phoebus') chariot, which, if it does not hold a man of great deeds, still holds one of great daring' (*Hic situs est Phaeton currus ariga paterni quem si non tenuit magnis tamen excidit ausis*).

and that fortune not only favored the defenders but also opposed the attackers, the ladder was considered not only useless but damnable as well. However, if one considered that there was only one ladder, this attitude was excusable.

Chapter 120

Wood for the siege, which had been searched for in vain, was found as if by divine intervention

The leaders consulted in the meantime and agreed to search in the shadows, to investigate the paths and the trackless areas and to collect wood from everywhere. None of the leaders was spared a part in this search. This was agreed and soon put into practice. But while the others labored in vain, Tancred was not kept from his desire. What I am about to describe is a type of miracle and anyone who considers this well would not deny that it was an act of heaven.

Tancred, at this time, was suffering badly from dysentery. Although he could barely sit on a horse, he did not spare himself from riding. This sickness frequently forced him to dismount, to go far off, and to search for a hidden spot. Suffering for a long while in this manner and with feet tired out from the journey, he decided to give up this labor and to return ingloriously. But then the accustomed torment struck him. So he withdrew, and climbed down thinking to escape the eyes of his comrades. But when he looked back, he realized that he had not gotten away. Therefore, he searched even further for a hidden spot but again saw people wandering about everywhere. He changed his spot a third and then a fourth time. Finally, after a long walk under a rocky outcropping in a circle surrounded by tall trees, he found quiet.[193] Pope! Who other than God can bring forth water from the rocks, make an ass speak, and create everything from nothing. He cured an army out of the infirmity of a smitten soldier. God cured him from his infirmity, and from this vile illness created an antidote that was more precious than any metal. After relieving himself and gaining back his strength, he noticed four pieces of wood on the opposite wall of the cave. One could not hope for anything more useful for the task at hand. For, it is said, that they were from the materials used by the king of Egypt in his conquest of Jerusalem. When he saw them, so great was his joy, that he could not believe it or trust his eyes. He got up and went over to touch them and see them more closely. Thereupon, 'Hey, hey, comrades, hurry here,' he shouted. 'Here', he repeated. 'God has given us

---

[193] Cf. Vergil, *Aeneid*, 1.310–11.

more than we sought. We were seeking rough wood and we have found it prepared.'

The companions appeared right away after being called whereupon they moaned with joy. Tancred hurried to send a messenger to console the disconsolate army. When this joyous news spread among the people, voices of joy and exultation were raised up in the tents of the Franks and they set out in a procession just as if they were performing litanies.

Chapter 121

Robert of Flanders is appointed as the guardian of the workers

Soon after, Count Robert of Flanders was chosen as the protector of the workers while they were engaged in their task, that is, while they collected the wood for the craftsmen, cut the wood when it was found, and brought back the cut wood. There was a grove in the mountains. The mountains were far off from Jerusalem, closer to Shechem, which was once called Sebasta, and before that Sychar.[194] At that time the road was unknown to our people. It has since become celebrated and is virtually the only road used by pilgrims.[195] The aforementioned count, having been sent out with 200 of his household troops, was exposed to innumerable thousands of the enemy, surrounding him before and behind, to the right, and to the left. He was no more worried about their squadrons and horns than he was about his own homeland and the local pipes.[196]

During the day, he hunted wild animals between and among the workers. At night, he feasted on their flesh alongside the workers. This labor was both useful and a pleasure to the lord. For their part, the laborers had a meal without fear. When enough wood had been cut, the count returned and wisely sent out armed men to guard the path ahead. This bold man followed with the rearguard while the crowd was diligently protected in the middle. He passed without loss through the archers of Damascus, the dogs of Arabia, and the spears of Ethiopia. His well-known good fortune, which always accompanied him, never let him down. It demanded hymns and celebration from many

---

[194] Shechem, originally called Sichem, was also called Sychar by the local inhabitants. The Romans named the town Flavia Neapolis. Today, the town is called both Shechem and Nablus, the site of Jacob's well.

[195] By the time Ralph wrote, Acre was the normal port for pilgrims and the road ran to Jerusalem in the way described here.

[196] The horns in this sentence probably refer to the composite bows of the Muslims, which were constructed from horn.

both at his exit and his return. Indeed, he deserved the favor and praise of everyone.

Chapter 122

On the same matter

There was a plain between the Christian camp and the valley of Josaphat. There was no place better suited to an assault by the attackers or any place that was more threatening to the defenders. The wall was a bit lower in this place, the towers less frequent, and the field, as I said, was wider. This area was empty of troops, to the amazement of the locals. But the foresight of the leaders had reserved this area for the last battle, until the wood tower was built from whose top the Frankish forces would fly onto the walls. Therefore, the silver firs, the cyprus trees, and the pines were hidden. Meanwhile, the besiegers established a false threat. Thus, the material that was unfinished was set up to the west so that later they could fight in the east.

Chapter 123

Dire hunger among the besiegers. The siege engines are readied and brought up to the walls

In the meantime, however, there was a lack of both grain and water. There was also fighting. The one was a threatening [danger], the other was present. The furor of Egypt, Palestine, Arabia and Damascus was raging fiercely. The hills were bristling and burgeoning around them. They were sprouting forth with spears and steel, which was their produce. Furthermore, it was rare, indeed, it almost never happened that grain from outside came to ease the hunger of the camp. Wherever you looked there were thin people. It was not possible for anyone to leave camp to search for something to eat. The people who before had been the besiegers would be much better described as the besieged. A single and universal complaint ran through the army: 'the battles in Romania (Anatolia) were in vain. The hunger at Antioch was in vain. The other labors we overcame were all in vain. Having crossed the entire sea, we understand that the sand of the seashore turns us into shipwrecked sailors.' You might even look on sadly at the relief available, which was pitiable even to their enemies.

There was a group that hated a life which called for death. There were some who hurried headlong in a joint rush toward the walls as if to the embrace of their wives. It was as if there were one thought for each of them, 'I shall kiss my desired Jerusalem before I die.' The kisses of these poor men were met by a storm of swords, stones and sometimes burning stakes that brought sudden death to those who tried to embrace the wall. But this devotion, once taken up, could not be frightened away. Often, yes very often, the death of some led others to this same embrace.

The siege had now passed into July and five weeks had gone by since the beginning of the struggle. The work was finished. The catapults were built, the siege engines were constructed and everything required by the present circumstance had been prepared. The posts, flooring and hurdles were ready to be connected, bound and raised, but had first to be transported. Night was chosen as the time to transport them and when the next day arrived, the limbs which were scattered about were reconnected to form one body. The camp was then moved to follow after the siege engines. The wall, which would be attacked in this battle, was now as apparent to the besieged as it was to the besiegers. The calamity now burdened the people of the city. Their minds were anxious and they were incapable of taking counsel. It had been thought that the huge mass of the wall had excluded any fear of a battle of this sort taking place. Furthermore, they had fortified that part of the wall very carefully with a great deal of wood, with stone throwers and with catapults to attack the enemy. This had been done in vain. When the attack was moved from that place to this, as was noted above, it carried fear in its wake. The only hope in these extreme conditions was to move the engines within the walls to where they could strike at the assault that had been redirected by those outside.

Chapter 124

A battering ram attacks the towers

Thus, both sides were prepared for battle, one side was shaking the walls and the other defending them. A digging ram sought to bore a hole at the base of the tower. Rocks dropped on the ram's neck to break it. There was one tower, made of wood, which approached the city. It was flying toward an unwilling object, a tottering tower against a stable wall. One rushed against an immovable object, the other stood to receive it. But if it had been possible, the wall would have retreated. The wonder of this spectacle deserves to be compared to a retreating elephant whom the fables recall grew frightened at the sight of a mouse. In the meantime, the clamor, roar and wounds did not cease. Rocks, javelins and arrows flew on both sides. Shields, helmets and hurdles resounded as they came together at the wall. Because of the sounds and the flying objects, neither the eyes nor the ears surpassed each other in their respective labors. The wooden mass (the siege tower) did not slow once it reached the chosen path. It pushed along the path which now lay open after the barbican had been smashed.[197] But when it reached the point where the iron of the spear points clashed against one another, the ram removed the obstacle standing before it as if it were a Greek herald clearing the path for his mistress. Now the only obstacle remaining was the little tower which was the object of the assault.

The walls did not permit the siege tower to go any further forward, the siege engines following behind did not permit it to go back. The nature of the gradient did not permit any maneuver to the right or to the left. In other words, there was no way of going forward, back or moving at all. Fire punished the side of the Norman tower where the sluggishness of its feet sank away from the strong point. Those inside the walls tried to use flames while those outside hurried to pour water on the flames. The tower remained unhurt.

Then, once again, there was another strike as the followers of Mohamet attacked the followers of Christ as dripping amphora might drink death after the mixture of pitch and sulfur had been set alight with a torch. Twice the tower was set afire and twice was doused with water. Mohamet was defeated twice and Christ was twice the victor. The elements recognized the author of these acts and at His nod the victory changed sides. With the way open again, the siege engines moved on again advancing with luck. But the third advance was lamentable. The wood, weakening under its burden, cracked and became unfit for service.

Chapter 125

The besieged foil the efforts of the siege engines through their artifices

A certain timber commonly called a *soliva* because it waded through the earth, was being used to support the left side of the siege tower. But it broke. Thus having been injured in one foot, the siege engine stood immobile. Unable to proceed and unwilling to retreat, it was content to stand still. Grief now returned, old not from use but from a new cause. The desolation was renewed and the old wound was back. They reasonably said, 'Hope is sluggish,[198] if only we had been unwilling to believe in this thing from which we have suffered once we gave it our trust. Is this the end which the thinkers

---

[197] It would appear that Ralph is referring here to the removal by the crusaders of fortifications that blocked the path of the siege tower.

[198] Cf. Ovid, *Heroides*, 2.9, 'hope has also been deliberate in taking its leave. We believe only slowly those things which cause pain to believe' (*spes quoque lenta fuit, tarde quae credita laedunt credimus*).

augured for us at the beginning?' However, amidst these groans, a battle line approached armed with scythes of steel on long poles with which to cut the ropes whose knots held the beams suspended from the walls that threatened us. Cutting them was accompanied by a loosening [of the beams], and this loosening was accompanied by their ruin.

When this defense was removed from the right and left towers, Tancred attacked the more remote of them with a storm from his stone throwers, while the Norman count attacked the closer tower. The defenders were so heavily engaged in this action that they did not hear shouting nearby. This was especially true of those opposing the Norman count who was the more deadly because he was nearer, and therefore the more hated. They would easily have succumbed to the attacks if the chaff placed about had not kept ruin from their catapult. For they had hidden the wall behind sacks so that the flying stones would not shake it. There was a great deal of labor and very little result. There were many tears and no laughter.

But who would not be moved to laughter, even in the midst of tears, by this warlike priest who, while the soldiers were growing tired, took up a ladder although he was not a fighting man and was dressed in his white stole? He did so in order that those who were crying might instead groan while carrying their burdens, and sing psalms amidst their tears. Such was his bearing, his work and his speech. Of the three, the sermon was the best. The strength of the soldiers, which had been growing weak from this labor, now picked up at this unaccustomed sight. They returned to the walls singing *Kyrie eleison*. This came from deep in their hearts and rose efficaciously to the ears of the Highest Judge. For the Lord heard the clamor of contrition and no longer sustained the blasphemies of the perfidious. 'He who divided the red sea into parts and led out Israel from its midst,'[199] now consoled his desolate people. Where hope of life had passed away, he preserved the possibility of victory.

They had tried many things in vain, but now it seemed fitting to try to imitate lightning and this permitted them to strip away the protections of the citadel like stripping off a cloak. Arrows which were accustomed to drink blood now spit out flames. Now, I say, they no longer thirsted to be extinguished or to extinguish, but rather to rage in flames. As the horn bows fired their missiles, you might have thought that the earth was raging in place of the sky. Burning iron dried out the air passing from below to above while flame vomiting spears, aided by wings attached to their shafts, penetrated and burned the chaff. There was no means of combating fires of this sort so that those who had not given way before the javelins or crossbows now gave way before the flames. When the walls were empty of the enemy, the attackers replaced their scaling ladders. Furthermore, a broad plank now served as a

---

[199] Psalms 136:13–14.

bridge from the siege tower to the wall so that the citizens came into contact with their enemies, wood came into contact with stone, and the wall came into contact with the siege engines. Once this had been done, an eager youth crept toward the city on his hands and knees as if crossing from storms into port.

Chapter 126

Bernard of Saint-Valery, Lethold, and Engelbert approach the walls

The first among the young men striding forth with a drawn sword, the glory of soldiers and also the glory of a renowned family, was Bernard,[200] you who call Saint Valery your patron, from whom you received your name and your surname. The wall met you and the meeting brought with it pain. The noble pair of brothers, Lethold, and your brother Engelbert following you, the second after the first in birth and in ascent. The count of Flanders who sent the ladders against the walls, sent them to the ladders. They divided up going to the wall, the one to the east and the brothers to the west. They tore apart the enemy, and having done so, pressed on. Whichever way they rushed a clamor followed them and him. The first neck left its shoulders after being cut off. It had met a death-dealing right arm. The third head rolled along. The trunk stood there while the still-helmeted head fell down. But soon the trunk followed it. So, the dead one met with the boot and the living one met with a sword.

Chapter 127

The city is captured

But now the battle grew more harsh. Now even greater numbers of people attacked the towers. The walls displeased their old citizens as the new ones came over the top. They were amazed at the weight of the victorious force, that this attack pressed on so heavily and with such harshness and force, that it rushed on so rapidly and struck with such force. The frightened defenders up to now had spurned flight. But they turned their trembling feet in retreat in face of the victorious assault. However, the victor, having gained entry, was separated from the

---

[200] This Bernard was the son of Walter, the advocate of the monastery of Saint-Valery-sur-Somme.

unmoving crowd. The assault on the walls – the prize – now weakened.
The lack of the necessary people delayed the desired assault up the
ladders. But a gate was found nearby. It was broken using only the
power of their shoulders against the hinge. Soon, the gates onto the
valley of Josaphat opened up to their strength. When the gates opened
up, everything was in their favor and nothing stood in their way.

Here, there, right and left, up and down, through bushes, homes,
roofs, fields and gardens, they launched their assault, killed, stole and
destroyed. Here it was cattle, there a house. Some seized gold and others
brass, deceived by its tawny and shiny appearance. Many people took
silver, certain others took gems, and others purple cloth. Many obtained
slaves. They rushed everywhere and everything was seized. However, as
it is commonly said, each person has his own great desire and the cure
for this desire takes precedence. Thus, after the superfluous baubles had
been acquired, each one found what his need required. Those who were
starving did not hunger for arms once an oven had been found. Nor did
those suffering from thirst wish for animals or money once they had
found water. One who lay wounded in a house rushed naked to obtain
clothing. The drunkard hurried to his goblets and the greedy man to his
treasures. The nobility continued in their labors while the crowd worked
to gain spoils. The soldier was covered in red [blood] from the dead and
the leader exhorted him and urged him on.

There were two powerful men there, both counts, both named
Robert, that is the count of Normandy and the count of Flanders. Duke
Godfrey, celebrated for his strength in battle, was also there. So too was
the generous count of Saint-Gilles. He had rushed from outside and
climbed the nearby towers. He had captured the tower that is called the
Tower of David, but not without a great slaughter of the many refugees
who had sought asylum in the tower after fleeing from the walls.

Chapter 128

Tancred

Although Tancred was a man, he was a lion rather than a man, and he
had the mouth and eyes of a lion and especially the heart of a lion. He
rushed on to do great deeds such that Ajax could not dream, nor that
Hector or his conqueror Achilles would dare.[201] This descendant of
Duke Guiscard acted with facility and ease. The sanctuary of what was

---

[201] Ralph is drawing comparisons here to the heroes of the siege of Troy.

now one church but which had been two, now belonging to the Lord but before to the Lord and Solomon, had a large circumference and faced the south.[202] It was large, had a great area inside, and was surrounded by high walls. A double iron gate had received almost the entire city, having fled the horror and battle in fear. These gates were adamantine, iron and hard, but he was harder still. Tancred struck them, broke them, crushed them, and entered. The innumerable crowd fled at his entrance and rushed into Solomon's five-sided courtyard. The slow fell to his sword while the fast fled from it. They blocked the gate of their escape and bolted it either in the hope of saving their lives or of a short delay before death. The victor turned toward the church of God and behold, the doors opened up to his banner held high.

Chapter 129

Tancred despoils the temple

A cast image, made from silver, sat on the highest throne. It was so heavy that six men with strong arms could barely lift it, and ten barely sufficed to carry it. When Tancred saw this he said, 'alas, why is this image here which stands on high? What is the purpose of this image with its gems and gold? What is the purpose of this purple cloth?' For it was an image of Mohamet, entirely covered with gems, purple cloth and shining with gold. 'Perhaps it is a statue of Mars or Apollo, for it could never be Christ. There are no insignia of Christ here, no cross, no crown, no key, no pierced side. Therefore, this is not Christ but rather the first antichrist, the depraved and pernicious Mohamet. If only his comrade were here, would that he came! For my foot would crush both of the antichrists here. Alas, alas, the fellowship of hell drinks in the Tower of the God and Pluto's slave is in the edifice of Solomon's God! Let this one fall quickly while that one also falls. Should he stand here arrogantly as if he had also conquered us?' The order was carried out immediately after it was given. The soldiers had never carried out any order as willingly as this one. The image was torn down, dragged out, torn apart and broken up. The material was precious metal but the form was vile. Therefore, something precious was taken from something vile.

---

[202] Ralph is referring here to the Dome of the Rock, which was identified by the crusaders as part of Solomon's Temple and known as the Temple of the Lord. This building gave its name to the military order known colloquially as the Templars.

Chapter 130

Tancred distributed the booty to his soldiers

The interior wall shined in its circuit from sheets of silver that were almost a cubit wide and just as long. Each one was about as thick as a thumb. This covering went in a long circle through the winding courts. The weight of the sheets was about 7000 marks. It was sitting there uselessly, but the wise man put it to use. He armed his unarmored men, he clothed the naked, and cared for the needy. He also increased the size of his military force, which was his only desire. He augmented his banners with the addition of foreign companies.

There were many columns under these gem-encrusted walls. Many were hidden below the silver and many below the gold. The extraordinary ornament created by the craftsman was an art that ought to be celebrated throughout the world. The material was a comfort to refined eyes. It had been hidden under coverings of this type, lying hidden under its metal covering as if avoiding observation and hateful of the light. Tancred's efforts brought back the light of day to the images, which now for a long time had suffered being enclosed in shadows as if in prison. And so removing the gold, he had eased the hunger of those in need and by uncovering the stone, he had brought new life to the limbs of Christ.

Chapter 131

Tancred cuts down the enemy

But once everything had been arranged that was to be arranged, and after the gems, metal and stone of the temple had been admired, Tancred said a prayer and took up his arms. He sought out those still resisting. Having penetrated their hiding places, either he rushed in or they rushed out. The enemy did not gain any time. Now the outer areas of the city were clear. The fields did not see any more of the battle. Tancred advanced and brought death to those in the interior.

The gates were opened. Then, the pools of blood demonstrated the capabilities of your sword and your prowess. There is not enough time to describe everything, either the mourning of those destroyed or the joy of the destroying crowd. Such great things arose from such awful ones. Mars raged in a thousand ways, along a thousand paths, in a thousand ruins. Anger rushes on, the sword devours, the enemy falls. Behold, holy anger, holy sword, holy destruction. Disperse, be dispersed you depraved people, you evil men. Shedder of innocent blood, the guilty man pours out his own blood. You who have torn apart Christ completely in his limbs, receive now the limbs that Christ's supporters return to you.

Chapter 132

The destruction of the city. The defeated enemies renew their courage

In the meantime, the sounds of battle were ringing throughout the city. The Christians gathered here and there, some for the hope of dealing death and others for the hope of gain. Soon, each one sought his own desire. Therefore, steel, iron, cedars, metal, copper, electrum and the beautiful strong doors of the Temple of Solomon fell, having been broken. They searched the hiding places and opened them up to battle. Why have you hidden yourself away, evil denier of Christ? What good will it do you to have closed the gates of the divine palace? Although you have closed 1000 entrances and hide behind 1000 closed gates, you are dragged through a 1000 openings. Behold, you attempt flight, your boldness having found fear! Just as the wolves devour the sheep once the gate of the pen has been broken, so too is this people exposed to slaughter by the Gallic sword. A few exiles slaughter an innumerable crowd. Some slit the throats of old men, others carry off children. Many desire to strip away ears decorated with gems. But having seen the slaughter, an avenger (Muslim defender) flew at the killers. Soon, however, he would be dead. Soldiers without number or order were roused from their hidden caves. They had the appearance of bees whom a herder has driven out with water or smoke.[203] They came out and attacked the passages. They struck whomever they found in the face, or the ears, or on the nose. But when they set free the shadows from their hiding places, a thousand arrows flew and the thousand flew like springtime hail. They attacked with clubs because they had not gathered their swords.

---

[203] Ralph is apparently referring to a goatherd or shepherd who is eliminating bees that might threaten his flock rather than to a bee keeper.

Chapter 133

The battle is in doubt. The faithful flee. Eberhard of le Puiset rallies those who have fled

The strength of the Gauls was both huge and small. They were a small swarm, but a robust swarm. Nevertheless, their spirits could not long hold out against such numbers. They gave way, and those who had retreated before were now upon them. And in as much as they had been broken, inasmuch as the doors were smashed, this aided them in pursuing the former conqueror. It aided those who had been cast down in accelerating their counterattack, and to deliver their own strike through open windows. The first group attacked the second, and the second returned the attack. First one group was driven off, and then the other. Thus, one group retreated before the other, and then the reverse. The supporters of Christ over the supporters of Mohamet, and then the squadrons of the supporters of Mohamet over the supporters of Christ. The end of the battle was in doubt. Thus, Mars played his games here, and gave his favor there.[204] Multiple retreats were played out on both sides. Then, finally, Eberhard of le Puiset, a man strong in battle, mentioned above, came rushing up. He was armed with a shield among his comrades who were all shieldless. This one shield stood against innumerable spears.

And then, with a great voice he exclaimed, 'Alas for Francia!, Alas for such a shameful retreat! For shame! Did we come to fight or to run? Boys are accustomed to engage in battles such as this. Girls are accustomed to root for the clash of arms. Indeed, there are often threatening blows in the midst of feasts.[205] Are you men of Francia? I do not think it dignified to give the name of French women to you who have feared to break these sheep pens and to slaughter the flock held within! Shake off your fear. Demonstrate the manliness of your homeland. I shall take up the first banner, let the others follow me.'

Thus gnashing his teeth, he roused them. But he inflamed those watching him even more with his actions. For he set off, protecting his chest with a shield and leading with his sword in his right hand. One man, a hero of Mars, attacked 1000. Roused by his voice alone, the young men were even more roused by the slaughter carried out by their leader. They all had the same anger, and one heart. They were all of the

---

[204] Mars is the god of war.

[205] This would appear to be a reference to a tournament.

same mind. So, they all supported the one who had been urging them on. They marched swiftly, following the one in the lead.

Chapter 134

The horrible slaughter of the infidels

The few were able to defeat infinite thousands. The smallness of their force did not hurt them any more than the large numbers helped the others. Great size proved to be a liability, as the greater the multitude and the more densely they were grouped, the weaker the crowd grew. The few pierced and pressed the dense crowd. The wounded hindered those who were still safe in a variety of ways. It sometimes happened that those laid low by their wounds obstructed those who had fallen without wounds. Thus, those who had been killed, killed the living in turn. The greater the crowd of people, the greater the harm. Certainly, the falling suffocated the standing, and the standing suffocated the fallen. The sword passed no one in peace. The sword tore up ribs, and necks, and cut through groins, backs and stomachs. The sanctuary was covered with vast quantities of blood. The glory of all of the craftsmen from throughout the world, was submerged in a lake at whose waves even its creator shuddered. How great, how great was the amazement at the interior of the temple. The doors, walls, seats, tables, columns, all were bloody. There was nothing without blood. The floor was completely covered by the slaughter. The walls were submerged knee high [in blood]. The gore was so great that waves stained the *penates*.[206] It was greater than the slaughter at Pharsalus under Caesar, or the Phrygian fields under the Greeks, or the fields of Latium under Marius and Sulla.[207]

Chapter 135

Tancred incurs the hatred of Arnulf. Arnulf's speech against Tancred in the presence of the leaders

But, in order that this festive day not go without a name, it took place when July illuminated the year, on the ides of July. This is on the sixth in the series of days.[208] It was the day before the fortieth day from the beginning of the

---

[206] Penates are Roman household gods.
[207] Ralph is referring here to epic battles from the classical world in which many thousands of combatants perished.
[208] The city of Jerusalem was captured by the Christians on Friday, 15 July 1099.

siege. O blessed Ides, glorious above all others. It was in you that those who had been ordered to spread the articles of the faith throughout the world were separated out. They were the beginning of the seed. Behold, the renewed seed now gathers its harvest in this same time. It was in the Ides during the morning that the Father sent out his household servants into the vineyard. Behold, it is in their evening that vines fill the cellar. O Ides, it is therefore just that you make the Ides renowned with your glory.

O Tancred, after the victory, you have found a struggle for the fruits of victory and after this struggle, you have found peace as the fruit of this contest. Jealousy grew up among the princes against Tancred because God had rewarded him more richly than all the rest. The eloquence of Arnulf, armed with his darts as if with those of another Ulysses, provoked the man, called him inside, and summoned the leaders. The leaders came together and a second Ulysses rose up.[209] Then, after fixing his gaze for a while on the floor, he spoke in this manner: 'Many things, o fathers, have urged me to subject myself to your will. Among these are the injuries which I have suffered recently. These have taught me how much a man might be separated from man, a benefactor from a thief, and a restorer of liberty from an invader. You have raised me up from my low position, you have made me known from my state of obscurity, you have made me a fellow receiver of tribute as if one of yourselves. Moreover, these graces are a new liberality flowing from the old grace of your ancestors. O leaders of royal blood, you have shown in me from what font you have sprung. You have been generous and enriched me. Not looking to your own interests, you have become poor.

'But Tancred persecutes me. He exercises a savage tyranny over me. He rages against me. What common consensus has granted to me, he denies. You have established me, you have vested me as the vicar of the pope, and he despoils me.[210] Therefore, o brave leaders defend your right, avenge your injury, punish this injury. Let no one think that this is my injury alone. It is yours, it is all of ours. I have been diminished and thus the injury to you has increased. He had caused me loss and you disgrace. For one who treads on something that has been granted surely condemns he who gave it. For it is written, "he who disdains the law spurns the king." Why would one who spurns God not spurn you? Why would one who does not spare altars spare you? Why would he allow you to go about with cloaks when he has stripped bare the temple of the Lord?

'The temple of the Lord, I say. It was not built yesterday or three days ago. It was not set out with anyone's permission at a particular place, time, or manner, or by any person. For it is firmly established that this is the house of

---

[209] Cf. Ovid, *Metamorphoses*, 13.1–123.

[210] At this point, Arnulf is claiming the legitimate succession from Adhemar and therefore the latter's position as the papal vicar on the campaign.

the Lord. The Lord himself founded it.[211] This is the place, which he called
the gate of heaven, where the patriarch Jacob learned truly that there was a
God. It was here that he saw the ladder touching the heavens with angels
climbing up and down.[212] As an infant, the Lord Christ illuminated this place
with his words.[213] As an adolescent, after driving out the money changers
with his holy zeal, he said, "it is written that this house is called a house of
prayer."[214] It would take a long time to list the accumulated praises of this
house as set out in the pages of the old and new [testaments].

'But if you had paid attention, o son of a marquis, you would, at any event,
have spared this place as if it were heaven on earth. You would have spared it
I say, as a place unique on earth, most like the heavens, if the earth can hold
something like the heavens. But allowances were made for a descendant of
Guiscard, for he followed in the footsteps of his ancestors. For who threw his
comrade from the walls while in the midst of an embrace and kisses? Surely, it
was Guiscard. And who pretended to be dead, while still alive, and had
himself carried to Montecassino to be buried while still in good health?
Again, Guiscard. Who, in order to make peace with his nephew first acted
warmly but soon acted very coldly? Guiscard again. Nevertheless, even he
was known as the founder of churches not as their destroyer. Nor did he
denude them having first endowed them. Pope! O descendant of Guiscard,
were you not aware that I am the servant of the house of God? Was it
prudent, knowing this, to show me contempt, to tread on my rights, to carry
out your evil acts, having profaned the sanctuary? Or if you sinned out of
ignorance, why did you not reverse your course once it was brought to your
attention? But if your sin was planned, why have your seizures stopped?
There are still other churches remaining whose altars are covered with gems.
Go ahead, rush in, steal them, throw out their servants, and take the place of
those you have thrown out so that Arnulf may be silent and Tancred might
try to persuade.

'But you, o leaders, I have served you well, I have labored with you, I have
never deserted you. Nicaea felt my presence from the very beginning of this
war, when, with my encouragement, striving overcame sloth. It was I who
urged on the young men and gave youth back to the old men. I roused the
resting siege engines that shook the walls. Soon after, in the valley of
Dorylaeum, when we were surrounded by enemies and, despairing of our
lives, when we saw death before our eyes, fear did not confuse my mind. I
offered no false counsel, and my actions were not without success. I
remembered to send for our comrades, to make known our situation to those

---

[211] Cf. Psalms 132:13.
[212] Genesis 28:12, 16–17.
[213] Cf. Luke 2:41–50.
[214] Matthew 21:13; Mark 11:15; Luke 19:45; and John 2:14.

who were unaware, and to gather our scattered forces. I considered the matter and I put into effect. Nor did I ever burden the shoulders of others fraudulently in order that mine might be free.

'I set out through thousands of the enemy with one man as my Achates for company.[215] He was lightly armed and unprepared for war. I evaded countless pursuers. I announced what had happened, I brought back victory, I conquered. That I was at Antioch, the enemy can witness. This day shall not have a description of that long struggle. I shall also remain silent about Marra because of the time. But let Arqah, at least, be remembered. I had a different type of flight from here than from the earlier case, but the fear was the same. A small skiff took me near the wall but beyond the naval forces of the enemy, along the shore of Maraclea, Tortosa, Valania, Jabala and finally Latakia. When I arrived at Antioch, after passing through a thousand dangers, I remonstrated at the delays of the leaders. But o leaders who were brought from there, I have you as witnesses for it was I who brought you. From that time up to the present Apollo (daylight) has not seen me in leisure, nor o Apollo have you ever seen me sleep. No table has seen my face. My soul has known no rest. While I serve and watch over the public good, I have grown old and I die. I could add much more to what I have set out already, o fathers. However, in order to bring this to a close, I will leave out a great deal and let my adversary answer my charges.'

Chapter 136

Tancred responds

After this, Tancred rose not sure whether he should follow the fervor of his spirit, or make an effort to convince the judges. Therefore, he began in this manner, 'you know, leaders where my efforts lie. I have been in the army. Neither persuasion nor verbal ability has promoted me, but rather my sword and spear. Therefore, I ask that you indulge me, in answering these charges, if I should pass beyond what is reasonable in this art that is unknown to me, that is if as a rough beginner I either pull too hard on the reins or leave them too slack.

'In my view, my opponent has reasoned in this manner. He has taken up this bold action of provoking me because he has all of his strength in his tongue just as a scorpion has in its tail. For shame, I say, for shame that his words should be from the tail of a scorpion.[216] Indeed, you yourselves have

---

[215] Vergil, *Aeneid*, 1.312.
[216] Cf. Pliny, *Naturalis historia*, 11.25.3.

heard, and no external witness is needed, that he attacked my family with great vehemence. He detracted from Guiscard, who was second only to Alexander (the Great) in audacity. This from a man whose family has never produced a leader to equal this great leader. The deeds of Guiscard are known throughout the world and no one could detract from them who had not striven to turn black into white and white into black.

'What is he saying? Is it the case that providing for the needy so that they can set aside their worries, that redeeming life with gold, that crushing the enemy with gems, or that creating soldiers from silver is what he, in his perversity and depravity, calls stripping the churches? Surely he is the one who travels about preaching in the parishes shouting, "tell me o bishops, what need does a saint have with gold". I have acted to assure the public good and to fight the infidel. Furthermore, I acted having been forced to do so by necessity with danger pressing and in a time of battle. Thus, I used the metal that was lying useless as if dormant so that this shining metal could be given to someone who would then serve better by fighting. I did not take pieces of it as necklaces for my nieces. I handed over everything and kept nothing. I put it into motion so that its productivity would grow. While it was stuck in immobility it did not increase. I sowed that I might reap. After the harvest I shall repay my creditor tenfold.

'Truly, it will not be Arnulf, acting as key-bearer of the temple, who will redeem these debts, since it is I who will gather the treasures of his storehouse. In the meantime, I shall try to blunt his talons. While Tancred fights on behalf of Jerusalem, Arnulf shall not despoil the temple of the Lord. Consider, o leaders, what is this if not an injury? While we were both outside, I chose this same man as a judge and asked him this question, "who shall occupy each of the houses and palaces?" I received the following response from him. He said, "it has been decided and universally agreed that whatever is under consideration shall be granted to him who first occupied it after entering the city". Perhaps he thought I had forgotten. But I have remembered and kept these matters in my mind. They are fixed there. It is shameful for a judge to change his mind in a matter of days and to deny today what he granted yesterday. Thus, he is like a slippery snake and similar to Proteus. With what bond shall I hold one changing his face in the manner of Proteus?[217]

'If he should try to usurp for himself the first entrance into the temple, he shall fall defeated in this as well. Perhaps one soldier shall act as a witness for him, but the army stands as my witness, a thousand who saw. I rushed in first. I broke the doors first. I went forward while he dared not follow. I fought in front of those [enemies] whom he dared not glance at from behind. But he

---

[217] Cf. Horace, *Epistolae*, 1.190, 'How shall I keep the face of Proteus from changing?' (*quo teneam vultus mutantem Protea nodo*).

uses his flights in his argument before us. He warned about the dangers, he made suggestions for a messenger to be sent, finally he carried a message. Who would be so dull, o leaders, that they would not see his fear in these acts? Surely, to be sent anywhere from danger is to be away from and free from danger. What does it matter that he persuaded, offered himself, and then finally left? Without any doubt, what we learned from this is that he fled. For, to give it its proper name, his withdrawal was certainly a flight. He cast a justifying word on his boast, but his entire intention and desire was to flee. Thus, having excused his fears, which he enumerated, and because of which he fled, let us consider what this sounds like: "Among the thousand manners of death, this death alone is feared, the one by which the frightened begin to die."[218]

'This struggle shames me o fathers. It is not my adversary, although he might not impute anything to himself, which forces me to this, but rather my reverence for you, which brought me to agree and which drives me to it. Now, I shall set aside the reins of my tired horse. You will decide now what action ought to be taken in this matter.'

Chapter 137

The judgment of the leaders

When the dissonance of these words had struck the ears of the leaders, they turned with equanimity to the calmness of Tancred's response. Having put aside their jealousy, they now searched for justice. They found a means by which Arnulf did not make his claims in vain but also in which Tancred was not frustrated in the gains achieved by the shedding of his own blood. They judged that the udders, which had produced so much milk, ought not to remain dry, especially since Tancred's generosity had not been lacking for other churches. Since he enriched the poor, it is surely fitting that the poor favor him in turn. What else? Following the advice of the council, the son of the marquis gave 700 marks back to the temple, and did so not unwillingly. Thus, in this manner, two men who had been at odds were rejoined. Both were renowned, both had become powerful from meager beginnings, and both were the subject of jealousy by everyone else, although neither one was jealous of the other except by chance. In regard to these two, I shall confidently set out what the Mantuan (Vergil) said about Hector and Aeneas: 'If the land of Gaul had sent out two other men such as these,[219] the Gauls

[218] Lucan, *De bello civili*, 3.689.
[219] Cf. Vergil, *Aeneid*, 11.285.

would now hold Memphis (Egypt) and Babylon as kings. Such was the gleaming power of their oratory, their bravery, their generosity, discretion, care, justice and prudence.'

Chapter 138

The Franks are victorious beneath the walls of Ascalon

Now two days had gone by since the events recorded above, and dawn broke on the fourth day, which was the day before the Sabbath. This day doubled their joy for it saw the Franks as victors beneath the walls of Ascalon.[220] The capture of Jerusalem had disturbed the entire kingdom of Memphis. All of Egypt trembled with rage, gathered 360 000 mounted soldiers, and sent them off to war. The number of foot soldiers was greater than the sands of the sea. But when news of the arrival of the troops was announced to the Franks, they rushed out as if they were starving men going to a feast. Our men poured out the blood of the enemy where and when I noted. The few defeated the many. However, the need to discuss Tancred requires that I pass by the details.

After the victory, when Count Raymond's banners had been raised, the people of Ascalon submitted themselves and their towers to him. For, while he had been in command at Jerusalem, the Tower of David had sent out its defenders unharmed.[221] That this man had kept his word was widely celebrated among these people. But then a dispute arose among the command council concerning who would be in command. The kingdom had fallen to Godfrey by lot but Raymond did not wish to accept this.[222] So, the newly captured city (Ascalon) returned to idolatry, spurning the reins of the count and the yoke of the king who had subdued it. This evil has not yet been remedied. And although many deeds have appropriately made Raymond illustrious, and even more illustrious deeds may await, his arrogant and vain acts carried out in his indignant state cast a pall on both his past and his future. Alas, you miserable man, you do not know what chains and slaughter you have unleashed on the innocent because you abandoned Ascalon, which is now the instrument of slaughter and chains. You do not press the guilty

---

[220] The crusaders defeated the Egyptians at the battle of Ascalon on 13 August 1099.

[221] During the capture of Jerusalem, Count Raymond had honored his promise of safe-conduct to the Muslim garrison of the Tower of David and permitted the soldiers to depart safely.

[222] After the capture of Jerusalem, Godfrey outmaneuvered Count Raymond politically. After Raymond refused election as king of Jerusalem, claiming that the city should be ruled by the church, Godfrey accepted election as the *advocatus* of the Holy Sepulcher. After Godfrey's death in 1100, his younger brother Baldwin was elected king of Jerusalem.

and you remove the yoke. This saddest day of your indignation hands on a pernicious problem to posterity.

Chapter 139

Tancred fortifies the stronghold of Beit She'an

But Tancred, who always kept active, always tried to better himself, and who always was humble before the loftiness of God, fought for the new king despite being richer than the others as a result of his gains from the temple. He did not chafe at this yoke nor did he fear being alone. The departure of many heavily armed mounted troops from the army so reduced the number of such soldiers from the earlier high point that barely 200 men, who were equipped with breastplates, remained to defend Jerusalem.[223] About 80 of these men were part of the Guiscardian's military household. He gathered valuable booty from all around on a regular basis but he also kept bandits away from the city, thus acting as the enricher of the citizens and the impoverisher of the enemy.

But it is certainly the case that his concern led this man to fortify the stronghold now called Beit She'an but which we have read was once called Bezamis.[224] It was far from Jerusalem, and was not fortified with stone, stakes, or even a ditch. Its poverty burdened the inhabitants and did not offer anything to travelers. But, other than this, the population of the area was expanding around a place that would become dangerous. For Tancred's boldness, just like that of a hunter viewing a meadow or a fowler examining a thicket, knew where great booty was to be found. Therefore, once he had built a wall all the way around Beit She'an, he raided the other towns in the area. He unhooked their plows and transferred the yokes from the draft animals to the farmers. He closed the roads to merchants, and, as a result, the gates of the cities as well. Haifa was afflicted in this manner. And despite being enclosed within walls and the sea, the city grew weak. First, he attacked with stone-throwing engines, and soon the city fell to his swordsmen advancing with ropes, ladders and along bridges [from siege towers].

---

[223] The majority of the crusaders who had captured Jerusalem left soon afterward to return home to the West.

[224] This town was called Scythopolis by the Byzantines.

Chapter 140

Bohemond and Baldwin head to Jerusalem

During this time, Bohemond and Baldwin, King Godfrey's brother, about whom I spoke above, wishing to fulfill their oath of going to Jerusalem, set out with a not insubstantial military force. When they came to the valley of the Camel and the neighborhood of Damascus, not only did they pass through Philip's Caesarea[225] but marvelous to say, they freely passed through their enemies who were rushing here and there to find them. This was the period of Lent.[226] When they reached Jerusalem they happily celebrated Easter (1 April 1100) there with King Godfrey.

At this same time, Daimbert, the bishop of Pisa, a most learned and eloquent man, arrived at Jaffa with a great many ships.[227] With Bohemond's aid, he was elevated as patriarch of Jerusalem. Arnulf, who was a man of great generosity, freely agreed to this although he had been elected to this dignity. He hoped that the other would be more successful in spreading Christianity than he might be. Four other bishops were ordained there as well, namely Roger of Tarsus, Bartholomew of Mamistra, Bernard of Artah, and Benedict of Edessa, who had come with Bohemond and Baldwin after being elevated to the priestly office.[228] After the Easter celebrations were over, Bohemond returned with his three fathers (bishops), bringing each bishop back to his own city. Baldwin returned with Archbishop Benedict of Edessa to his county of Edessa.

Chapter 141

Bohemond liberates the city of Melitine from a siege. However, once the battle is begun, he is led away after being captured by the Turks

When Bohemond heard reports that the city of Melitine was surrounded by Turkish forces, he immediately gathered his army and set out to try to liberate

---

[225] Philip the Tetrach (4BC–AD34) was the son of Herod the Great noted in Luke 3.1.
[226] This was the month of March. Easter in 1100 was on the first day of April.
[227] Daimbert, the archbishop of Pisa, used his command of a large naval force and the support of Bohemond to wrest the patriarchal see away from Arnulf of Chocques. Daimbert was patriarch in Jerusalem for three years 1099–1102. Daimbert was deposed by the papal legate Robert of Paris on 8 October 1102.
[228] The consecration of these bishops took place at Jerusalem because Antioch still had a Greek patriarch, John IV.

it although it lay ten or more days journey from Antioch.[229] When the Turks learned that he was in the area, they gave up their siege, by design, and as is their practice, withdrew. They had more success, at least over the short term, when retreating rather than when attacking because they were accustomed to shoot arrows while in flight and thus wound their pursuers. When Bohemond approached the city and did not see the Turkish force, it was recommended to him that he enter the city for a short time and rest. Afterwards, when his men had been refreshed, he should set out to fight the Turks.

But he did not accept this counsel. Instead, acting on his own stupid audacity, he said, 'far be it that Bohemond now do something that he never remembers having done. They have acted like foxes who seek the shadows as soon as they hear the dogs barking.' Therefore, he set out against the Turks, and soon joined in a battle against them that he never should have entered. While they were fighting, Bohemond was captured and bound. This was a source of great joy to the supporters of Mohamet and misery to the Christians. He was then carried off in chains to Romania (Asia Minor) to the Danishmend king.[230] After his capture, Antioch remained in a state of misery, as there was no one who could help or offer consolation.

Chapter 142

The death of King Godfrey

A miserable event followed in the footsteps of the previous one, on account of which Jerusalem suffered even more. For Godfrey, a great king and a fearer of God, died soon after Bohemond was captured.[231] One year had gone by from the beginning of his reign until his death. Before he passed on, however, while he was still bound in his bodily illness, he called Patriarch Daimbert, Arnulf, and others to him. He said to them, 'Behold, I am about to enter the path of the universal world. While I am still alive, I would have your counsel about who should be appointed to rule in my place in Jerusalem.' But they answered, 'We place our trust in your providence. Whomever you choose for us, we will obey him without any doubt.' So he answered, 'if this is the decision that is taken, I judge that it is fitting for my brother Baldwin to take

---

[229] Melitine was ruled by an Armenian named Gabriel whose daughter Morfia had been married to Baldwin Le Bourg, the cousin of Baldwin of Boulogne who was elected king of Jerusalem in 1100. Baldwin Le Bourg at this time was the ruler of Edessa. Melitine is about 190 miles/304 kilometers north-east of Antioch.

[230] The Danishmend capital was at Sebastia (Sivas) in what is today central Turkey on the Kizilirmak River.

[231] Godfrey died on 18 July 1100 and Bohemond was captured in August of the same year.

up this highest office'. When they heard Baldwin's name, they all immediately agreed, praised the choice, and swore, with a firm oath, to obey him. They recognized him to be a man who was generous with money, well versed in war, humble in his affect, and exceptionally magnanimous. It was as if, as we say, nature had carved him out with her own hand. He was at this time, as noted above, in Rages, which is called Edessa, where he was established as the prince and where he had been for some time.

Chapter 143

Baldwin succeeds Godfrey in the kingdom of Jerusalem. Tancred takes over Antioch and conquers Mamistra, Adana, and Tarsus[232]

But in the meantime, after the aforementioned king was buried at Golgotha, a messenger was sent to Edessa, so that Baldwin might come to Jerusalem once he was summoned, since he had been named the successor to his brother's scepter.[233] This raised up the flames of great dissension and war. But Tancred's departure to take over the government of Antioch, which was caused by the same necessity that had required the summons to Baldwin, preceded this conflict. The heirs thus took their places, Baldwin at Jerusalem and Tancred at Antioch, both rushing eagerly toward fame. The younger were not less virtuous than their elders, although each one burned with jealousy toward the other.

His new-found rank weighed upon the son of the marquis because it seemed to him that he was more of a host than a prince. It was necessary for him to make himself more worthy because his rule as prince was likely to be short. He expected it to end once Bohemond returned. Laboring under these concerns, he first drove out Baldwin from command of the army.[234] Baldwin was among the powerful at Antioch and resented this new yoke. He had obtained the command of the garrison at Antioch under Bohemond. Now this fact, and his new role as prince of Edessa, which had been granted to him had roused his spirits, as is customarily the case. When Tancred had accomplished this act, he was soon energized to expand the boundaries of the principality, to the point which Bohemond had ruled shortly before but which the Greeks had since contracted. Therefore, he fought a brief but sharp

---

[232] This campaign began in April 1101.

[233] Golgotha/Calvary, the site of the Holy Sepulcher, became the traditional burial place for the kings of Jerusalem.

[234] This is not Baldwin, the brother of Godfrey, but rather that Baldwin's lieutenant and cousin, Baldwin Le Bourg, who served as the governor of Edessa. Baldwin Le Bourg was elected king of Jerusalem in 1118 as Baldwin II.

campaign against Mamistra, Adana and Tarsus, subjecting them, now for a second time, to his rule, since they had fallen away the first time through his predecessor's lack of caution.

Chapter 144

Tancred attacks Latakia[235]

Then, turning to Latakia, he attacked with all of his strength. This place, which was strongly defended with natural defenses, resisted this man, against whom iron, steel, rock and every other human effort had failed. It could be seen from the ruins that this city had once been noble, having churches, a large population, riches, towers, palaces, theatres and all of the other things which make a place great. Aside from Antioch, no other city had within its circuit such great signs of ancient nobility. The multiple series of columns, aqueducts which ran over rough terrain, towers built toward the heavens, statues lying around in fitting places, all of which were well constructed from precious materials. All of these noteworthy works, still present after so much time and so many ravages, provide evidence of its past from its present, its former state from its destroyed remains, and its large population from its current state of abandonment. It extended eastward up to a small hill and westward to the sea. Along one side there was a plain. Its circuit was either walled, or surrounded by ruins. The large population feared nothing, and in fact was an object of fear to other peoples nearby. In its day, it had decided against including much of its area within walls, content instead with a few fortifications.

But I return to the small hill which now provided the only defense against enemies. This difficult and steep hill received on its spacious top the citizens who had fled the plain after being frightened by the terrors of battle. Its difficult ascent would have been enough, even without walls, to repel besiegers. But since it was crowned with a wall, it offered a two-fold strength against adversaries, one wrought by nature and one by human efforts. Protected within these walls, the Greeks watched Tancred's approach. But this leader, who was knowledgeable in war but also eager, sent out many skirmishers so that they might capture anyone who came out or to induce them to come out. But the Greeks, who as usual were very vigilant, were careful so that no one was captured wandering outside nor were any of them provoked into going out. They considered anyone who left the protection of

---

[235] Tancred began a year-and-a-half-long siege of Latakia in the summer of 1101.

the gates to be mentally unbalanced. When they looked out on those outside their towers, they trembled even though they were protected.

From this behavior, Tancred determined that they were afraid. He exclaimed, 'hey, my companions, let us attack this sheepfold. You see it as difficult, but you know that it is empty. It is full of riches and empty of men. Any real soldier would be embarrassed to be shut up within gates. Let us attack the hill. I say this wall will give way before our axes or our ladders.' The prince gave his order, the soldiers attacked. They rushed up to the walls. Hammers, mattocks, axes, and every other tool of this sort beat at the gates. And although they were double gates and made of iron, they could not bear it, and trembled as if a single gate made of twigs. Seeing that iron and stone, and even nature itself was falling to these blows, the citizens left the safety of their enclosure and took up arms. Heavy stones rained down from the towers. Neither side lacked thrown spears. No one inside the walls remained at leisure. Fear of death drove away fear of the enemy. Indeed, the closer this effect came, the more effective they became in driving off its efficient cause.[236] Moreover, the nature of the place itself encouraged the people to take part. It was possible for anyone of either sex and any age to drop stones from the towers. In turn, arrows flew against the towers. They frequently pierced eyes and hands. Thus, action took place on both sides until it was necessary to rest when both strength and quivers were exhausted. This was especially true since the iron and steel, while breaking down the gates, also flew apart and were broken in turn.

Chapter 145

Count Raymond besieges Tripoli. He demands aid from the emperor. After being captured he is carried off to Antioch along with his treasure

Many, many battles were fought over the course of this year.[237] Count Raymond, who desired to aid the Greeks, was driven off. The leaders of the Turks were driven off. Finally, Jerusalem received aid in a moment of great distress. One person did all of these things. But Tancred did not give up the siege of Latakia, but rather maintained it. As we said, he drove off the Persians, the Egyptians, and the Provençal count (Raymond of Toulouse). The last named count, a man of truly amazing audacity, besieged Tripoli, one man against many thousands.[238] He had about 400 Christian troops,

---

[236] This discussion of cause and effect gives insight into Ralph's education, which obviously included instruction in logic.

[237] It would appear that the year in question was 1101.

[238] Following the election of Godfrey as ruler of Jerusalem and the crusader victory at Ascalon in August 1099, Raymond left the newly established kingdom of Jerusalem.

including both heavily armed mounted soldiers and foot soldiers. Trusting in
this number, he began to fortify with a wall and towers a small hill near to the
city. He named it Mount Pilgrim, usurping for himself a title that was
common property. Remaining there, he launched numerous assaults against
the city. The townsmen, for their part, almost destroyed this stronghold. It
was a rare day that did not see blood from both sides spilled on the plain that
separated them. One side was energized for battle by its great wealth and the
other side by the smallness of its force and by its poverty. In circumstances
when there are few troops, this very rarity fires their spirits. However, when
there are many soldiers it is easier to tolerate the shedding of their blood as
simply a factor in the horrors of war.

   But, while the stronghold and the city were defying each other, the
diminution of his force frightened Raymond. This in turn compelled him to
leave and beg the Greek emperor for aid. He brought with him the
apocryphal lance, mentioned above, which had sent its discoverer to temporal
and eternal flames. This, I say, he brought with him to Alexios as a gift. He
was richly rewarded in return. Grateful for what he had brought, [Alexios]
was even more grateful that [Raymond] had come in person. For, when going
to Jerusalem, he had not wanted to ask for aid, even when invited to do so.
Now he returned as a supplicant. While before he had turned a deaf ear when
asked, now he was a good listener asking for aid.

   Hatred, was the common factor which brought them together. Antioch was
an enemy to each man. Thus, I say, Raymond was sent back with great gifts
to fight their common enemy, the son of the marquis. Men consider the
matter on earth, and God, who is seated above the cherubim, judges the
matter in heaven.[239] Alexios, you sent the treasures to Tancred, when
Raymond's galleys, loaded with your gifts, almost sank. After passing by
many places, accompanied by unhappy auspices, they were carried with
happy auspices to the treasury of your enemy, that is to the nearby port of
Tarsus. After being buffeted by storms, they could not avoid falling into the
hands of their enemies. When word of this came to the ears of the prince

---

He went to Constantinople in 1100 and entered Byzantine service. He subsequently
joined the Western forces (called the crusade of 1101 by scholars) as a representative of
Emperor Alexios. Following the destruction of this crusading force by the Turks,
Raymond again returned to Constantinople. Raymond then joined with the remaining
leaders of the failed 1101 expedition with a rendezvous planned at Antioch. It is in this
context that Raymond, who was still in Byzantine service, was captured by Tancred's
supporter Bernard the Stranger, as is discussed in the text below. Ultimately released
after promising to leave Antioch in peace, Raymond joined the crusader forces that
captured the city of Tortosa in 1102. This city subsequently served as a base of
operations for Raymond in his efforts to capture Tripoli and establish the county of
Tripoli ultimately gained by his son William Jordan in 1109.
   [239] The cherubim are the second choir in the highest level of angels, along with the
seraphim and thrones.

(Tancred), he ordered that the count and the Greek treasures be carried to
Antioch, to serve him, that is so he could disburse them. However, the count
was not held for long. He abjured or swore whatever he was ordered to. After
taking his oath, the gates were opened up for him. In this manner, the count
saved his life but also severely limited his options. Thus, matters are
transformed by the will of fate, so that the poor become rich and the rich
become poor.[240]

Chapter 146

Latakia is captured after a year and a half

But Tancred always persevered in the task that he had set himself. Once he
began something, he never deserted it. He could besiege Latakia and would
not leave until was captured. Now, however, a year and a half had gone by,
when God inspired him with the means by which the city might be captured.
The besieged were accustomed to lay ambushes for their besiegers. In the
middle of the day, they would sometimes burst out in an attack and disturb
those who were sleeping, often with death and plunder. Once the alarm was
raised, the roused Franks armed themselves. But, in the meantime, the men of
Latakia had returned uninjured after carrying out their attack. They fell upon
the army, once, twice, a third time. But they showed the path by which they
carried out their attacks because they often took a not dissimilar route.

In order that he might overcome this stratagem with a stratagem of his
own, Tancred set an ambush for the ambushers. He ordered that a tent be set
up whose capacity was greater than that of any which anyone had ever heard
or seen before. The tallest possible pine tree was to be found which could
serve as a center column to sustain a very heavy weight. Tancred spoke and it
was done. A tree was found, its spacious curves were set in a circle and its
branches were enclosed and bound. The townsmen who saw this prideful act
thought that this bit of pageantry was intended to surpass the palaces in the
city. But at daybreak, Tancred summoned his heavily armed troops and
placed them in the shadows astride their horses. When the time was right,
they were to charge into battle without any delay, using their spurs.

At the rising of the sun, Tancred sent a substantial portion of his army to
gather grain, and did so under the eyes of the enemy. When they had left, he
ate and then gave the appearance of going to sleep thereby promising the
hope and opportunity of plunder to those who were looking on. From their

---

[240] It is noteworthy that Ralph refers here to the will of fate rather than to the will of
God.

heights, the townsmen looked out at the silence and hoped that, as they were accustomed, they might discomfort the army and then escape through a quick retreat before the enemy's sluggish efforts at retaliation could be realized. Leaving only a few men behind, almost all of them set out. The simulated opportunity had fooled the incautious townsmen. They rushed out to gather booty. Then, burdened down, they ran into each other as they returned to their gates. Now, those who had been prepared and hiding in the shade immediately attacked once the path was clear. They held the gates against those who were returning. Tancred then rushed upon those who were locked out and captured or killed them without delay. The remaining guards were few in number and terrified. They had no trust in the walls or in themselves. They sought peace and offered to hand over the walls to those approaching if they could have an agreement about their safety. This was satisfactory to the prince. Thus, after long labors, he returned home to Antioch.[241]

Chapter 147

The archbishop of Milan and the count of Poitou are defeated by the Danishmends. Bohemond is ransomed

At that time, Anselm, the archbishop of Milan, and Count William of Poitou fought against the Danishmends in Romania (Asia Minor).[242] The archbishop was killed and the count barely escaped from the Turks. He fled, impoverished, hopeless, and naked, to Cilicia. There, he approached and found Tancred. The one who was discovered to have been destitute of everything was taken in and provided with an abundance of all good things. Thus comforted, he headed to Mount Pilgrim. Going to Jerusalem, he accepted an escort from the count (Raymond).

At this time, raising Bohemond's ransom weighed heavily on the people, especially on Count Baldwin (of Edessa), who was a particular enemy of

---

[241] Latakia was captured by Tancred when Tzintziluca, the emperor's commander, and the Greeks, surrendered.

[242] Anselm of Buis, the archbishop of Milan, set out for Jerusalem in 1100. But after fleeing from the Turks, he died at Constantinople in 1101. William of Poitou, also known as Duke William IX of Aquitaine, led a large force of his countrymen in the campaign subsequently called by scholars the crusade of 1101. Following the utter defeat of the Aquitanians and their Bavarian co-crusaders at the battle of Heraclea in early September 1101, Duke William fled and eventually reached Longiniada, the port of Tarsus, where they were given aid by Bernard the Stranger, a supporter of Tancred. The Danishmends were the Turkish dynasty ruling the city of Sebastia. The Danishmends, in alliance with the forces of Aleppo and Harran, defeated the various groups of crusaders who marched through Anatolia in 1101.

Tancred. Baldwin belabored the Antiochenes with warnings, pleadings and reproaches, so that they would gain Bohemond's freedom. The recently elevated Patriarch Bernard also made great efforts as if to repay Bohemond who had gained his release from prison.[243] Nor did Tancred stand in the way of these efforts, although it seemed that Bohemond's return would be a hindrance to his continued prosperity. Partly through these, and partly through other favorable circumstances, Bohemond returned, having been redeemed for a sum of 10 000 *Michaels*.[244] Tancred returned to him what he had received and also what he had not received. The first he did willingly, the second unwillingly. He was forced to give over Latakia, Mamistra, Adana and Tarsus, which he gained by dint of his own effort, to the one who had been freed from chains and irons. Thus denuded of all of his properties and even the company of the army, he had to beg for two small towns.[245]

Chapter 148

The Assyrians go to war and surround Edessa.[246] A battle ensues[247]

In the meantime, the Assyrians went to war and surrounded Edessa and its neighborhood with an infinite multitude. When asked for aid, Bohemond did not delay. He crossed the Euphrates accompanied by the patriarch (Bernard), Tancred and Joscelin, who at that time ruled the city of Marash, bringing whatever troops he had.[248] When the Turks heard about Bohemond's advance, they left Edessa and went off a short distance, still avid for battle, but pretending otherwise. They simulated flight with a certain adroitness so that they could attack their enemies without warning as they followed behind. The one side was to pass along known paths to safety while the other side headed toward danger along unfamiliar roads. The one side proceeded toward supplies, while the other side carried on into hunger. The one side was to advance toward reinforcements, while the other side continued toward losses. Thus, they went on for a period of three days, until they passed beyond

---

[243] Bernard of Valence, who had been Adhemar of Le Puy's chaplain, was appointed by Bohemond to serve as the Latin patriarch of Antioch in 1100 and held this office until 1135.

[244] This is a Byzantine gold coin.

[245] Bohemond's treatment of Tancred may have been related to Tancred's less than vigorous efforts to raise the funds necessary to pay Bohemond's ransom.

[246] The Assyrians here are Turks.

[247] This is the battle of Harran that took place on 7 May 1104.

[248] Joscelin of Courtenay was the leading supporter and first cousin of Baldwin Le Bourg.

the city of Harran [Carrhes] with one side deceiving and the other side being deceived. This went on until they reached and crossed the river Chobar.

The delay in battle was now sufficient for the Turks. They gave up their deception and prepared for war with their mouths and with their hands. They thought that our men would be played out, that there was no hope of escape now that they had crossed the river, and that their strength was gone. Not long after the thought came the deed. The Christians were marching along in three columns. Bohemond held the right and Count Baldwin held the left. Neither one was wearing his armor, both were unprepared, and both were unaware of the plans of the enemy. Tancred was stationed in the middle. He was prepared, ready and armed.

The Turks, who were not far in front of them, almost as if they were serving as a vanguard, had scouts nearby who reported on the situation among the Franks. As the fourth quarter of the day began and three quarters of the day had gone by, the Franks began to make their camp in the order noted above.[249] When the Turks learned from their scouts who was prepared and who was not, they launched a sudden assault. They avoided Tancred's force and attacked the armies of Bohemond and Baldwin. Neither one was able to put on his armor so they fought with bare heads and chests. The Antiochenes struggled to resist, but uncovered as they were, they were forced to abandon their baggage. Then, while the enemies were busy with their baggage and rich goods, our men caught their breath. Thus, although they were skilled in war, it was the loss of their property which saved their bodies. They considered themselves lucky to have lost their goods.

Chapter 149

Baldwin is led away as a captive. Benedict is captured and rescued by Tancred

But then the men of Edessa suddenly failed. They were not able to protect their baggage or themselves. Baldwin was captured and led away in bonds. The unlucky archbishop Benedict was also captured and carried off. Both of the chained men had baggage loaded onto their shoulders. But when the latter was being led away in front of Tancred's force, he shouted, 'Tancred, Tancred, help me, may the suffering of Benedict move you to pity.' When the son of the marquis heard this shout, and recognized whence it came and who it was, he charged out, freed him, and led him back to safety. He provided the liberated man with a mule. Because he said that he would aid him, he

---

[249] The day is divided into two twelve-hour portions beginning at sunrise and sunset. The beginning of the fourth portion is the beginning of the tenth hour after sunrise.

consoled the trembling man and stayed with him assuring him that there was nothing to fear. At that point, the approaching night and the arguments of his soldiers opposed Tancred's desire to go into battle. The same objection also restrained Bohemond who preferred to hold off fighting until the next day. In the meantime, the darkness of the night enclosed the world. So, after sending out their scouts, the leaders went to sleep. However, the common troops, who did not have available the comforts of the court, considered ways of fleeing as they feared the fate that they saw set out for them on the next day.

Chapter 150

The Christians retreat

The river stood in the way of their retreat. It had one ford. The remainder of its course was blocked by steep banks. Guards watched this one area as if it were a gate so that it would not offer a means of escape to the terrified people. They could keep those attempting to flee away from the ford if there were only a few of them. However, when there were many, this was not possible. The orders of the commanders were disregarded when the fear of death disturbed the troops. So, they rushed toward the prohibited gates and the overflowing crowd grew larger. Some threw boards from one bank to the other in a different spot in order to use them as a bridge. The guards were forced to retreat in face of this force.

The guards then roused Bohemond and complained about the force used against them which ended in their flight. The news also roused Tancred. Both of the leaders now prepared to retreat having learned that they had been abandoned by their men. Some went on ahead while Tancred delayed to remain behind. He would take up the role of a wall against the spears of the enemies following behind. Others prepared to flee. Some used their bridles and others their spurs. God took mercy on his people. The Turks remained unaware of the retreat. They remained in a deep sleep while the careful flight of the Christians adorned the paths with precious baggage. They threw away clothing, tents, silver and gold vessels, and whatever else was heavy and could delay them. They even cast aside their weapons, which were the protectors of their lives. Rain made the roads bad transforming dust into mud. The mounted soldiers and foot soldiers were impeded by the slippery path and by the burdens that they were dragging behind them.

Patriarch Bernard was there. He fled with those who were fleeing, and his mud-soaked mule was held back with those who were delayed. No one opposed him. But it seemed as if there were an infinite number of enemies around with drawn swords and bows. His eye was disturbed by the fear around him that was manifest no less in their spirits than it was obvious on their faces. Therefore, calling on his fellow participants in this retreat, he called out, 'listen to me my sons, hear your father. Cut away this oar which hangs from your poop. It is not only not directing your course, it is holding you back. Cut it off I say. I shall not blush, while in this storm, to press the back of this animal after it has been cut free and lightened. Cut them free. Just as God cuts away your sins, I absolve everything from those who cut it away.'

Many passed by with closed ears, for a blind fear closed them. No one cared for another, each person afflicted by his own misery. Now, one fellow, removing himself from the fleeing troops accepted this remedy in exchange for the aforementioned remission [of sins]. Thus, two matters were absolved with one act. The soldier was absolved of his sins, and the beast was absolved of its burden. When the soldier cut off the burden, he was sowing blessings, and reaping them as well, since the patriarch blessed him with his mouth, his heart and his right hand.[250] Thus, the soldier was a reaper, having reaped both the burden and the blessing at the same time. They rode together to Edessa, the archbishop riding with the man who had given back to him the ability to ride.

Chapter 151

Edessa, after it has been saved, is given to Tancred. The enemy attacks Artah after capturing the nearby towns

The people gathered here and the leaders came in last. They conferred about whom they ought to appoint as a successor to Baldwin, who would be able to carry this heavy load. Tancred was chosen as worthy, and he remained there to rule. Bohemond returned to Antioch. When the Frankish defeat became known through the cities, Cilicia, Syria and Phoenicia rejoiced, both those who had been subjected, and those who might face subjection. The latter shed fear from their hearts while the former shed the yoke from their necks. Tarsus, Adana and Mamistra returned to their own rule.[251] They invited in the Greeks and expelled our people. The Turks attacked Artah and devastated the entire region up to the Orontes River. Finally, a huge number of Greek ships filled the port at Latakia. The ships were filled with weapons as well as with both craftsmen and troops, so that they could both wage war and undertake building operations. Having brought both hewn stone and masons, they began to build. There was abundant material from the tumbled-down walls for those needing stone. The port was fortified, and the building project went up.

---

[250] Cf. 2 Corinthians 9:6.
[251] These cities were reoccupied by Byzantine land and naval forces.

Hardly had the news reached Bohemond than, impelled by a hope that the work was not yet done, he marched out and found it completed. An old tower, named after Saint Elias, had stood above the gate. It was now only separated from the new construction by the gate. The Greeks now fortified this as well, and connected it to their fort. Now, with the citadel built over the gate, the latter served both as a passage to and fro, and as a defense against entry by hostile ships.

Chapter 152

Bohemond recalls Tancred

Bohemond, seeing that everything was against him, returned to Antioch. Soon thereafter he discussed the state of the principality with his men. He recalled Tancred, with whom, above all he shared the burdens brought about by necessity. Having been summoned, Tancred did not delay because he never delayed in doing anything. After the assembly was gathered in the basilica of Saint Peter, Bohemond spoke in the following manner, 'the work set out for us at this moment, o leaders is great indeed. If we neglect it we shall perish. The peoples come against us in force. The Greeks and the Turks enclose us all around. We have irritated the two richest powers in the world, Constantinople and Persia. The East terrifies us by land, and the West terrifies us by land and by sea. Moreover, lest I leave it out, Artah, which had been the shield of Antioch, now stretches the bow and directs the arrows. We are few and even our small numbers are shrinking on a regular basis. Our forces were greatly reduced by the loss of the count of Edessa. Pay close attention and consider attentively what should be done at this crucial moment. I shall briefly set out what I believe. We must search for help from the men across the sea. The people of the Gauls must be roused. Their bravery will liberate us, or nothing will. Use me, I say, use me. I shall act as the agent in this matter. To secure your safety, I will not set aside this task. This labor is most welcome to me, so that through it I can provide rest for you.'

When he finished and sat down, Tancred rose and spoke in this way, 'O leaders this matter has been set out prudently, and clearly. You have heard about the strength of the enemy, our weakness, the origin, and also the end, the causes, and the remedy. Our lord prince Bohemond had set these matters out beautifully, well, and correctly.[252] He has not disdained to name a medicine for this illness or to offer himself as the one to obtain it.

---

[252] Cf. Horace, *Ars poetica*, 428.

'But o leaders why should it be thus? Is there no one else among us who can be sent, someone who having been sent out, or rather, who is far from us, cannot be called on thereafter? When a pack of wolves surrounds a sheepfold, it is the task of the shepherd to be present, not absent. When he is present, he opposes the danger, he calls the dogs, he chases off the thieves, he liberates the flock. But, when he is gone, the barking stops, the plunder increases. When he is quiet, the flock is dispersed. The listener will justly and greatly chide my stupidity when he hears that with Bohemond gone, Tancred will remain at home.

'But, perhaps, I am held by this idea, and I am forced to make clear what is in my soul after hearing what has been said. It is my clear will, and I shall not keep silent about my desire. For the common good, I will expose myself to the danger. I shall go forth safely bound by this task. In order that my request might find support, I promise before God that I shall carry out this task with zeal and I will return quickly. Furthermore, that drunkenness might not upset my intention, I shall be content with water and shall give up wine until I return to Antioch. Let only it be permitted to me to remain two days under this roof, something which before was a matter of shame to me. I shall freely take these burdens upon my shoulder, and shall undertake even heavier burdens if you impose them on me.'

Bohemond objected at this point, 'the matter which we are now considering is of great weight, and will barely work even with a person of great experience. It is our purpose to raise great forces. This is not something which just any man can do. One must have experience to undertake important deeds. It takes a great wind to tear an oak tree out by its roots. They will not listen to a Tancred. Those rulers now settled in peace will barely listen to a Bohemond when called on to undertake the labor of an exile. Therefore, lest anyone else's temerity stand in the way of my intention, I propose to go. This cannot be altered. The matter is settled. This desire must be completed, and my devotion shall complete it by the sword. The mercies of Saint Leonard have absolved me. I shall fulfill my vow of visiting him or I shall die in the attempt.'[253]

---

[253] The shrine of Saint Leonard, patron saint of prisoners, was at Noblat near Limoges.

Chapter 153

After leaving Antioch, stripped of all of its wealth, to Tancred, Bohemond departs

Everyone became still and no other objections were raised to the prince's will since everyone knew the proverb: 'The law follows the king where the king wishes to lead the law.'

Therefore a fleet was prepared. They were ten galleys as well as three other ships with only one bank of oars that are commonly called *sandaliae*. Bohemond was satisfied with this number. He passed in sight of the Greek fleet, leaving Antioch to the son of the marquis. He carried off the gold, silver, gems and clothing. The city was left to Tancred without protection, wages and mercenaries. Honest men have related to me that Tancred was left in such penury that he abstained from wine and contented himself with water. When he was encouraged to have a little wine to treat his stomach, he said, 'leave me be to abstain with the abstainers. I have decided not to partake of the fruit of the vine until there is enough to give to everyone. Far be it for me to be swelled up in drunkenness while my fellow soldiers droop from famine.'

Chapter 154

On the same matter

Almost 40 days had gone by when there came a large supply of grain and a great deal of gold rained down from the sky. One of the citizens, having heard about the poverty of the court, was moved by pity and came to Tancred. He demanded a reward and at once obtained it so that he would lift this penury. He said, 'this city has hundreds of citizens, each of whom has a money pouch which could easily pour out thousands of gold coins. If they are asked, they will not hold them back. Ask my lord, I shall give you the names of those whom you should ask.'

Tancred followed this advice. The men were named so that they could be written down. They were written down so that they could be summoned. They were summoned so that they could be asked. And having been sent inside, they were asked. Urgent necessity was named as the cause and was used to excuse the current requests. The promise of reward supported this claim. They also did not remain silent about the enemies who were nearby, who could not be driven off except by armed men. It was also noted that these armed men could not be sent out unless there was gold. All of these reasons flowed together so that the aforementioned requested sum of gold was obtained at last.

When Tancred had obtained the gold, the son of the marquis was comforted, and he, in turn, comforted the soldiers. He reinvigorated those who had been cast down, he armed those who lacked armor, and he replaced those who had died. While the supply of money lasted, he did not cease to increase his military forces. Antioch, which had lain prostrate, now began to recover. From being terrified, it was becoming terrifying. Artah was attacked immediately. This place, along with others, had attacked its mother. Indeed, it was both the bitterest as well as the closest of all the places in Syria. Tancred surrounded this place first and, at his thrust, its towers were barely able to stand up under a bombardment of stones. When Raduanus [Ridwan], the king of Aleppo, heard this, he marched out with 30 000 soldiers against the small force trusting in his multitude.[254] The men of Artah joined him and all of them opposed Antioch.

Chapter 155

He drives Raduanus from Artah (1105)

Between Antioch and Artah there was a rocky plain through which horses could ride but could not run. If one were forced to run, the hoof would not protect the foot, and the horseshoe would not protect the hoof. The sharp rocks would puncture the horse's feet and both the horse and rider would fall to the ground. Tancred, who was aware of this, withdrew a little way, and permitted the enemy to advance so that the difficulties of the place would make it hard for them to retreat. Raduanus either neglected this matter or was ignorant of it and so he attacked the Christian force. The Christians held their position as if torpid and held their place until their spears were ready. Then, when the Turks had passed the rough ground, Tancred charged into their midst as if having been roused from sleep. The Turks quickly retreated hoping, as was their custom, to turn about while fleeing and shoot. However, their hopes and their tricks were foiled, and both the spears of the Christians and the path itself made sport of them. The first pressed them, and the second slowed their course. The spears struck them in the back and the path arrested their flight. Their horses were useless. They threw away their quivers and bows and put their trust in their own feet. When their horses failed, they were left to rely on themselves. They were human and yet they wished to be deer. In order that he not fail completely, Raduanus shot arrows at some of the Christians. For the remainder, however, they turned in flight. Some of his archers escaped injury but many were killed.

---

[254] Ridwan was the Seljuk Turkish ruler of the city of Aleppo.

Chapter 156

Tancred returns as a victor to Antioch. He besieges Apamea[255]

Tancred took Artah as a victor. Then, after garrisoning the place, he returned to Antioch. The faithful were comforted by the spoils taken from the infidel and were awakened as if rising from the dead. It was pleasing that the fortune of the renewed prince had also been renewed. But he could be compared to a hawk that had been denied the ability to fly for a long time and whose spirit had grown weak from its long imprisonment. When it is finally set free, if fortune has ordered that it be sent to seize some prey, these are secondary matters to the hawk's desire. If it catches sight of a flock of cranes, he attacks its handler and flies up to attack. Tancred was inflamed with an equal ardor. When he obtained his victory, he grew rich from the spoils of Aleppo.

Now, about to attack New Latakia, he was warned that the old city had been reinforced with numerous troops.[256] He, himself, set out for Apamea with the rest of his army. And so it was done. Tancred repaid the Greeks in kind who had set up a fort opposed to his fort. Now he blockaded the garrison with his own garrison. He surrounded Apamea with a small but strong force. They were all prepared for death, just as he was prepared for death. Nearby stood the towns of Sysara, Hama, Raphanie and many other towns and cities. All of them were full of threats and filled with the enemy. The Christians besieged one city, and many cities besieged the Christians. When they needed grain, they were not able to search for it unless they divided the army in two. One part remained while the other set out. Thus divided, they were able to turn aside dangers that they could hardly keep at bay while united. They ascribed this to God rather than to human strength. Christ fought openly for the Christians.

Chapter 157

The great need of the men at Latakia

Tancred received a report concerning the desperate straights of his men at Latakia. Although he had shipped them supplies, they now faced shortages from which they would suffer. In the near future they would either have to get grain or the military force would have to withdraw. The great number of the enemy prohibited any advance since they tirelessly watched the roads. The

---

[255] Tancred captured Apamea in 1106.
[256] The siege of Latakia began either in late 1107 or early in 1108.

prince was disturbed by the news because he knew that only hunger could deliver cities. A starving people does not know terror.[257]

He considered a variety of matters. He considered whether he preferred what he could have in the future to what he now held, or what he now held to what he might have in the future. It was difficult to give up the siege of Latakia after so much effort. It was difficult to give up Apamea since it would be taken so easily. It seemed impossible that he could undertake one task without giving up the other. But courage, which is the only thing that makes impossible things possible, comforted this man. He informed those making the request that he would quickly come to their aid. He encouraged the soldiers who were to remain to protect the camp saying, 'hear me, o martyrs of Christ. Prepare to have your blood pour out and to pour out blood for Him. Remain steadfast. You have begun well. Finish it well. Do not allow your small number to frighten you. Victory is not a matter of numbers but comes from God's strength.'[258]

---

[257] Lucan, *De bello civili*, 3.58.
[258] Ralph's history ends here and clearly is incomplete.

Bibliography

Manuscripts and Editions

Codex ms. 5373 Bruxellensis ol. Gembleaux, folios 84v–150v.
Edition by Dom Martene in *Thesaurus novus anecdotorum*, 3 (Paris, 1717).
Edition by L. A. Muratori in *Scriptores rerum Italicarum*, 5.
Edition in *Recueil des historiens des croisades: historiens occidentaux*, III (Paris, 1866).

Sources

Baudri of Bourgueil, *Historia Hierosolymitana, Recueil des historiens des croisades*, IV (Paris, 1879).
Comnena, Anna, *The Alexiad of the Princess Anna Comnena*, trans. Elizabeth A. S. Dawes (London, 2003, first published 1928).
———, *Alexiad*, trans. E. R. A. Sewter (London, 1969).
Dudo of Saint Quentin, *De moribus et actis primorum Normaniae ducum*, ed. Jules Lair (Paris, 1865), trans. Eric Christiansen (Rochester NY, 1998).
Faits et gestes du Prince Tancrède, trans. M. Guizot in Collection des mémoires relatifs a l'histoire de France, 23 (Paris, 1825).
Gesta Francorum et aliorum Hierosolymitanorum, ed. and trans. Rosalind Hill (London, 1962).
Hagenmeyer, Heinrich, *Die Kreuzzugsbriefe aus den Jahren 1088–1100* (repr. Hildesheim, 1973).
Isidore of Seville, *Etymologiarum sive originum libri xx*, 2 vols, ed. W. M. Lindsay (Oxford, 1911, repr. 1957).
Raymond of Aguilers, *Historia Francorum qui ceperunt Iherusalem*, trans. John Hugh Hill and Laurita L. Hill (Philadelphia, 1968).

Scholarly Literature

Albu, Emily, *The Normans in their Histories: Propaganda, Myth and Subversion* (Woodbridge, 2001).
Asbridge, T., *The Creation of the Principality of Antioch, 1098–1130* (Woodbridge, 2000).
Bachrach, Bernard S., 'Dudo of Saint Quentin as an Historian of Military Organization', *Haskins Society Journal*, 12 (2002), 165–185.
Bachrach, David S., *Religion and the Conduct of War* (Woodbridge, 2003).
Birkenmeier, John W., *The Development of the Komnenian Army: 1081–1180* (Leiden, 2002).

Blatt, Franz, *The Latin Josephus 1: Introduction and Text* (Aarhus, 1951).

Boehm, L., 'Die "Gesta Tancredi" des Radulf von Caen. Ein Beitrag zur Geschichtss-chreibung der Normannen um 1100', *Historisches Jahrbuch*, 75 (1956), 47–72.

Brault, Gerard, *The Song of Roland: An Analytical Edition*, 2 vols (University Park, 1981).

Buisson, Ludwig, 'Heerführrertum und Eroberrecht auf dem ersten Kreuzzug', in *Zeitschrift der Savigny-Stiftung für Rechtsgeschichte, Germanische Abteilung*, 112 (1995), 316–44.

David, Charles Wendell, *Robert Curthose, Duke of Normandy* (Cambridge, Mass, 1920, repr. New York, 1982).

Edgington, Susan, 'The First Crusade: Reviewing the Evidence', in *The First Crusade: Origins and Impact*, ed. Jonathan Phillips (Manchester, 1997), 57–77.

Foreville, R., 'Un chef de la première croisade: Arnoul Malecouronne', *Bulletin Philologique et Historique du comité des travaux historiques et scientifiques* (1953–54), 377–90.

Glaesener, H., 'Raoul de Caen historien et écrivain', *Revue d'histoire ecclésiastique*, 46 (1951), 5–21.

Hanawalt (Albu), Emily, 'Norman Views of Eastern Christendom: From the First Crusade to the Principality of Antioch', in *The Meeting of Two Worlds: Cultural Exchange between East and West during the Period of the Crusades* (Kalamazoo, 1986), ed. Vladamir P. Goss, 115–21.

Haskins, Charles Homer, *Norman Institutions* (New York, 1918, repr. 1967).

Kantorowicz, Ernst H., *Laudes Regiae: A Study in Liturgical Acclamations and Medieval Ruler Worship* (Berkeley, 1946).

Mutafian, Claude, 'Lenjeu Cilicien et les prétentions normandes (1097–1137)', in *Autour de la première croisade*, ed. Michel Balard (Paris, 1996), 453–63.

Nicholson, Robert Lawrence, *Tancred: A Study of his Career and Work in their Relation to the First Crusade and the Establishment of the Latin States in Syria and Palestine* (Chicago, 1940).

Payen, Jean-Charles, 'Une légende épique en gestation: les "gesta Tancredi" de Raoul de Caen', in *La chanson de geste et le mythe Carolingien: mélanges René Louis*, 2 vols, (Saint-Père-sous-Vézelay, 1982), vol. II: 1051–62.

——, 'L'hégémonie normande dans la *Chanson de Roland* et les *Gesta Tancredi*: de la Neustrie à la chrétienté, ou Turold est-il nationaliste?', in *Romance Epic: Essays on a Medieval Literary Genre*, ed. Hans-Erich Keller (Kalamazoo, 1987), 73–90.

Peters, Edward (ed.), *The First Crusade*, 2nd edn (Philadelphia, 1998).

Quint, Maria Barbara, *Untersuchungen zur mittelalterlichen Horaz-Rezeption* (Frankfurt, 1988).

Russo, Luigi, 'Tancredi e i Bizantini. Sui *Gesta Tancredi in expeditione Hierosolymitana* di Rodolfo di Caen', *Medio evo greco*, 2 (2002), 193–230.

Rowe, J. G., 'Pascal II and the Relation between the Spiritual and Temporal Powers in the Kingdom of Jerusalem', *Speculum*, 32 (1957), 470–501.

Index